BULLFIGHT

para Antonio y Nicolás
andaluces, aficionados y amigos

GARRY MARVIN

BULLFIGHT

Basil Blackwell

First published 1988

Basil Blackwell Ltd
108 Cowley Road, Oxford, OX4 1JF, UK

Basil Blackwell Inc.
432 Park Avenue South, Suite 1503
New York, NY 10016, USA

British Library Cataloguing in Publication Data

Marvin, Garry
  Bullfight.
  1. Bull-fights——Spain
  I. Title
  791'.82'0946   GV1108.5
  ISBN 0-631-15471-X

Library of Congress Cataloging in Publication Data

Marvin, Garry.
  Bullfight/Garry Marvin.
  p. cm.
  ISBN 0-631-15471-X
  1. Bullfights.   I. Title.
GV1107.M414 1988
791'.82—dc19   87-26927 CIP

Typeset in 10 on 12½ pt plantin by Columns of Reading.
Printed in Great Britain by T.J. Press Ltd, Padstow

Contents

In the bullfight the Spaniard has found the most perfect expression for defining his human quality.

Rafael Campos de España

Spain is the only country where death is the national spectacle.

Federico García Lorca

Introduction

This book is an accessible, interpretive account of the bullfight for
anyone who seeks to understand why men risk their lives to perform
with and to kill wild bulls and why this should be *la Fiesta Nacional* (the
National Celebration) of Spain.[1] The first thoughts for it came,
appropriately enough, in Ronda, a city in the province of Malaga in
Andalusia, which is revered by many as the birthplace of *toreo* (the art of
bullfighting).[2] It was there that I saw my first *corrida de toros* (bullfight),
and although I was not immediately converted to being an *aficionado* (an
enthusiast or fan) I did become intrigued to understand its status as a key
Spanish cultural event. As an anthropologist I was struck by the fact
that, although the available enthnographies of Spain mentioned the
corrida and its importance as a celebratory event, as far as I could
discover no detailed anthropological study of the event itself had been
carried out. The cultural significance of the event was suggested by its
general popular image as something quintessentially Spanish, by the
considerable attention paid to it within Spain, and because of its status as
an elaborate and spectacular ritual drama which is staged as an essential
part of many important celebrations. My reading suggested that many
Spaniards perceived the *corrida* to be a uniquely Spanish art form based
on and incorporating particularly Spanish values, and that the *torero* (the
bullfighter) the man responsible for demonstrating these values, had long
been a heroic figure who occupied a special place in Spanish popular
culture. It was with the intention of understanding those values, the
images associated with them and how they were responded to, that I
embarked on this study.

The greater part of this research was carried out in Seville,[3] which is,
along with Madrid, the most important Spanish centre of the taurine
world. Not only is Seville the setting for one of the most important

weeks of *corridas* in the year, the April Fair, but it is possible to see *corridas* there throughout the season. It is also a city where one can find bullfighters – *toreros* – and their managers, impresarios, the controlling officials and *aficionados* – very many *aficionados*. For two years (and then for many months after that on almost annual return trips) I lived in Seville, where I devoted myself to the world of the *corrida*. My time was spent attending *corridas* all over Andalusia; with *toreros* as they trained and talked about their art and prepared for performances; on ranches learning about the life and character of the fighting bull; in interviewing anyone who had a part to play in performing, in organizing or controlling this world; and most of all in bars with *aficionados* talking about what the *corrida* meant to them. In particular I spent several hours each day in the *Peña Taurina Curro Romero* in Camas, near Seville. This is a private men's social club founded by a group of *aficionados* and dedicated to Curro Romero, one of Spain's greatest artistic *toreros*, who was born in the village. Here men came to drink, play cards or dominoes, read the newspaper or just to talk. It was from the men in this club that I received my most important lessons in the appreciation of the *corrida* and what sense it made in their lives, and it was there that my aesthetic taste was formed and my appreciation was refined for the artistic style epitomized by Curro Romero. Finally, I talked incessantly about bulls, *toreros* and *toreo* with a wider range of friends and acquaintances during my years in Seville.

My interest throughout the research was definitely in understanding the nature of the *corrida* in its totality (rather than simply the art of bullfighting which occurs within it) and its significance in this culture. The more I became familiar with the literature the more it became obvious that, despite the wealth of material dealing with the *corrida*, there was no detailed anthropological analysis of the nature or meaning of the event. The lack of such an analysis seemed to constitute an important omission in the ethnography of Spain, and particularly the ethnography of Andalusia, the area I knew best and where the *corrida* was of particular importance. This book does not pretend to be a complete ethnography of the *corrida*. Instead it concentrates on the meaning and nature of the *corrida*, particularly in terms of its structure; something which involves an analysis of the setting of the event, the role of the human performers and the nature of their performance, the role of the animals, the relation between those animals and the humans, and its character as a celebration within the wider context of celebratory occasions.

My perspective has obviously been influenced by the way I conducted my research and by my concern to understand the event in depth. I spent most of my time with people who are interested in or actively involved in the *corrida*. Such people are mainly men, and thus I spent most of my time with men, talking about an event which they considered to be a particularly masculine event, and one they perceived to be necessarily based on masculine characteristics and qualities. I have talked to many women about the *corrida*, but I have certainly come to understand the male attitude better and more completely. If I had not conducted my research in the way I did, I do not believe that I would have been able to achieve an understanding of sufficient depth.

Although my focus has been on the *corrida* itself, it is not possible to understand it without taking into consideration its social and cultural setting. As Brandes has said:

> the actual content of any given item of expressive culture is inseparable from the way it is employed and the entire social context in which it is articulated. (1980: 9)

It is because authors have failed to make a careful analysis of the *corrida* in terms of its socio-cultural setting that so much nonsense has been written about it both in English and Spanish. It is a dramatic, emotional, elaborate and complex spectacle and there is a danger, to which many writers have succumbed, that one will launch into flights of fancy when writing what purports to be analysis. Such pieces of writing perhaps tell us more about the minds and imaginations of the authors than they do about the event itself. Throughout this study I have attempted only to draw meaning out of the event rather than read meaning into it. I have tried to retain a sense of the importance of the emotional and dramatic impact of the *corrida*, an impact which results both from the spectacular framework of the event and the performances within that framework; but also to go beyond that to attempt to understand what it is about the *corrida* which creates such an emotional impact on members of the audience, how it achieves its effect and what it 'says' to the audience. One can only fully understand the *corrida* if one's interpretation of it is set firmly within the cultural context which gives it meaning, something which involves getting to know those who attend and those who perform, and setting their experience of the *corrida* in the framework of their culture and cultural attitudes. As Geertz says, 'one cannot understand men without knowing them' (1975: 30).

Although the *corrida* is an event which is held all over Spain, (indeed one of its names is *la Fiesta Nacional* (The National Celebration)), I decided to concentrate on the region where it is most popular, Andalusia.

In this way, I felt I would be able to examine the *corrida* much more closely in terms of its relation to a particular regional culture in which it occurs and in which it is richly elaborated. The alternative would have been to spread my interpretation more thinly and attempt a pan-Spanish perspective, which would have to have dealt with the question of regional variations and why it is more popular in some regions than others. I am fairly sure that many of the comments I make about the *corrida* and my general interpretation of it are valid for Spain as a whole, and certainly the structure and rules of the event are everywhere the same; but as each of the regions is culturally distinct, and because my knowledge of Andalusia is more detailed than my knowledge of any other part of Spain, I have restricted my comments to that region.

It is necessary to make another autobiographical point here, for it is something which perhaps informed my research and subsequently this book. It was not particularly difficult to convince the men in the club where I worked or the other *aficionados* and *toreros* I met of my enthusiasm for the *corrida*, because I was not expressing interest simply to obtain information. By that time I had become an enthusiast and greatly enjoyed the event. Some of my friends and many of those with whom I have talked about the *corrida* have found this enthusiasm difficult to understand and some have even thought it immoral. Extreme positions are adopted with regard to the event: it is either passionately defended as a great and noble art or it is equally passionately censured as a brutal and deplorable blood sport. The result is that very few people attain a balanced understanding of it. Although I do not wish to discuss the morality of the event (no such discussion appears in this book), I suggest that it would have been difficult to spend several years involved on such a project, which brought me into close contact with all aspects of the event and certainly involved watching the slaughter of several hundred animals, if I detested it and condemned those who watched or participated. I further suggest that I was able to produce a balanced and, I hope, sensitive account of the *corrida* because of my position of being an enthusiast, without being carried away with the romantic and exotic image of the event, as most foreign and many Spanish enthusiasts have been. It is important that my interest started as purely anthropological, that I wanted to understand how a particular event fitted into a particular socio-cultural context, and what the event and context revealed about one another. My *afición* (enthusiasm) only came with greater exposure to the event, with friendships formed with those involved in it and great respect for those who went into the arena.

During recent years friends have tolerated my talking endlessly about bullfights, and I would like to thank them for being patient with my particular obsession. To some, however, special thanks are due. John and Marie Corbin first taught me anthropology, suggested the project to me and have continued to take an active interest in my work; it is their research in Andalusia which provided me with the basis for my own research. The president and members of the *Peña Taurina Curro Romero* made me welcome in the club, did me the honour of making me a member and invited me to dozens of bullfights with them. In the *peña* I particularly want to thank Antonio Torres, who always obtained tickets for *corridas* even when they were sold out, and Nicolas Vargas, who dedicated himself to my general education in the appreciation of things *andaluz* and to my education as an *aficionado*. Antonio Marcelo Herrera and his family made me welcome at the Cortijo de la Sierra and have, with many of the staff of that ranch, particularly Diego Reina and Antonio Guardiola, taught me much about the fighting bull in the country. I am grateful to Francisco Gatto who helped me with translation difficulties and Liliana Eslava who helped work out the original diagrams. I would particularly like to thank Richard Fardon, Ladislav Holy and David Riches at St Andrews for their comments on earlier versions of this work, and Bob Davis, who had a more difficult task than he thought. Margaret Kenna and Chris Stray became involved in all of this in a very special way; my debt to them is enormous. Finally I would like to thank Sean Magee at Basil Blackwell who has taken great interest in this work and has been supportive and encouraging at all the stages from manuscript to printed text.

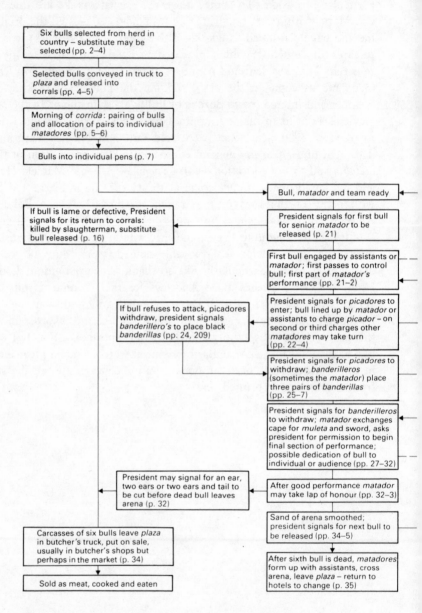

Six bulls selected from herd in country – substitute may be selected (pp. 2–4)

Selected bulls conveyed in truck to *plaza* and released into corrals (pp. 4–5)

Morning of *corrida*: pairing of bulls and allocation of pairs to individual *matadores* (pp. 5–6)

Bulls into individual pens (p. 7)

Bull, *matador* and team ready

If bull is lame or defective, President signals for its return to corrals: killed by slaughterman, substitute bull released (p. 16)

President signals for first bull for senior *matador* to be released (p. 21)

First bull engaged by assistants or *matador*; first passes to control bull; first part of *matador's* performance (pp. 21–2)

If bull refuses to attack, picadores withdraw, president signals *banderillero's* to place black *banderillas* (pp. 24, 209)

President signals for *picadores* to enter; bull lined up by *matador* or assistants to charge *picador* – on second or third charges other *matadores* may take turn (pp. 22–4)

President signals for *picadores* to withdraw; *banderilleros* (sometimes the *matador*) place three pairs of *banderillas* (pp. 25–7)

President signals for *banderilleros* to withdraw; *matador* exchanges cape for *muleta* and sword, asks president for permission to begin final section of performance; possible dedication of bull to individual or audience (pp. 27–32)

President may signal for an ear, two ears or two ears and tail to be cut before dead bull leaves arena (p. 32)

After good performance *matador* may take lap of honour (pp. 32–3)

Sand of arena smoothed; president signals for next bull to be released (pp. 34–5)

Carcasses of six bulls leave *plaza* in butcher's truck, put on sale, usually in butcher's shops but perhaps in the market (p. 34)

After sixth bull is dead, *matadores* form up with assistants, cross arena, leave *plaza* – return to hotels to change (p. 35)

Sold as meat, cooked and eaten

Figure 1   La corrida de toros: a diagrammatic outline

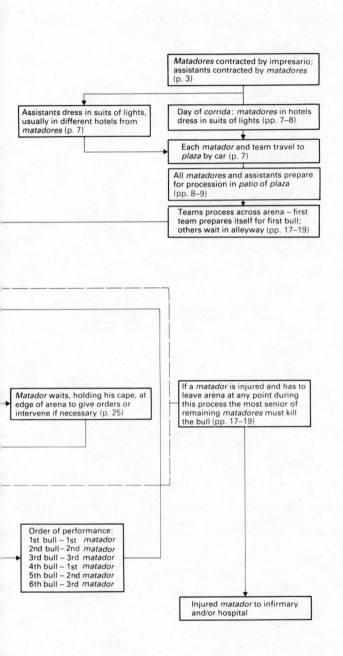

Matadores contracted by impresario;
assistants contracted by *matadores*
(p. 3)

Assistants dress in suits of lights,
usually in different hotels from
matadores (p. 7)

Day of *corrida*: *matadores* in hotels
dress in suits of lights (pp. 7–8)

Each *matador* and team travel to
plaza by car (p. 7)

All *matadores* and assistants prepare
for procession in *patio* of *plaza*
(pp. 8–9)

Teams process across arena – first
team prepares itself for first bull;
others wait in alleyway (pp. 17–19)

Matador waits, holding his cape, at
edge of arena to give orders or
intervene if necessary (p. 25)

If a *matador* is injured and has to
leave arena at any point during
this process the most senior of
remaining *matadores* must kill
the bull (pp. 17–19)

Order of performance:
1st bull – 1st *matador*
2nd bull – 2nd *matador*
3rd bull – 3rd *matador*
4th bull – 1st *matador*
5th bull – 2nd *matador*
6th bull – 3rd *matador*

Injured *matador* to infirmary
and/or hospital

1

The *corrida* described

The confusing array of some two dozen men similarly dressed in sparkling costumes, the occasional trumpet calls, the music and cheering and the apparently chaotic and ever-shifting arrangement of men, capes, bulls and horses in a sand covered arena in the bright summer sunshine often leaves non-initiated spectators bemused and without any sense of how the event they are watching is progressing. The actors in the arena change every few minutes but it is difficult to recognize who has just changed with whom or even whether or not there has been a change; at one moment there are three men using their capes to tease the bull before ducking behind the fence of the arena to escape it, at another there is just one who does not attempt to flee. Men on horses appear and once again there are a number of people in the arena. The men who had the capes suddenly appear without them but with coloured sticks which they thrust into the bull, but are these the same men? Bulls appear alive and at the gallop through one gate and a short while later they are dragged out dead through another, but it is difficult to understand what has happened to cause this change. The names *picador*, *matador*, *banderillero*, *torero* and even *toreador* are recognized by many English speakers, but few, even of those who have seen *corridas* in Spain, are clear about the differences between them or understand their role in the *corrida*.

In fact the *corrida* is a highly ordered, structured and tightly controlled event. The bull passes through various stages and in order to have any understanding of the significance of the *corrida* it is necessary to understand these stages and the roles of the men who act on the bull during each of them. The central aim of this chapter is therefore to make clear how the human and animal actors come together to witness or perform in this event and how the sequence of events which constitutes the *corrida* unfolds. To an *aficionado* each *corrida* is unique, but this uniqueness is from the point of view of stylistic, interpretive or emotional content, whereas this account will stress form. It is an account of a *corrida* of the most usual type, in which six bulls between four and six years old (*Reglamento Taurino Español* 1972: article 74) from the same ranch are played and killed by three *matadores de toros* with the assistance of their respective teams.[1] In order to include the widest range of elements of the form the account will be set as if in a first class *plaza de toros* (bullring) of which there are eight in Spain.[2] The actual description here is based not simply on knowledge of the literature but also on personal attendance at some 250 *corridas* in Spain, most of them in Andalusia and more especially in the *Plaza de la Real Maestranza* in Seville. It must be pointed out, however, that what follows is a descriptive outline of only the major features of the *form* of the event and the *processes* within it; if every element of what should happen or what could happen were entered into, the detail would swamp any sense of these general features (see figure 1).

The contracting of bulls and *matadores*

Prior to the commencement of the performing season (some time in the early spring) the impresarios of the major *plazas* where many *corridas* will be held during the year must contact bull breeders and contract enough bulls for the *corridas* they know that they are certain to present. They will not book all the animals they might need because, although a rough estimate will have been made of their needs, they will probably be uncertain as to exactly how many *corridas* they will present in the year. They must certainly begin negotiations as early as possible because there is considerable competition to secure the best bulls from the best ranches.

The important impresarios have an intermediary, usually called a *conocedor* ('an expert', from the verb *conocer*, to know) who has particular expertise in the selection of bulls, and it is he who goes to the ranch to see what bulls are available, and to negotiate for the best on behalf of the impresario. In a normal *corrida* six bulls from the same ranch are used, and the *conocedor* must try to reach agreement about which six animals will be set aside for him. If he is representing an important impresario who is staging *corridas* in major *plazas* where it is prestigious for a breeder to have his bulls used, the *conocedor* will have considerable influence over which animals are put aside for him. If, on the other hand, he is representing an unimportant impresario he will probably have to simply accept what he is offered. Once the bulls are chosen they will remain on the ranch until just before they are needed.

Having contracted the bulls for the season, the impresario must contract the *matadores* to perform with them. If he is contracting relatively unimportant or uninfluential *matadores* he has no real problem, because the competition among *matadores* to be able to perform is so intense that those offered the opportunity to do so are rarely in a position to debate the terms of their contract with the impresario. If, on the other hand, he is seeking to contract *figuras* (a *figura* is literally 'a figure' or personality, and in this context a star) who are in great demand, there are more difficulties. Some *matadores* will not perform on the same programme as other *matadores*, some will not perform with bulls from certain ranches, some will *only* perform with bulls from certain ranches, some want to know what the individual bulls are like before they agree to perform with them and, as might be expected, there is also the question of the fee which they require. In all they have a considerable influence in the way that the programme is put together. The impresario does not contract the assistants; this is the responsibility of the individual *matadores*, who also pay them. Some, particularly those who perform often, will have permanent teams, whereas those whose season is less certain will contract assistants on an ad hoc basis.

Once the impresario has made up the programme, he must present details of it to the civil authorities and ask for permission to hold the event. For an ordinary *corrida* (there are a few extra regulations for certain special *corridas*) he must also present documentation which certifies the good state of the *plaza de toros* itself, the medical facilities available, and the state of the corrals where the animals are held and of the stables and the butchery department; proof that those performing are registered with the *Sector Taurino del Sindicato Nacional de Espectáculo* (the Taurine Section of the National Entertainment Syndicate), have proper contracts, and, if they are under twenty-one, have written permission from their parents or guardians allowing them to perform; certificates with details of the health and pedigree of each bull; a sales certificate from the breeder; and a certificate stating that the bulls have never been used in a *plaza de toros* before.[3]

Nearer the day of the *corrida*, the *conocedor* must go to the ranch to see that all is well with the bulls and to close the deal with the breeder. A considerable time might have elapsed between when they were chosen and the date on which they are to be used, and in this time accidents might have occurred. An animal might have become sick, it might have damaged a horn or, because bulls do fight in the fields, one might have been wounded or killed. It is also possible that the *conocedor* and the breeder agreed to select the six bulls from a group of eight or nine possible animals, and the decision then has to be made as to which six to select. The regulations state that in addition to the six bulls to be used in the *corrida* there must be at least one reserve bull (two in the major *plazas*), so unless there is already a bull in the corrals of the *plaza* the *conocedor* will often chose a seventh bull from the same ranch. (This is not, though, necessarily the case; the reserve bull often comes from another ranch.)

Transportation and examination of the bulls

The *conocedor* or a trusted representative of the impresario will be present at the loading of the bulls into the truck to take them to the *plaza*, an event which usually happens the day before the *corrida* if the journey from the ranch to the *plaza* is not a long one, and a couple of days before if it is a long journey. This gives the animals time to rest and recuperate in the corals. The breeder does not have to provide the truck; a specialist in the transportation of bulls will be contracted by the impresario. The loading can be a tricky operation because each bull must be put into narrow individual crates on the truck and they are rarely willing to go into them easily. In the process of being separated from the herd, rounded up in the field, herded into the corrals and finally into the chutes which lead to the truck, the bulls become progressively more nervous and thus aggressive, and there is always the risk that they will attack each other or charge the walls or barriers and thus damage themselves. If this happens, substitute bulls must be found. Once they are all in their crates the bulls are ready to leave the ranch for the *plaza*, a journey on which they are accompanied by the *mayoral* (the senior ranch hand who is responsible for the care of the bulls; he too is sometimes called a *conocedor*). The bulls often have to travel great distances in these crates, and a journey from the south coast to one of the most northern cities such as Bilbao or Santander may take a couple of days. Nowadays they are sometimes flown in their crates to South America for important *corridas*.

Once the truck arrives at the *plaza* the bulls are released one at a time into a corral. Here they are examined by two veterinary surgeons, in the presence of representatives of the civil governor, of the impresario, and of the bull breeder, for physical defects such as lameness, blindness and broken or malformed horns. They are also examined for *trapío*, a term used of the general form and bearing of the animal. The meaning of *trapío* is difficult to define but it refers to the fact that the essential 'fighting-bull quality' of the animal should stand out. It is a term and a quality which *aficionados* will argue about endlessly and it will be examined in detail in the section dealing with the animals themselves. Faulty animals can be rejected and reserve animals substituted at this stage. If the impresario or the breeder are dissatisfied with any of the decisions there is an arbitration process which can be set in motion. The bulls are also weighed to be sure that they meet the weight requirement of the *plaza*.[4] After the examination they are given a little hay and water and are left in the communal corral.

The breeder's representative and the representative of the impresario keep watch over the bulls from the time they arrive in the *plaza* until the time they are required in the arena. This is in order to stop any fights between the animals, should they occur and to prevent anyone tampering with them. It has been known for bulls to be weakened by the administration of drugs such as laxatives, by having sandbags dropped on their backs or by their horns being meddled with. This procedure is called *afeitando* (literally, 'shaving') and consists of sawing off the points of the horns and then reworking them into a new point; the workmanship is covered by rubbing dirt on the cuts. The point of this is partly that the bull is reluctant to strike anything solid because the horns are now sensitive, but also and more importantly, because it affects the bull's aim. Bulls are able to strike very accurately with their horns and the effect of removing a section of horn is similar to what would happen if one shortened the length of a trained boxer's arm by an inch without telling him (although this of course would be physically impossible); the result in both cases would be a misjudgement of how to hit the target.

The *sorteo*

At midday on the day of the *corrida*, the *sorteo* (sorting into lots) takes place to divide the animals into three roughly equal pairs and to assign these to the three *matadores*. The choice of each set of animals is made by the communal agreement of each of the *peones de confianza* (trusted assistants, usually the senior *banderilleros*, the assistants who perform on foot) of each *matador*, again in the presence of those who attended the inspection of the bulls. The managers of the *matadores* may also attend Gilperez García and Fraile Sanz: article 77).

What is attempted at the *sorteo* is to obtain acceptable pairs so that one *matador* does not have two advantageous nor two disadvantageous bulls. For example, a bull with large horns will be paired with one with small horns and the heaviest with the lightest. Once the pairs are agreed on, the ranch numbers of the two bulls of each pair are written on cigarette papers, the three papers are rolled up individually and placed in a wide-brimmed hat (the *sombrero de ala ancha*) with another hat on top to form a lid. The hat usually belongs to the breeder's representative because, traditionally, he will be the one wearing the *traje corto* (the formal Andalusian country clothes) of which the *sombrero de ala ancha* forms a part; but the regulations do not actually state whose hat it has to be, nor do they stipulate who is to hold it.

The assistant of the most senior *matador* makes the first draw, selecting one of the papers and calling out the numbers of the bulls allocated to his *matador*. The assistant of the next senior makes the next draw and calls out the numbers, and the most junior assistant takes the remaining piece of paper. Each of the assistants decides which of the two bulls his *matador* will take first, and the official lists can then be drawn up.

Matadores are ranked according to the date when they took the *alternativa*, the graduation ceremony at which they move from the rank of *matador de novillos* (*matador* of young bulls, *novillos* being three- to four-year-old bulls) to full *matadores de toros* (the bulls for these *matadores* being four- to six-year-olds). The significance of the *alternativa* will be considered in detail in the chapter dealing with the career of the *torero*. In a *corrida* the *matadores* perform in order of seniority – the age or popularity of a particular *matador* does not effect this. When the lists are drawn up, the animals selected for the senior matador will be in first and fourth place, those of the next senior in second and fifth, and those of the junior in third and sixth.

This is an account of how the *sorteo* ought to take place. There are, as might be expected, various tricks and forms of pressure to ensure that the most influential *matador* receives the best or the least difficult animals; such animals are described as the *más cómodos* (literally, 'the most comfortable'). One trick described to me involved a small piece of lead shot being rolled into the paper containing the numbers of the best bulls, so that it could easily be chosen by the senior assistant; on another occasion it was explained to me how the junior *matador* who had the best of the selection was persuaded to swap them with the senior man. This is not to claim that the *sorteo* is always, or even often, manipulated, but merely that it can be.

Once the bulls have been paired and assigned they are lured out of the communal corral one at a time and into individual pens, *chiqueros*, where they wait in the cool and dark until they are required in the arena. The doors are locked and on each is written the number corresponding to the animal's position in the *corrida*; that is, not its ranch number but simply a number from 1 to 6.

The *matador's* preparations

The *matadores* rarely go themselves to see the bulls but rely on the information given to them by their assistants. The way any individual *matador* spends his time on the day of a *corrida* is a matter of personal taste, but the majority attempt to sleep late and then remain in the hotel room after a light lunch and attempt to sleep again. Some *matadores* abstain from food entirely before a *corrida* because they are too nervous to eat; some, however, claim that this is also beneficial should they be caught by the bull and need an operation, because with an empty stomach there will be fewer problems with the anaesthetic.

About two hours before the start of the *corrida* the *matador* is woken by his *mozo de espadas* (literally his 'sword servant', this man is his general, non-performing assistant, and does indeed prepare his swords, and his capes, for him). He showers and then begins to dress with the help of his *mozo*. It is a complicated procedure to dress a *matador* in his *traje de luces* (literally, 'suit of lights'), largely because of the tightness of the costume. Once he has on his shirt, his underwear (incidentally, there are no protective pieces in the suit of lights) and the two pairs of pink stockings, he has to be assisted into his trousers. Not only are the trousers (technically known as *taleguillas*) tight and restricting but they are also very high waisted, and it is important that everything be well tucked in. Particular importance is attached to the proper tying of the tassels of the trousers at the point where they join the stockings just below the knee. These tassels are known as *machos* (literally, 'males') and it is the responsibility of the *mozo* to tie them just tight enough to secure the trousers around the leg.[5] The other items which complete the suit of lights are a tie, an embroidered waistcoat (which is not always worn), a thickly embroidered short jacket, a coloured waistband which covers the top of the trousers, a pair of slippers like ballet-slippers and a hat known as a *montera*.

Some *matadores* allow close friends and associates in the room for this dressing; some allow them to enter at the beginning of the dressing and then expect them to leave before the end; some allow no visitors at all. The dressing is accompanied by a growing seriousness and reserve on the part of the *matador*, often culminating in a few moments of silent prayer in front of the religious medals and pictures which are set out on a table for him. Some *matadores* have quite an elaborate collection and the table is set out like a shrine, whereas others have very few, perhaps just a personal medallion. Some will also drink a cup of coffee and smoke a final cigarette. These are the last few quiet moments for the man before he steps out in public as a *matador*

The two mounted and three foot assistants (*picadores* and *banderilleros* respectively) who make up the *cuadrilla* (team) change in another, usually cheaper, hotel. The foot assistants are often driven to the *matador's* hotel to meet him, although they do not go up to his room but wait for him in the foyer. Usually two cars are used to convey the team to the *plaza*, with the *picadores* leaving earlier so that they can check the preparation of the horses. On arrival at the *plaza* the foot assistants and the *matador* carry their parade capes folded inside out over the left arm, and each holds his hat for the short walk into the *plaza*. They enter the *patio de caballos* (the horse yard where the procession forms up – see figure 1), although on the way they may have to shake hands with and say a few words to admirers who often wait at the gate of the *plaza*.

While the performing members of the team wait in the *patio*, the non-performing members take the boxes of capes into the *callejón* (the alleyway which runs all the way around the arena – see figure 1) where they are prepared by the *mozo*. He must fold the working capes correctly so that they can be handed quickly to anyone in the team who has theirs torn away by the bull. The *muletas* (a red cloth which is used in the final section of the performance; a further description is given later in this section) have to have their supporting sticks screwed into them; several of these must be prepared in case the *matador* should drop one and is unable to retrieve it. The swords, which have been sharpened, are checked; again, several are prepared in case the *matador* misplaces one as he enters to kill.

Off the *patio* there is a room which can be used for prayer. In the major *plazas* such as that in Seville there is an actual chapel, and there is always a priest in attendance at the *corrida*, should he be needed, to give the last rites; something which is fortunately rarely necessary these days because of improved medical facilities. The caretaker of the chapel in Seville told me that all the *matadores* entered, usually with their assistants, if only for a few moments. She further told me that this was to offer a prayer not just for their own safety but also that they might be able to acquit themselves well in front of the public. This is very much in line with what most *matadores* replied when asked about fear. They said that they certainly did fear the bull, but much more than that they were worried by the responsibility of the task of performing in public. In many ways the public posed a more fearful threat for them than did the bull.

Up to this point the *matadores* and *banderilleros* have carried their elaborate dress capes with the plain coloured lining facing outwards. Now they wrap the capes right side out, around their bodies, with the right arm free and with the material tucked in such a way that the left arm is wrapped in the cape somewhat like an arm in a sling, with the left hand grasping the loose ends. These capes are elaborately embroidered and incorporate religious images and floral or geometric designs; the *matadores'* capes are more lavishly decorated than those of the assistants.

Other preparations

On arrival at the *plaza*, the *picadores* must check their horses. The day before the *corrida* these animals are examined by the veterinary surgeons to check that their weight and height correspond to the regulations (Gilperez García and Fraile Sanz 1972: article 1983) and that they are fit. The horses are supplied by a specialist horse contractor or are owned by the impresario; they are not owned by the individual *picadores*.

On the day of the *corrida*, the *picadores* meet at the same time as the *sorteo* to choose, by seniority, the animals they will ride and the saddles and protective padding (supplied by the impresario) they will use. Once the animals have been examined and chosen, a thin red cord is put around the neck of each animal and is sealed with a metal tag so that there can be no substitutions. Some time before the *corrida*, the horse will be injected with a tranquillizing drug, the thick mattress padding which covers much of the animal is belted into place, the ears are stopped with cotton wool and loosely tied shut, and a black scarf is tied over the face to cover the right eye so that the horse cannot see the bull. It is the right eye which is covered because it is on this side that the horse is made to face the bull. The saddle is put on and the horse is then ready for the *picador* to exercise it a little in the *patio* before the parade.

The other animals prepared at this time are the two mule teams which are used to drag the carcass of the dead bull to the butchery department in the *plaza*. These animals are usually decorated in some way; in Seville, for example, they have thin coloured blankets, usually of red and yellow (the Spanish national colours, colours which are also symbolically associated with blood and sand in the context of this event), bells and coloured flags.

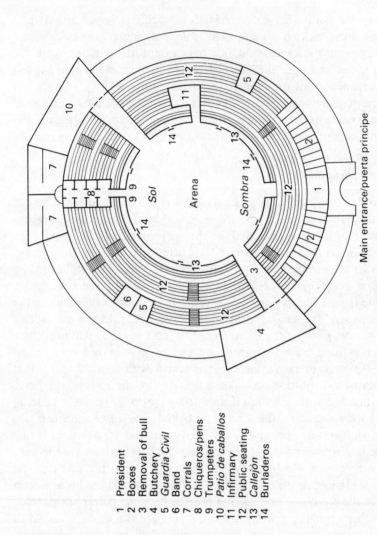

1 President
2 Boxes
3 Removal of bull
4 Butchery
5 *Guardia Civil*
6 Band
7 Corrals
8 Chiqueros/pens
9 Trumpeters
10 *Patio de caballos*
11 Infirmary
12 Public seating
13 *Callejón*
14 Burladeros

Figure 2 General outline of the main features of a *plaza de toros*

The *plaza* – the physical features

The constitution of a special arena for the *corrida* did not really begin until the late seventeenth and early eighteenth centuries, and then only in the larger towns. If a town did not have a special arena, then a main square would be blocked off with planks of wood and carts and the *corrida* held in the space thus formed. Even today it is still possible to find villages where this occurs. The *plaza de toros* (literally, the 'place of bulls') is usually owned by the town council and is rented out to an impresario for a number of years, after which it is put out to tender again. The *plaza* in Seville, however, is somewhat unusual in that it is owned by *La Real Maestranza de Caballeria* (a society of noblemen founded in the eighteenth century to promote the skills of horsemanship) and permanently rented out to one impresario.

Any *plaza* is basically an unroofed circle of banked seats around a sand-covered arena. The architecture of any particular *plaza* has distinctive features but there are a number of basic similarities in all *plazas*. This description of the *plaza* in Seville gives the main features (see figure 2).

The arena cannot, according to the regulations, be more than 70 m in diameter nor less than 45 m. The boundary of the arena is marked by a wooden barrier 1.7 m high, which is broken at several points by narrow gaps that allow access into the arena. About 0·5 m in front of each of these gaps is a section of barrier about 1·5 m long, which allows the performers to slip to safety behind the main barrier without the bull being able to follow; these refuges are called *burladeros* (from the verb '*burlar*', 'to deceive'). The barrier is also broken by four double gates. One opens on to the short passageway under the seats on the shady side of the *plaza* that leads to the *puerta principe* (the main gate). Some members of the audience use the *puerta principe* to gain access to their seats, but the connecting gate into the arena is only used if the *matador* is carried into the streets after a triumphal lap of honour in the arena. Another gate connects with the *patio de caballos*, through which the parade enters at the beginning of the event and which the *picadores* use throughout. The third gate is opposite the *patio de caballos* and is used by the mule teams to drag the carcass of the dead bull out to the butchery department. The fourth gate is opposite the gate to the *puerta principe* and connects with the corridor through which the bull enters the arena.

Between the first row of seats and the barrier is the *callejón*, which runs all the way around the arena and in which the teams and officials stand. Within the *callejón* are other *burladeros* behind which those in the *callejón* can protect themselves should the bull leap the barrier from the arena. When this does happen it becomes a source of great amusement for the crowd, because all those in the *callejón* attempt to leap to the safety of the arena, by which time the bull is being forced back into the arena and there is a struggle to get back to the *callejón*. In Seville there are *burladeros* for the *toreros* themselves, for members of the medical staff, for the police, for the *matadores'* managers, for the impresarios, for the official photographers, and for the various groups of employees who service the arena during the course of the event. The back wall of the *callejón* is 2·2 m high (that is, it is almost impossible for the bull to jump it) and is topped with a fixed steel cable. Immediately behind it is the first row of seats; the seating is then banked upwards to the outer edge of the *plaza*. Although it was said above that the *plaza de toros* was an unroofed building, there is in fact a narrow roof over the very top set of seats.

High on the shady side of the *plaza* there are a few boxes for members of the *Real Maestranza* and visiting dignitaries. It is here that the president of the *corrida*, the man who controls the event, has his box, almost directly above the passage leading to the *puerta principe*. In the *plaza* there are areas set aside for the trumpeters, the band, the *Guardia Civil* and an infirmary, all of which vary according to the *plaza*.

Sol y sombra

The *corrida* takes place in the afternoon at a time after the worst of the heat of the day and yet while there is still sufficient light. The regulations stipulate that a minimum time of 30 minutes must be allotted for each bull, and this time, multiplied by six, must be balanced against the time of the setting of the sun. The sinking sun throws one part of the *plaza* into shade at the beginning of the event and other parts come into the shade during the afternoon. *Plasas* are therefore divided, for the purpose of ticket prices, into *sombra* (shade), *sol y sombra* (sun and shade – an area which starts in the sunlight and, with the movement of the sun, goes into shade), and *sol* (sun). The seats in the sun are the cheapest and those in the shade the most expensive.

The high price of tickets (those for the *corrida* are expensive in comparison with other events such as theatre, cinema, concerts or football) and the difference in price between the sun and shade tickets (a ticket for a main block seat in the shade is usually double that of a similar seat in the sun) makes a division between the richer and poorer members of the audience, expressed in terms of seating, inevitable. The cheapest seat in a *corrida* during the April Fair week in Seville costs nearly three times the price of a cinema ticket, and the cheapest seat in the shade costs more than a good seat to see either of the two first division football teams in Seville. An average working man's lunch in a bar is certainly cheaper than a ticket for the *corrida*. Although one could make a rough correlation between ticket purchase and social class, there are other factors to be considered, for the less well-off *aficionados* will often pay a little extra to sit in the back row in the shade rather than in the main block in the sun. This is not only because it is more comfortable but because it is the accepted practice to attempt to climb the fence dividing the main block from the upper section so as to move forward into the unoccupied seats, and in some *corridas* it is possible to move into the very front rows. Although one can often move from the cheapest seats in the sun to the more expensive seats in the sun and from the cheapest seats in the shade to the more expensive seats in the shade, a large, unclimbable fence prevents one from moving from the sun side to the shade. It is not generally considerations of prestige which govern this buying of the cheapest shade seats by the poorer *aficionado*, but the purely technical criterion that most of the activity in the arena takes place on the shade side and one therefore has a better view. Some areas in the sun actually do go into the shade without them being labelled *sol y sombra*, and many *aficionados* attempt to buy them if they must buy sun-side tickets. If one travels to other towns for *corridas* one soon becomes an expert in where the sun goes and at what time in the various *plazas* of the region, and one buys tickets accordingly.

The affluent buy the expensive front row seats in the shade as much for public display and social prestige as for an *aficionado*'s desire to see the event at close quarters. The extent to which they do so depends on the *corrida*, for it is still extremely prestigious to have a front row shade seat during the famous *corridas* held during the town celebrations in the *Feria de Abril* (April Fair) in Seville. Such seats, because of their high price, usually remain unsold for the less important *corridas* and for the *novilladas* (junior events – for detailed discussion see chapter 2) held most Sundays during the season. I say unsold rather than unoccupied because empty places are soon filled by people who have bought cheaper tickets and have moved forward. For example, although I and a group of pensioners from the club where I researched had season tickets, during the years I was in Seville we only had to occupy those seats for the most popular *corridas* during the fair and on two or three other occasions. On other occasions we could move into the seats in the first few rows.

The traditional literary image has the poor, unruly but 'true' *aficionados* tightly packed in the discomfort of the sun section, and the affluent, less knowledgeable, less committed gentleman spectators in the shade; with the obvious implication that the real spirit of appreciation is to be found in the former. This might be true of the once-a-year *corrida* in a small town, or to some extent in a major *plaza* on a socially prestigious occasion, but from my observations there is not such a rigid division in the level of informed opinion or excitement and interest between the sun and the shade sides. Obviously a social division is reflected, because of the prices of the tickets, but this does not necessarily reflect a division of knowledge or appreciation.

The audience at a *corrida* – sex and age

To obtain a complete picture of the audience composition according to age, sex and social and economic status would have involved a large research team to carry out questionnaire work of such a scope and complexity as to put it beyond the range of the research resources of this study. Neither has it been possible to work from any Spanish surveys, official or otherwise, because they simply do not exist. Although it is therefore difficult to make detailed comments about attendance, it is possible to make some general, impressionistic points (but see chapter ten for comments on the importance of the role of the public).

Attendance at the *corrida* is nor restricted to people of any particular category or group; anyone who purchases a ticket may attend. Middle-aged and older men predominate in any *corrida* audience, but the actual composition on any occasion will vary according to the quality of the programme (this being judged in terms of the reputation of the *matadores* and/or of the ranch from which the bulls have been chosen), the time of year, the *plaza*, and whether it is a *corrida* within a *feria* (a town fair).

While the audience is predominantly male, women do attend *corridas*, but rarely unescorted. A woman accompanies her husband, fiancé or boyfriend rather than her father, uncle, or brother. A woman thus attends as part of a couple which is, in an important sense, on public display. Few commentators, with the exception of the most conservative traditionalists, argue nowadays that women should not attend *corridas* at all. Generally the traditionalists argue that while women most certainly should not be allowed to take an active part in the arena as performers, they do have an important passive role in the audience, gracing the event with their beauty and acting as ideal recipients of the *matador*'s dedications. Although they do comment and make judgement on the *matador*'s performance, women are not expected to shout these out as do the men; this would be regarded as unseemly behaviour. It is the men in the audience who make the public assessments of the men and bulls in the arena.

Children do attend *corridas* but never unaccompanied; they are usually taken by an *aficionado* grandfather, father or uncle. There is a law of 1921 which prohibits the attendance of children, accompanied or otherwise, under the age of fourteen, but this law is rarely observed. A society dedicated to the abolition of the *corrida* has on occasion successfully forced impresarios to comply with this law, but this is rare, and it is expected that the law will actually be repealed.

The *corrida* – signalling the start

About an hour before the start of the *corrida*, the atmosphere begins to build up in front of the *plaza*. People begin to gather to meet friends and to talk about the prospects for a good afternoon, to buy tickets if they don't have them (on days when the ticket office displays the sign '*No Hay Billetes*' ['no tickets'] there is always a busy trade in black-market tickets), to buy cigarettes, cigars, maybe the traditional red carnations for decoration on a suit or dress, a glass of fresh water, a packet of sunflower seeds or a cardboard sunshade. It is always noisy and lively, there is always a throng of people. It is what the Andalusians call *vida* (literally, 'life', but in this context 'liveliness', a proper atmosphere of human socialising), and there is also the sense of excited expectation; all of which creates the proper *ambiente* (atmosphere or emotion) in which the *corrida* should take place.

A few moments before the appointed time for the start, the *presidente* (the president or the presiding official) enters his box, accompanied by one of the veterinary surgeons who inspected the bulls, and a technical assessor, who is usually a retired *matador*. The veterinary surgeon sits on the president's right and the assessor on the left. The function of these two men is to give advice to the president during the *corrida*. There are very strict rules as to who may be president. If the *corrida* takes place in Madrid, it should be the Director General of Security, in other provincial capitals it should be the Civil Govenor and in other towns the mayor. If these officials cannot attend, the responsibility can be delegated to an official of the police force, to an assistant of the mayor or some other suitable person.

In Seville the president at any *corrida* is one of three appointed presidents, all of whom are senior police officials, who take it in turn to preside. Many commentators have complained about this system on the grounds that the president is always a representative of the state and quite often a high ranking one whose role, as the regulations suggest, (Gilpérez García and Fraile Sanz 1972: articles 65 and 66) corresponds to or parallels that of the most important officials in the urban setting, and he is thus an authority figure (rather than an informed but impartial assessor) who may have little of the knowledge or experience needed to carry out the task. The fact that he is a representative of the state has often made him a target of abuse from members of the audience. This was especially so during Franco's rule in Spain, when the president was one of the few officials at whom it was possible to hurl abuse publicly and yet remain relatively safe from exposure in the anonymity of the crowd. Even today it is possible to hear this. To achieve maximum effect, the disgruntled *aficionado*, who thinks that the president has committed an error of judgement, waits for a moment of quiet (usually before the next bull is about to enter) and then lets out a ringing '*¡Señor Presidente. Hijo de la gran puta. Cabrón!*' ('Mr President. Son of a great whore. Cuckold!'), to the amusement of the public and the annoyance of the police who try to spot the culprit. This, during the Franco dictatorship, must have been a potent public insult.

The tasks of the president are: (i) to keep order in the *plaza* (both in the arena and among the audience; (ii) to see that the regulations for the event are adhered to; (iii) to cue the action and sequence of events; and (iv) to reward and punish the performers. Both (iii) and (iv) involve judgement and assessment of qualities of performance, and while he does have two experts with him he is in no way obliged to accept their advice. It should be noted that although the president controls the event once it has started, he has no say in the composition of the event. In contrast the impresario organizes the event and chooses the animals and performers, but has no control over it once it has started.

The *corrida* begins exactly on time (traditionally the only thing which does in Spain) as the president lays a white handkerchief for a few seconds over the balcony of his box. The president's directions are indicated by the colour of the handkerchief shown. White is to signal the start of the event, to change acts (in the sense of telling the performers to finish one set of actions and move on to the next), and to give awards; red is used to order the placing of *banderillas negras* (see below); green to return a defective bull to the corrals; and blue to order the triumphal lap for an exceptionally good bull once it has been killed. The coloured handkerchiefs are the visible expression of the president's decisions; these are then given audible expression by the trumpet calls. The trumpet calls do not vary according to what is being signalled, as do military bugle calls, but remain the same throughout the *corrida*, and one therefore has to have knowledge of the event to understand from the context what has been signalled. In some *plazas* drums accompany the trumpets, but in Seville there is only a single pair of trumpets. The trumpeters do not form a part of the band, neither do they sit with the band; they are positioned above the entrance to the corridor leading to the bull pens (see figure 1), directly facing the presidential box. Although the position for the trumpeters is not the same in all *plazas*, they are always in a position from which they can see the president.

At the beginning of the afternoon it is the band which takes up the president's first signal with the white handkerchief, and as they begin to play the first line of the procession moves into the arena. The whole parade (see figure 3) is led out by the two *alguaciles* – the president's constables, dressed in costumes of the time of Felipe II – who are mounted at this stage of the proceedings. Those in the procession wait as the *alguaciles* advance slowly across the arena to a position below the presidential box to ask his permission to lead the procession forward. They do this by raising their hats; he responds by half-raising himself from his seat and giving a slight bow. The two then make a tour around the arena from opposite sides. Originally the *alguaciles* were responsible for clearing the arena of spectators before the procession, this being necessary because members of the public were able to walk about the arena before the event began. Today this is not permitted, and their sweep of the arena can best be interpreted as the agents of authority taking control of that space. The two return and take up a position at the head of the procession, which has been forming up at the edge of the arena and in the passageway which leads to the *patio de caballos*. The performers make the sign of the cross, turn and salute their companions with the words '*¡Que Dios reparta la suerte!*' ('May God divide the luck!', that is, divide it equally between us). The procession moves out.

The first line, three abreast, after the *alguaciles* are the *matadores*. Viewed from the position of the president, coming towards him on his right is the most senior *matador*, on the far left is the next senior and in the middle is the most junior. The seniority of the *matadores* determines the order of performance and the most senior *matador* acts as the *director de la lidia* (director of the performance). It is his responsibility to liaise with the president if there is a problem, to keep order among the teams, and if one of his companions is seriously injured and is unable to

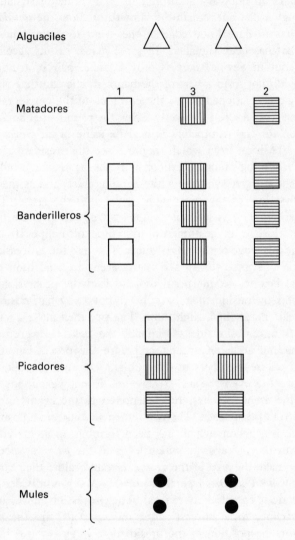

Figure 3 The procession

continue with the performance, then it is his task to kill that bull. Should he be injured himself it is then the responsibility of the next most senior to fulfil these duties. It must be noted, however, that the *director de la lidia* can in no way override the authority of the president.

Behind the three *matadores* come the *banderilleros*, three per team, who walk in single file behind their respective *matadores*; and behind them the *picadores*, two per team, who process in pairs across the arena, the first pair being those of the senior *matador*, and so on. Finally come the mule teams which are used to drag out the dead bulls.

The *alguaciles* lead the parade to the barrier on the far side of the arena where all salute the president by bowing slightly and touching their hats; the president returns the bow. All the *toreros* wear their hats in the procession unless it is the first time they have performed in that particular *plaza*, in which case they parade bareheaded as a mark of respect. The team now separate, remove their dress capes and go into the *callejón*. The dress capes are hung open on the back wall of the *callejón* or, as a mark of honour, they are taken to a special friend in the audience and are spread out in front of him or her.

As the teams disperse and the *picadores* return to the patio, the *alguaciles* come forward once again to a point just below the presidential box to receive the key which opens the gate to the corridor leading to the bull pen; yet another signal of the authority of the president. Traditionally the president should throw the real key and an *alguacil* should attempt to catch it in his hat. This does not happen any more in Seville, where the key is merely a token (it does not actually open the lock) and is handed to the *alguacil* by an official in the *callejón*. The *alguaciles* then gallop to the far side of the arena and give the key to the keeper of the door to the bull pens. They then exit from the arena via the *callejón* to the *patio*, where they leave their horses, and from this moment they remain on foot in the alleyway. At least one of them is always close to the action in the arena to ensure that there is no infringement of the rules and to convey any instructions from the president to those in the arena. They are in contact with the president by means of a telephone connected between his box and the *callejón*.

Music and the events of the *corrida*

From the moment of the first signal of the president, the band (in Seville a brass band with percussion some twenty strong) plays a *pasodoble* a two-step march and dance traditionally associated with the *corrida*, and they continue to play this until the president signals for the first bull to be released. In Seville the band always plays the same *pasodoble*, one dedicated to this *plaza*, but uses a varied repertoire later in the *corrida*. The first signal of the president is the only occasion on which he directs the band to play; at all other times the conductor decides when it will play, although this decision is based on certain norms. The regulations state that the band may play according to the tradition of each *plaza*: in Madrid, for example, it is only played during parade, during any lap of honour and during the removal of the dead bull, but not during the performance. Generally, though, music is played for the parade, whenever the *matador* is performing well, if he decides to place his own *banderillas* (see below), for any laps of honour he might be awarded and when the dead bull is dragged out.

Music is rarely played in the first part of the performance when the bull has just been released, because it is such a short section and the *matador* does not usually engage the animal for a long enough period for there to be any real sense of a sustained performance, even though he may take some fine *lances* (the passes with the cape – see appendix). On only two occasions in my experience of some 250 *corridas* have I heard the band play in this section, and on both occasions it was because the performance was outstanding. The music usually starts in the final section when the *muleta* (a red cloth which is smaller than the *capote*) is used, and then only if the performance is considered to be a fine one. One often reads in press reports of *corridas* that a *matador* was '*premiado*' with music, meaning that the band played as a type of prize (*premio*), an award or mark of approval for a particularly good performance. The music also gives *ambiente* and reinforces the emotion generated by a good performance in the arena. To some extent it actually helps to create that emotion in the first place, for the *matador* usually responds to the music by committing himself even more.

The conductor decides when the band is to play, a decision based on his assessment of the *matador*'s performance, although he may be encouraged by the audience and influenced by their response to the performance. The audience is very quick to criticize and abuse the band if they do not play when they, the audience, consider that there is something worth while happening in the arena. The *matador* cannot ask for music, but on several occasions I witnessed a scene in Seville when the *matador* dedicated a bull to the band, which then began to play almost immediately, much to the amusement of the crowd to whom it was obvious that this was a reciprocation for the dedication and that the dedication itself was designed to secure this response. Music, then, during the performance is a mark of approval, and as soon as the *matador* loses control the music stops, signalling an immediate negative evaluation. The music also stops as the *matador* prepares to kill, here indicating the seriousness of the occasion.

The first bull

As soon as the president signals, again with his white handkerchief, for the first bull to be released, the trumpets sound and the band stops abruptly without even finishing the phrase being played. Out of sight of the audience the door of the pen containing the first bull is swung open as is the gate from the corridor to the arena. Above the gate through which the bull will enter is a board announcing the weight of the bull. Some *plazas* display the registration number of the bull and its name and age, but in Seville most of this information is given on a small poster fixed outside the *plaza*, close to the main gate. In first class *plazas*, just before the bull is released a man standing above the animal and using a long pole pushes a barbed dart, to which are attached the colours of the ranch, into the neck muscle. This decoration of the bull is the first part of a complex process of decorating or adorning it.

The members of the first team have in the meantime picked up the large capes set out by the *mozo de espadas* and prepare to receive this first bull. Normally the assistants make the first cape passes while the *matador* waits near one of the gaps in the fence to note the peculiarities of the animal, its willingness to charge, its favoured side of attack and the other characteristics which will help him decide how to structure his performance.

According to the regulations the *banderilleros* should only use one hand to hold the cape when engaging the bull. This style is known as *de brega* (from the verb '*bregar*', 'to struggle' or 'to slog away at something'). The aim is not to create artistically or aesthetically pleasing passes but merely to gain the bull's attention, to persuade it to follow the cape and thus to manoeuvre it to that part of the arena where it is needed. The specification of this one-handed style ensures that the assistants should not be able to outshine their *matador* by making graceful passes which might possibly be better than his; the utilitarian role of the *banderillero* is thus emphasized. In fact the assistants do usually use both hands, but without attempting to be graceful, because although the *de brega* style is not artistic in the sense that the *matador*'s passes are, it is extremely difficult to manage the cape with one hand. It is, indeed, so rare to see an assistant performing *de brega*, and doing it well, that it *does* become a performance worthy of praise and is greeted with warm applause from the audience. If an assistant attempted to make fine passes he would be severely criticized by the audience and would probably be censured by the *matador* for showing himself off rather than working to highlight the *matador*'s performance.

The playing of the bull by the assistants lasts only a few minutes and ceases as the *matador* steps into the arena and tells the assistants to leave the bull for him. Armed with his few moments' knowledge of the bull's characteristics, he begins to construct his performance. The bull is still fresh and disorientated and it requires a fine sense of timing to be able to drift the cape a few centimetres from the bull's horns without the animal catching it, and at the same moment to slow the bull down, during the course of the *lance* (pass with the large cape – see appendix). *Aficionados* will often marvel that whereas most artists have time to reflect on the material which they will use for their creation, and most performers (dancers, for example) have time for rehearsal, the *matador* has almost no time to prepare his performance or understand how to mould his partner. Within a few moments he has to decide how best to create that carefully sculpted relationship between himself and the bull, a relationship mediated by the cape.

Instead of letting the assistants play the bull for them, certain *matadores*, who base their style on a more than average supply of courage and daring, will sometimes receive the bull on their knees near the exit from the pens. This is a hazardous enterprise because of the uncertainty of how the bull will come into the arena. However, if well timed the effect is most dramatic, as the *matador* at the last moment pulls the cape up off the sand and over his shoulder with one hand, a movement which takes the bull close past his head and kneeling body. If it is mistimed the result can be disastrous, for the man is in a position in which it is difficult to control the situation.

The president decides how long this section will last (it is rarely more than a few minutes) and he then signals for the *picadores* to enter. The first *picador* takes up a position on the shade side of the arena a little to the left of the president's box, and the second takes up a position opposite him across the arena. Two concentric circles are marked out by dye or paint in the sand of the arena; one of these is 7 m, and the other 9 m, from the barrier. The *picador* must place himself between the barrier and the 7 m line (but close to the line) and the bull must be manoeuvred by cape movements from wherever it in in the arena and placed, facing the horse, between the centre of the arena and the 9 m line. There is thus a minimum distance of 2 m between the bull and the *picador* when the bull charges. If the bull is willing to charge from a greater distance this is even better, for it is a sign that it is a strong and aggressive animal and as such it is much admired by the audience.

The horse is largely covered by a jointed set of thick padding so that it is not injured by the bull. This has not always been the case; until 1928 horses had no protection and it was common for several to be killed during the course of a *corrida*. The *picador* also has some protection on both legs, in the form of metal plates extending from the thigh to the toe. He is armed with a pike consisting of a spike fixed to the end of a long pole. There are regulations about the length of the spike, which varies according to the category of the event, the spike in a full *corrida* being longer than that for a *novillada* (see next chapter for details of the differences in these events). All the spikes have a triangular metal point above which is a crossbar which prevents the spike being pushed in beyond the regulation depth.

The task of the *picador* is to provoke the bull into charging the horse by calling it, by waving the pike or by clanking his armoured leggings to attract its attention, and as it approaches, to push the spike into the *murillo* (the enlarged hump on the neck). The corresponding *matador*'s responsibility is to manoeuvre the bull for the charge and to remove it when he thinks that it has received enough *castigo* ('punishment' – see appendix for a discussion of this term), but he may leave this task to one of his assistants.

The regulations state that the bull should receive the spike three separate times. After the first wounding it should be led away from the horse and lined up for a new charge. It is assumed that, at the end of the first charge, the animal has not yet associated the charge with the pain from the spike, but that on the second charge it has made this connection; and so if it charges for a third time it is interpreted as doing so deliberately, thus showing itself to be a brave animal. A sign of an especially good bull is if it is willing to lower its head and push hard when in contact with the horse, for it is felt that such an animal is freely opening its neck to the attack of the *picador* and is not attempting to reduce the pain it is suffering by closing up the wound. This section of the event is particularly important for the bull breeder because it is here that an essential quality of his animals is revealed, something which is important in connection with the breeding of future stock. The president can order the *picador* to withdraw even if the bull has not received three spikes if he considers the animal to be excessively weakened. The *matador* is also able to ask the president to order the withdrawal of the *picador* for the same reason. This is done by the *matador* turning to the president and raising his hat to him; the president is not obliged to grant this request.

A *matador* may ask for the withdrawal of the *picadores* because he wants the bull to have enough strength for the rest of the performance, and this can be lost if the bull suffers too much at the hands of the *picador*. A *picador* who places the spike illegally or who pushes into the animal excessively can severely damage it, a fact which some *matadores* find to their advantage. It was reported to me that *matadores* will occasionally tell their *picadores* in private to weaken the bull as much as possible. This will be very unpopular with the crowd and at the time the *matador* might well be yelling at the *picador* and telling him to leave it alone. The *picador*, however, ignores this theatricality and continues the punishment.

On the second and third charges the *matador* may allow each of his fellow *matadores* in turn to manoeuvre the bull into position and to remove it from the horse, an opportunity which allows them to attempt a few elegant cape passes; this is particularly important if they have been able to do nothing with their own bull. The removal of the bull from the horse and the series of passes to line it up for the next charge is known as a *quite* (from the verb '*quitar*', 'to take away' or 'to remove').

The detailed technicalities of placing the spike need not detail us here. Suffice it to say that the intention is to weaken the bull's neck muscle in order that the *matador* can work closer to it because the head is held lower. The spike does inflict a considerable wound and this releases blood, which tires the animal and consequently reduces some of its strength and makes it a little more manageable.

A bull which shies away from the *picador* and does not receive the spike at all is considered unworkable and therefore unfit for the proper sequence of events. In such a case the president signals for *banderillas negras* (*banderillas* are the decorated barbed sticks which are placed in the bull, described more fully below, and *banderillas negras* are black and have longer and double harpoon points) to be placed, a task for one of the *banderilleros* in the team. Because the spike on these is longer than normal, some of the blood-letting normally achieved by the *picador* can be achieved by this means. More importantly, however, they signify unfitness in another sense, in that the bull is not behaving like a proper fighting bull, and they constitute a stigma which the bull has to carry for the rest of the event. Not only is the bull thus stigmatized but the *banderillas negras* also denote great disgrace for the breeder.

At the end of this section, again signalled by the president's handkerchief and the trumpets, the *picadores* leave the arena in an anti-clockwise direction (although the one closest to the *patio de caballos* may turn directly into that gate) thus passing under the presidential box, and they salute him as they pass. Later in the *corrida*, when the *matador*'s second bull is to be spiked, there is a change of *picadores* so that the one who received the first bull does not receive the second, but instead takes the reserve place.

Once the arena gates have been shut behind the *picadores*, the president signals for the foot assistants to place the *banderillas* (literally, little flags). These are wooden sticks 70 cm long and tipped with a small harpoon-like spike 6 cm long that holds the *banderilla* in the hide of the animal (unlike the spike of the *picador*, which is pushed into the animal and then withdrawn). The wooden sticks, which are always placed as pairs, are individually wrapped around with bright coloured paper, each of the two having the same colours. The regulations state that three pairs of *banderillas* will be placed, but the president can use his discretion to reduce this, and the *matador* can appeal for this section to be stopped short of the regulation number if he feels that the bull is being overly weakened by the amount of running it has to do in this act.

This act is considerably more lively than the previous one because the *banderillas* are slammed into the bull with both man and animal on the run. The first *banderillero* takes one of the sticks in each hand and goes towards where the other assistants are controlling the bull. The assistants attempt to line the bull up so that it is facing the *banderillero* but at a considerable distance from him. Behind the *banderillero* one of the other *matadores* moves his cape to attract the attention of the bull, and behind the bull and slightly to one side of it is another assistant who is ready to protect his colleague's exit after placing the sticks. Once the *banderillero* has the attention of the bull he begins to run towards it and the bull should begin to charge at him. The *banderillero* has his arms raised with the sticks held just below his own head height with the spiked ends pointing down. At the moment of contact the man should have his feet together on the sand and should lean over the horns to place the *banderillas* in the neck muscle of the bull. Having done so he should be able to spin to safety along the flank of the animal. If the *banderillas* are well placed the bull is almost stopped in its tracks, and after a few quick steps to get clear of the *banderillero* should be able to walk calmly away without the bull following him. This is the ideal and rarely happens; what is more common is for the bull to pursue the man until it is distracted by the capes of the other assistants, who are strategically placed to protect their colleague, or until the man reaches the safety of the barrier.

The technical reason for placing *banderillas* is to enliven the bull after the sluggishness induced by the loss of blood and the battering it received from the *picadores*; it is also claimed that the careful placing of the *banderillas* can correct certain defects in the way the animal charges. For interpretive purposes it is also significant that this section constitutes a further adornment of the bull. The significance of the colours used to decorate the wooden sticks of the *banderillas* (as opposed to the *banderillas* themselves decorating the bull, a point which will be dealt with later) is explicitly recognized. If the *corrida* takes place on an important regional or local day, then the regional colours might be used on one pair with the Spanish national colours and other local colours on the second and third. As an example, I was told that should the British Queen attend a *corrida* in Seville the three sets of colour combinations would be a red, white, and blue pair for Great Britain, red, yellow and red for Spain, and green, white and green for Andalusia. Black, as was mentioned above always signals disgrace.

A *matador* has the right to place his own *banderillas* but few include this in their repertoire. However, if a *matador* does decide to place his own then he is likely to place all white ones and this, combined with the fact that *banderilleros* never place single colour white *banderillas*, marks the process as something special. Colours other than white may be used by *matadores* placing their own, but this is rare and might well suggest that a special message is being communicated. For example, a Mexican *matador*, performing in Seville, placed *banderillas* with Mexican national colours and other pairs with Spanish national colours.

If a *matador* decides to place his own *banderillas*, then a combination of elements marks this as a special occasion. He removes his hat before performing, in contrast to the assistants who always wear theirs. He has no assistants in the arena to help him guide the bull to where he wants it (or to help him in case of difficulties) and this positioning of the bull becomes a major part of the performance. In all, the whole of this section becomes more elaborate and stylish, it lasts much longer than normal and, something which is very special, the band plays the entire time that the *matador* is performing whatever the quality of that performance.

The assistants usually place *banderillas* in an unstylish and workman-like manner and avoid any risk to themselves. One can, however, see the pairs placed finely and skilfully by particular assistants and these individuals are often well known. If the *banderillas* are well placed by an assistant the audience will readily applaud, but in keeping with his status he may not acknowledge the applause until instructed to do so by his *matador*. The applause here is for a skilled craftsman, rather than for an artist as in the case of the *matador* as *banderillero*.

The *banderillas* having been placed the president signals the commencement of the final section, in which the *matador* plays and finally kills the bull. If it is his first bull of the afternoon the *matador* must obtain the president's permission to kill it. He exchanges his large cape for the *muleta*, a large, almost circular piece of red flannel with a yellow lining, folded over a short stick which is fixed into it in such a way that the cloth falls in a half circle on either side of it. The word *muleta* literally means 'crutch', and in this context refers to the support given to the material by the stick. With this and his hat and sword in hand the *matador* approaches a point in the arena below the presidential box, and with the hat held high in his right hand he salutes the president with a few words, such as, '*Buenas tardes, señor, con su permiso...*'). ('Good afternoon, sir, with your permission...'). He then leaves his hat with his *mozo* and prepares for the final section of the performance and the kill.

This greeting to the president constitutes the obligatory *brindis*. The word is from the verb '*brindar*', 'to toast, to dedicate, to offer or present', even though it actually constitutes a formal request for permission to continue, an imposed sign of deference to authority, rather than a true dedication, and the *matador* certainly does not dedicate the bull to the president. Once he has completed this formal procedure there is nothing to prevent the *matador* dedicating the same bull to another person, and with his second bull he does not have to make any acknowledgement of the president. It is worth distinguishing between the obligatory *brindis* to the president and the personal one, which is more elaborate. The correct form of this is for the *matador* to approach the section of the barrier nearest to the chosen person, to lean across the alleyway and to make a short speech, in which he explains what has prompted him to choose that person and offers his performance and the death of the bull to the dedicatee.[6] He then turns his back to the person and, over his right shoulder, he throws the person his hat, which he or she keeps until the end of this performance. When the bull is dead he collects his hat and traditionally (although this does not seem to be the case now) receives a small gift from this person later.

If the *matador* dedicates to the public as a whole he steps into the centre of the arena, holds the hat high in his right hand and turns a complete circle, thus saluting the whole audience; once again he throws his hat over his right shoulder. If the hat lands with the brim down this is a sign of good luck; if it lands with the brim up this is a sign of bad luck. The 'true' dedication involves the *matador* not even bothering to look back at the hat. Some place it in a very deliberate fashion on the ground as if they were making sure that good luck accompanies them, and others lean down to turn it the way they want it to fall – brim downwards; both of these actions provoke an amused response in the crowd. The most elaborate variation I personally have witnessed was when the hat was thrown over the shoulder and landed brim uppermost, at which the *matador* leaned down, took a handful of sand, kissed it and, without changing the position of the hat, placed the sand in it. In this little ritual he seemed to be paying homage to the inherent good nature of the place or the ground on which he was performing and, by implication, the people associated with it.

A *matador* will only make a personal dedication or a general dedication if he feels sure that he is likely to produce a good performance; a personal dedication followed by a fiasco in the arena can make the dedicatee look foolish. It is also possible that an audience will refuse a dedication by whistling and booing, if they feel that the bull is not of a sufficient quality to be dedicated.

The dedication over, the *matador*, using the sword and the *muleta*, begins the final section, in which he attempts to develop the aesthetic quality of the performance and his domination of the bull before killing it. The regulations state that he should use a steel sword throughout this section but he can claim on medical grounds (usually an injured wrist is given as the reason) an exemption from this and permission to use an imitation sword made of wood and painted to look like steel, only changing it for the real one when he intends to kill. The real sword is heavy and many *matadores* find it uncomfortable to use, but those who use the real one throughout argue that by not having to change swords at the last moment they do not have to interrupt the rhythm of the performance.

The timing of this last section is most rigidly controlled by the president; from the time of picking up the *muleta* and sword the *matador* has fifteen minutes in which to perform and kill. If the bull is not dead after ten minutes the president signals an *aviso* (a warning) and the trumpets sound out; they sound again three minutes later to indicate that there are two minutes left, and finally when those two minutes are up. If the bull is still not dead at this point the *matador* must retire to the barrier and the bull is lead out of the arena to be killed in the corrals, or, if it is unable to walk that far, the *puntillero* (literally 'he of the *puntillo*', a broad-bladed slaughterman's knife) of the *plaza* will attempt to kill it in the arena. This is the ultimate signal of disgrace for the *matador* for it indicates that he has failed completely for his task. This happens rarely and in all the *corridas* I have attended I have only witnessed it once.

As previously mentioned, music is played during this section if the *matador*'s performance is judged by the crowd and the band to be a good one. The first indication of approval from the audience is a general murmur of appreciation with the odd cry of '*¡Muy bien!*' ('Well done!') coupled with applause; if the emotion increases, '*¡Muy bien!*' will give way to the famous cry associated with the *corrida* and with *flamenco*: '*¡Olé!*'. Although this means 'well done' or 'just right', when associated with a performance it is a spontaneous shout, not as conscious an evaluative judgement as 'well done'. '*¡Olé!*' is the unpremeditated emotional response to something fine. As one friend described it, it is something which simply burst out, '*que no se piensa*' ('which is not thought'); and another said that '"*Olé*" *es algo que no pasa por el cerebro*' ('"*Olé*" is something which does not pass through the brain'), which emphasizes that it is a product of emotional rather than rational processes (see chapter 4 for further discussion).

The audience is also quick to abuse and to express its disapproval; in fact throughout the *corrida* there is a continual torrent of praise, abuse, criticism, insult and general comment from the audience, directed at both the animal and human actors. A bull, for example, will be reviled for being ugly, cowardly or treacherous. (A detailed consideration of these qualities is given in chapter 6.) As well as criticizing the *matador* for incompetence, the audience also insults him by suggesting that he should not be there at all. The arena is the place for *toreros* and a *torero* must be truly male, so the insults make use of sexual imagery which denies the *matador* his maleness and hence, by implication, his right to be in the arena at all. (This point will be more fully considered in chapter 9.) The public in Seville is also famous throughout the taurine world for one other reaction; total silence. There is a positive silence, one of expectation, in that *plaza* when it is thought that the *matador* is preparing to do something extraordinary; but the negative silence, when the *matador* is performing so badly that it is not even worth booing, is more enduring. People do not call out; they don't even take any notice of what is going on in the arena. It is as if the *matador* were not there, and most *matadores* said that they preferred booing or criticism to this silence which denies their existence.

To return to the action in the arena: although the assistants will keep the bull under control while the *matador* is going through the ceremony of dedication, when he is ready to take over they leave the arena. The *matador* performs alone at this time and the assistants stand just in the *burladeros* waiting to rush to his assistance should he get into difficulty, or to bring the bull towards him should it flee to the far side of the arena. The *matador* has a repertoire of passes from which to draw those for his performance. Individual passes, however, are not enough to constitute a good performance: what the audience is looking for is the performance of the passes necessary to dominate the animal, and the intelligent and graceful linking of one pass to another to form a smooth whole. In terms of his postures and comportment in the arena the *matador* should ideally combine tranquility with flexible grace; the audience not only criticize the *matador* who dodges around to avoid the bull but also the one who stands artificially rigid. It is said that ideally his back should be straight but flexible, his chin tucked in towards the chest, the waist flexible, the leg facing the charge of the animal advanced, and the wrist supple so that the bull can be guided gracefully past the *matador*'s body with the *muleta*.

As well as the passes themselves, there are also flourishes called *adornos* (from the very '*adornar*', meaning 'to decorate or embellish') at the end of a good set of passes. Some *adornos* are regarded by traditionalists as somewhat vulgar; for example, kneeling in front of the bull and biting the end of one of the horns or stroking the forehead of the animal. A particularly famous *adorno*, invented by Reverte in 1910 and popularized by Arruza in 1944, is the *teléfono*, in which the *matador* leans his elbow on the forehead of the bull with his hand on his ears as though he were making a telephone call. The most classical *adorno* is a proud, almost disdainful posturing with the chest thrust out towards the stilled bull; the *matador*, with an almost contemptuous look, then turns his back on the animal and swaggers away – a movement which demonstrates the complete domination of the animal by the man.

A *matador* will watch the bull very carefully during the performance with the muleta because he needs to balance the increasing tiredness of the animal against his desire to make as many passes as possible with it. He cannot wear the bull out completely because at the moment he decides to kill it the bull must still have enough strength to charge at him. This is only really a consideration with bulls with which a *matador* can perform well. With many it is difficult to perform because of their quality, and with many the *matador* is able to do little because of his own inabilities; in either case he is likely to keep this section as short as possible.

The kill should be performed when the animal has been stilled and *cuadrado* (squared up) by the *matador*. The *cuadrado* position with the front feet together is important, because it causes the shoulder blades to open, and there is thus a gap formed through which the *matador* attempts to push the sword in order to reach the vital organs. The *matador* sights along his sword and moves the *muleta* towards the bull's face and to the right across his own body. The movement encourages the bull to charge in that direction as the man leans over the horns to plunge the sword in and spin to safety on his right leg along the right flank of the bull.

If the sword has gone in correctly and it seems that the bull will die quickly, the *matador* orders all the assistants away (they usually come into the arena as soon as the sword has gone in) and remains close to the bull until it falls. A classic posture for the *matador* at this moment is to have the *muleta* folded under his left arm and his right arm extended towards the bull, a position somewhat reminiscent of a flamenco dancer at the end of a dance, and indicating the end of his performance. Some *matadores* at this moment stroke the curly hair on the forehead of the dying bull in an almost affectionate manner, as though they were saying a fond farewell to the animal; indeed many said to me that they feel this at the end of a good performance, in which the bull has been less an enemy to be overcome and more a collaborator with whom they have established an artistic partnership.

If the animal is still on his feet and it is obvious that the sword thrust has been ineffective, then the *matador* or one of his assistants must retrieve the sword and start again; he cannot simply thrust in another sword. If on the other hand the sword has been effective but, although almost ready to die, the bull needs a *coup de grâce*, then the *matador* uses a *descabello* (a sword-like implement with a short crossbar some 8 cm from the tip, the tip itself being a sharp-pointed broad blade) for the task. He and the assistants encourage the bull to lower its head by flinging their capes close to the ground under its nose and, once the neck is extended, the *matador* thrusts the *descabello* vertically down into a spot at the top of the neck, severing the spinal cord as he does so. The bull should fall immediately although some *matadores* need several thrusts with the *descabello*.

Even if the bull falls cleanly, somebody needs to finish it off to ensure that it is completely dead before it is dragged out of the arena. This task is accomplished with the broad-bladed knife already referred to, the *puntillo*, which is pushed into the same spot as the *descabello*. The *matador* is not responsible for this; it is a task to be performed by one of his team or by someone hired by the impresario. In Seville a *puntillero* is employed and is dressed in the costume of a foot assistant. In some *plazas* the *puntillero* is not dressed in any particular costume and is usually a local slaughterman or butcher hired for the day. While this is going on, one of the assistants removes the sword from the bull and hands it to the *matador*, who slightly raises it and bows to the president as he crosses the arena.

There is a graded set of awards at the end of each individual performance if it is judged to have been a good one. The simplest is for the public to cheer and applaud and for the *matador* to step into the arena to acknowledge this; if he has performed badly the crowd will boo and whistle and he will stay in the shelter of the *callejón*. If the applause is prolonged he will collect his hat and large working cape and take a lap of honour with his *banderilleros*. The next step is the award of physical trophies – the bull's ears and tail, awarded separately. Technically the only parts of the bull which may normally be cut and handed to the *matador* are the ears (see Gilpérez García and Fraile Sanz 1972: article 68), in exceptional cases the tail may be awarded but it is totally prohibited for hooves to be cut as awards. The public decides whether the first ear shall be awarded by waving their handkerchiefs. If the majority of the audience do so then the president *must* award this ear. The second ear is entirely the president's to award, and although he may take note of the reaction of the audience and the advice of his assessors he is in no way obligated to accede to their requests. If the public does not ask for the first ear to be given the president may not award the second ear however much he might think it is merited. Despite the fact that it is the president who decides on the award and an assistant who physically detaches the ear from the bull, in common usage it is said to be the *matador* who cuts the ears of a bull. Meeting friends in a bar one might ask if Curro cut ears in Seville that afternoon; one does not ask if he was 'awarded' ears.

It was mentioned earlier that members of the audience have always enjoyed shouting abuse at the president, who is a representative of state authority. Quite often this sort of attack is because the president has not awarded an ear despite the fact that the majority of the audience are demanding it; something which is a common enough occurrence. If he refused to do so despite the protest of the crowd there will be vigorous applause for the *matador*, who might well have to take two laps of honour, and then, just before the arrival of the new bull, there will be an outbreak of whistling, booing and abuse directed at the president. On the other hand, in minor *plazas* or where there are weak presidents the assistants can often force a decision on the president by cutting the ears and then holding them up for his approval. Although the number of ears that a *matador* cuts gives some indication of the success of his performance during the season, *aficionados* know that the quality of the audience in a *plaza* determines how easy it is to cut ears there. In some *plazas* where there is a regular attendance of dedicated *aficionados* there will be far more exacting standards than in others, and so, for example, a performance which was awarded two ears in Marbella on the holiday coast might have achieved little more than applause in Seville or Madrid.

The highest ranking trophies are presidential and thus official. This status is reflected in the article in the regulations which states that if, once in possession of a trophy, the *matador* takes any notice of a minority in the audience which disagrees with the award, and throws the trophy on the ground, he will be fined (Gilpérez García and Fraile Sanz 1972: article 68). In other words, public contempt of the president's decisions can be punished. The *matador* cannot side with a section of the audience against authority and he cannot show his disagreement with the presidential decision by ridding himself of the award. One perfectionist *matador* did, however, manage to do exactly that in the 1979 season in Seville without being fined. He was awarded two ears, an award which he apparently thought was too great for the performance he had just given. He accepted both ears and bowed his thanks to the president; he then placed one ear on the fence and bowed again as if to say 'Thank you, but I really do not deserve the honour you do me', and he made the lap of honour with only one.

The president signals for the awards with his white handkerchief and one of the assistants cuts them; the trumpets do not sound on this occasion. The trophy or trophies are handed to one of the constables (yet another signal of the official status of the award), who presents them to the *matador*. They both remove their hats and embrace, and the *matador* bows to the president before beginning his lap of honour. The ears are rarely kept by the *matador* unless for some reason the *corrida* has been of particular significance for him; they are usually thrown to members of the audience. During the lap of honour objects are thrown to the *matador*. Some of these he picks up himself and throws back to the owners; some are picked up by the assistants and handed to the *matador* to be thrown back; and some are thrown back directly by them. It would seem that at least part of the explanation here is that it is almost like having the autograph of a famous person – the *matador* has 'signed' it by touching it, and in a sense he has made that object special. Traditionally wineskins are thrown; these are drunk from and returned. The wide-brimmed Andalusian hat is also an appropriate object to throw and have returned, while cigars and flowers are kept by the *matador*. Nowadays many other objects are thrown, including articles of clothing, handbags, and presents of various kinds.

Before this lap of honour can begin the dead bull must be removed from the arena. The *banderillas* and ranch colours are pulled out and the animal is hitched to a set of chains dragged by one of the mule teams. If the bull's performance is judged to have been exceptionally good it might be awarded a lap of honour, once again the petition for this comes from the crowd and is authorized by the president showing a blue handkerchief, on which people will stand and applaud the bull; something which enhances the breeder's reputation. If this happens the breeder, if he is present, or the foreman usually steps into the arena to acknowledge the applause. Such a lap of honour is rare, though, and the bull is normally taken directly to the butchery department. Its departure from the arena is often marked by applause if it was thought to have performed well, and whistles and jeers if it did not live up to expectation or if it behaved in a particularly treacherous manner.

In some *plazas* and on some special occasions the meat goes to a charity, but normally the impresario sells it to offset some of the cost of the bull. This can only recoup a fraction of what he paid for the live animal, because the main value is in the pedigree that produces fighting ability, a quality which disappears as soon as the bull dies. The carcass is cleaned and jointed into six, and the parts are weighed in order to get a complete weight for the bull. There is an expected ratio between the dressed meat weight and the live weight; if the difference is too great it suggests some malpractice, such as forced feeding or forced water intake at the last moment in order to make the bull appear larger and to make its weight acceptable for the *plaza*. If this is suspected an investigation might be held. The heads of the dead animals are set aside so that the veterinary surgeons can examine the teeth, for this is the only reliable way to check the true age. Fines can be imposed on breeders who are thus shown to have supplied bulls which do not truly conform to the regulations. Also at this time if it is suspected that the horns of any of the bulls have been tampered with they are cut from the head, sealed in boxes and sent to an official veterinary laboratory where they can be examined under a microscope. This form of malpractice can also be fined.

As the bull is dragged from the arena there are a few preparations before the next one is released. The sand must be raked smooth by a team of workmen employed by the impresario, and if the circles have been obliterated in parts they are repainted from a watering can. Any faeces from the horses or the bull are collected, as is any excessively bloodied sand. Sometimes carpenters are needed to strengthen a section of the barrier quickly if it has been weakened by the bull crashing into it.

Once the president is satisfied that all is in order he shows his white handkerchief, the trumpets sound and the next bull is released into the arena to be played by the second *matador* and his team. For the rest of the afternoon the three *matadores* take turns to give their performances.

At the end of the afternoon, enthusiastic supporters of a *matador* who has been exceptionally good may attempt to seize their hero and carry him on their shoulders for a lap of honour. The maximum honour is for him to be carried out of the plaza through the *puerta principe*. It is a rare honour and, once again, it is only the president who can order the gates to be opened, something he will only do if the *matador* has cut a minimum of two ears during the afternoon.

The most usual way for the *corrida* to finish is for the teams to form up and walk across the arena, bowing to the president as they do so. There is no formal parade and the teams do not keep to the same pattern as at the beginning; a *matador* will leave as soon as his team is together. The *picadores* do not join because they are always on the far side of the arena near the horse *patio*. As they cross the arena the *matador* walks slightly ahead of his team; they have their dress capes folded inside out over their arms and they often carry their hats. If a *matador*'s performance is judged to have been extremely poor, members of the audience might well throw cushions at him. Although regarded as bad taste by most *aficionados*, it is certainly an added piece of entertainment for many.

The *corrida* officially finishes when the president leaves his seat. For the public the *corrida* is completely over, and they go home or to bars and clubs to discuss the afternoon. The *matador* returns to his hotel to shower, change, relax or move on. The president must complete the official papers relating to the afternoon's proceeding. All details of the animals, the names of the performers, trophies, fines and any unusual incidents are recorded to be sent to the controlling government departments. All that remains is for the *plaza* assistants to clean up and the butchers to finish their work.

2

Related bull events

It has been suggested by some commentators that there is a pervasive spirit of *taurofilia* (love of bulls) in Spain. This might appear to be a strange characterization but there is a significant element of truth in it, for throughout Spain there are events based on contests between humans and bulls which constitute an essential central feature of many of their days of celebration. Such events take an enormous variety of forms, especially those in which members of the community and bulls confront each other in the sealed off streets and squares of towns and villages. Although they all have two essential elements in common – that they take place in an urban setting (or at least in the zone of human habitation) and that the central feature is a confrontation and contest between humans and animals – they cannot easily be analysed or compared as varieties of a single cultural phenomenon without detailed consideration of the local context. It is possible, however, to point to a fundamental difference between those which are formal professional events, governed by rules and marked by elaborate ceremony, in which there is a distinction between the performers and the public, and those which might be equally complex and rich in terms of cultural resonances but which are regionally and locally specific and make no such performer/public distinction. In this section the aim is to give a brief account of some of the major *formal* events, and the emphasis will be on those which have structural elements similar to those of the *corrida de toros*. The central concern here is to set the *corrida* in this wider context in order to provide a point to refer back to when examining the significance of it in the context of celebration and *fiesta*. The events dealt with here will also be referred to in the following chapter, which is a historical outline of the *corrida*.

Corrida de novillos or *novillada*

Corrida de novillos literally means 'the running of young bulls', *novillos* being three- or four-year-old animals, whereas the *corrida de toros* are four- or five-year-olds. Although the formal term is *corrida de novillos*, the usual way to refer to this event is by the popular term *novillada*.

In outward appearance there is very little difference between a *novillada* and a *corrida*, and untrained observers would probably fail to be able to tell which they were watching. The only significant difference comes in the *novilladas sin picadores* (*novillada* without the mounted assistants), the most junior form of the professional event, in which those performing will normally be very young and the bulls really no more than large calves. In the *novillada con picadores* (*novillada* with the mounted assistants), the differences from a full *corrida* are that the bulls are younger and lighter and that slightly deformed animals may be used, something which is not permissible in a *corrida*. *Novillo* bulls which have damaged or deformed horns can be used, as can bulls which are blind in one eye, and these are announced as *desecho de tienta* (rejected from the testing) on the posters advertising the event (for details of this testing see chapter 6).

Just as the bulls used in *novilladas* are not full grown, so too the *matadores* who perform in them are not yet fully fledged. They are known as *novilleros*, or officially as *matadores de novillos* (killers of junior bulls). Although they have not yet taken the graduation ceremony (see chapter 7) and attained the full status of *matadores de toros*, they do not dress or perform in any way differently from full *matadores*.

The *novillada* has not always been simply a junior form of the *corrida de toros*. Prior to the twentieth century, *novilladas* often involved comic or pantomime elements, women were allowed to participate in them and generally *novilladas* were not treated with the seriousness that they are today. De Cossío (Vol. I: 658), points out that it is difficult to differentiate in the reports prior to the eighteenth century between the various forms of the *fiestas de toros* (celebrations with bulls), and it is particularly difficult to differentiate between *corridas* and *novilladas*. Generally, many different forms of caping of bulls in *plazas* of unimportant villages and towns were called *novilladas*. Often in these the bulls were caped by non-professionals, had their horns padded and were not killed. Before the middle of the eighteenth century, such events were usually held off-season from the *corridas*, in the winter or late autumn, and it was only in the late eighteenth century that they came to be held in the summer.

De Cossio (Vol 1: 660) claims that an important element in the development of the serious treatment of *novilladas* was a programme in 1801 in which the bulls were announced as *con puntas* (literally 'with points', meaning that the bulls' horns were not blunted or padded). Even though they still contained elements of masque and pantomime until the mid-nineteenth century, *novilladas* gradually came to be regarded as the junior event to the *corrida* and the event in which future *matadores* began to learn their craft.

The *corrida de toros* commands respect as the most serious and impressive of all bull events in Spain, and as such the ideal is for a town or village to celebrate an important day by staging one. Nowadays, however, this is virtually impossible for any but the larger towns because the costs are so high. For example, six bulls from a ranch with a reasonable reputation could easily cost £20,000, and a top ranking *matador de toros* performing in a major plaza could command between £5,000 and £25,000 for an afternoon. Of course, less impressive bulls and *matadores* who are not stars are not so expensive, but they are still usually too expensive for a small town. As Boado and Cebolla write: 'Only the saints of important towns enjoyed the privilege of a formal *corrida de toros*. The villages on the whole contented themselves with *novilladas*' (1976: 42).

Throughout the season in Seville, although *corridas* are held to celebrate important days, it is *novilladas* and not *corridas* which are held virtually every Sunday; once again this is because the cost of mounting *corridas* is prohibitive, even in a city the size of Seville. *Aficionados* will attend most of these to look at the new generation of *matadores* but many Spaniards who are only casually interested will attend few *novilladas*, which feature almost unknown performers. Numbers at *novilladas* will be swollen by the summer tourists, who attend just to see a 'bullfight', the most famous of Spanish spèctacles. For them the difference between a *novillada* and a *corrida* is irrelevant; it is the fact that it is a 'bullfight' event which is important. In midsummer in Seville, when most of the Sevillanos have left the town and gone to the mountains or to the coast to avoid the worst of the heat, the programmes are not of enough interest to encourage the casual attender into the *plaza*, and the tourists can almost outnumber the Spaniards. If the programme is good, however, one can expect the *plaza* to be quite full. Indeed, if the *novilleros* performing have a particularly interesting record the *plaza* can be fuller than for a *corrida de toros*.

Toreo cómico

Toreo cómico (comic *toreo*) is not simply a comic version of the *corrida*. With its mixture of musical numbers, sometimes some dances, pantomime, slapstick and the playing of young cows or bulls, the event seems to contain at least some of the elements and to resemble the form of the nineteenth-century *novilladas* mentioned above, except that the modern event uses calves rather than *novillos*. All the important *ferias* and some of the smaller ones which have *corridas* have one performance of this pantomime event, but it is rarely found outside the context of *feria*. The most famous company which performs in Spain and many Latin American countries is that of *El Bombero Torero y Sus Enanitos* (The Fireman *Torero* and his Dwarves). Three or four calves may be killed during the afternoon in an event which has elements of slapstick, and one of the sections in which the dwarves perform is a complex parody of a *corrida*.[1]

There is one section which is more serious than the rest, in which a slightly larger calf is released for an *aspirante* (aspiring *torero*) or a very junior *novillero* who wears a full suit of lights. The form of this section is exactly the same as that for a *novillada* without *picadores*, and the president controls the sequence of events in this section in the same way as he would in a *novillada*. This part of the afternoon, *la parte seria* (the 'serious part') as it is referred to in the regulations, should occur at the beginning of the event, and the *aspirante* and assistants must process into the arena ahead of the other performers of the comic section.

One important section of the comic event includes such figures as a fireman, a Chinaman, an American baseball player and Charlie Chaplin playing and killing a couple of calves. Although rules govern what may be done to the calves these rules are often not adhered to in this section; *banderillas* might be thrown at the animal in the way that darts are thrown at a dartboard, or they might be placed in the calf as one of the characters leaps over it and the animals are often manhandled.[2] The kill is performed in ways which would be completely prohibited in a *corrida*; for example, the performer might hold the animal while he puts the sword in, or he might even push the sword in and out in time to the music.

A major section of the event is that in which the dwarves (and they are actually congenital dwarves) perform a parody of a *corrida*. They wear suits of lights and the '*picadores*' ride hobbyhorses, using brooms instead of pikes. The comic *corrida* is of interest anthropologically in that it is an event which involves a process of reversal and inversion, and it also shows up which sections or actions of the formal *corrida* are well enough known by a general audience to be parodied. For example, the performers in this event delight the audience by aping the swaggering movements and by exaggerating the postures of *toreros*; they also imitate the particular mannerisms of famous *matadores* such as El Cordobés or Paquirri. The performers are unusual characters, because, judging from the way they are spoken about, as dwarves they are not perceived as fully developed human beings, and yet they are performing as *toreros* (which is seen as a role for only the truly human and truly masculine), a role which they perform in a way which would be unacceptable for a normal *torero*. This they can do because they are only playing a part; no one would regard them as real *toreros*, and because of their size and disability, and the fact that in a sense they are not perceived as full human beings or at least not fully adult, they pose no threat to the definition of '*torero*' and can act in a very un-*torero*-like manner and satirize all the cherished images of what it is to be a *torero*. For example, instead of standing still and dominating the bull they dodge about or even run away from it and allow themselves to be chased by it; they hide behind one another or crouch down in the sand and cover their heads with their hands or cape – something which often results in them being buffeted by the animal. Whereas the *torero* is expected to control his fear, to be brave and stand his ground, these *toreros* do exactly the opposite; they give in to their instincts and openly demonstrate their fear and flee. Having engaged in such 'cowardly' behaviour, the dwarf *toreros* usually return to the swaggering and arrogantly brave style of a 'normal' *torero* until they panic and flee again. In their performance they reveal and accentuate what a *torero* might well feel but which he must disguise or control. Such antics delight the crowd; individuals laugh and applaud the very things which they would jeer and abuse if done by a *matador* or any *torero* in a *corrida*.

The *toreo cómico* is certainly not an event for *aficionados* and it is often referred to as a *diversion*, an 'entertainment', a term which would never be used of a *corrida*. Although attended and enjoyed by adults, it is regarded as essentially for children who certainly form the majority of the audience. The event is very popular and on the occasions when I attended in Seville the *plaza* seating over 12,000, was completely full.

La corrida de rejoneo

In a *corrida de rejoneo* (a *rejón* is the type of lance used in this event), the equivalent performer to the *matador* is the *rejoneador*, who performs from horseback throughout. The *rejoneador* (wearing *traje corto* Andulusian equestrian dress, which will be described and commented on later in this section) is assisted by one or two foot assistants who wear the same suits of lights and use the same work capes as the *banderilleros* in the *corrida de toros*. In fact such men are usually *banderilleros* for a *matador* when they are not performing in *rejoneo*. It should be pointed out that the horses used in this event belong to the individual *rejoneador* and are not the same sort as used by the *picadores*. They are expensive pedigree horses, usually of Spanish, Arab or English blood, and are trained in the 'high school' style. Once they have been thus trained they have to be further trained to perform in the arena where they have to work close to the bull. These horses are neither padded nor blindfolded; it is the combined skill of the rider and the training and agility of the horse which stops the latter being caught. A *rejoneador* may ride up to six horses during the course of a performance with one bull, because some of the mounts will be more specialized in certain parts of the event.

From horseback the *rejoneador* first places *rejones de castigo* (punishment lances) in the bull. These consist of a long steel blade, covered with decorative coloured paper, attached to a wooden lance so that as the blade enters the animal it breaks away from the stick and thus releases a small flag which is attached to the base of the stick. The performer raises the stick to show the flag, which demonstrates that the blade is in the bull; the flag is sometimes used almost as a cape to lead the bull away from the back of the horse if it comes too close. Three *rejones de castigo* are usually used and they perform a similar function to the spike of the *picador* in that they begin to weaken the bull.

The *rejoneador* then places *banderillas* in the bull; these are exactly the same as those used in the foot event. They are usually placed individually, although if the rider wishes to demonstrate his very special horsemanship, he (the male pronoun is used here because although, as will be mentioned later, there are a few female performers in this event, most performers are men) will place them in pairs, one in each hand, and will guide the horse using only his knees. He might also choose to place *banderillas* which are half the length of the normal ones, and thus work closer and closer to the bull. As the high point of his performance he might place a small rosette attached to a spike, a movement which involves him leaning so far over the side of the horse and being so close to the bull that he almost has to touch it.

The bull is finally killed by thrusting a lance (again covered with coloured paper) into the same spot between the shoulder blades that the *matador* aims at with his sword. If the *rejoneador* fails to kill the bull from horseback, he might dismount and use the sword and *muleta* to control and kill the bull. Some *rejoneadores* have *sobresalientes* (in theatrical terms, 'understudies', usually aspiring *matadores* dressed in the normal suit of lights) in their team, and if they fail to kill from the horse they will signal for the *sobresaliente* to do so while they wait alongside on horseback. Alternatively, depending on what they feel is the proper behaviour for a *rejoneador* at this point (some seem to think it degrading to dismount) and depending on whether they are competent with the sword, they will dismount and do it themselves.

As in the *corrida* and the *novillada*, it is the president who controls this event; but it is highly significant that his control is somewhat different from that in the foot event. Here he takes his cue from what the *rejoneador* is ready to do, something which very much underlines the segnorial or lordly quality of the event. In both the *corrida* and the *novillada*, the procession at the beginning of the event takes but a few moments – the length of time it takes for all the performers to walk across the arena. The procession of the *rejoneadores*, however, is much more elaborate.[3] They do indeed process slowly across the arena to salute the president, and their foot assistants stay at the barrier, but then the riders trot around the edge of the arena once or twice to present themselves to the audience, and then reform in the centre of the arena to perform attractive drill sequences with their companions. Garcia-Baquero et al., writing about seventeenth-century *rejoneo*, described this as 'the public ceremony of the possession of the ring' (1980: 45), and this is still exactly the impression which is given today. This is not something which happens in the *corrida* with *matadores*; the *matadores* never greet the audience and they certainly never make such a display before the event. The *rejoneadores* themselves decide how long this display of horsemanship will last, and then they withdraw from the arena, leaving one of them to face the first bull. The president waits until he sees that the rider is ready and then he signals for the first bull to be released; again, this is in marked contrast with the foot event, where the president signals for the bull to be released and the *matador* must be ready.

This is not the only way in which the presidential control is different in the two events. The *rejoneador* decides how many *rejoneos* he is going to put into the bull, and when the president sees that he has finished, he then signals for the change of act; the same occurs with the *banderillas*. In between all this the rider is able to make elaborate displays of decorative horsemanship around the bull; he is never ordered on to the next section. The only point at which the time is strictly controlled by the president is in the last act, when the rider picks up the *rejón de muerte*, the 'death lance') (although once again it is the rider and not the president who decides when he shall pick it up), at which point he only has a certain length of time to kill the bull before the president signals for an *aviso* ('warning' – see Gilpérez García and Fraile Sanz 1972: article 131).

Unlike those in the *corrida* or the *novillada*, the bulls for *rejoneo* are treated before they enter the arena, in that they have the tips of their horns sawn flat. It is possible to perform this event with the horns intact but this is very rare, and most *rejoneadores* are not willing to expose their extremely valuable horses to the risk of being caught and gored by a bull with sharp horns.

The bulls for this event may be either *novillos* or full *toros* (although they are not mixed on the same programme), and are announced as such on the posters. The important thing is that the type of animals used does not vary according to the status of the *rejoneador*, because there is no equivalent of *novillero* and full *matador* among Spanish *rejoneadores*. Whether full *toros* or *novillos* are used depends on the wider context. For example, it is usually only in a series of *corridas* during an important *feria* such as those of Valencia, Seville or Madrid that there will be a complete *corrida de rejoneo*. The more usual practice is to have one *rejoneador* within a *novillada* or a *corrida*, so that if the main event is a *novillada* the animal for the *rejoneador* will be a *novillo*, and if it is a *corrida* a full *toro* will be used; on a complete programme of *rejoneo* the animals will be full *toros*.

If the *rejoneador* is performing as part of a *novillada* or a *corrida*, then he will take precedence in the procession and will perform first; an important factor, for that precedence emphasizes the relative status of the *rejoneador* and the *matador*. The only occasion on which the *rejoneador* will not perform first is if the arena is in a poor state because of rain. In such a case the president can decide that the horse would do too much damage to the sand, to the detriment of the foot performers, and he will thus order the *rejoneador* to perform later in the programme, usually in the middle.

Rejoneadores perform in a slightly finer or more elaborate version of *traje corto*, the Andalusian equestrian dress. This consists of tight, high-waisted trousers which come to just below the knee, brown riding boots, a short, tight jacket, white shirt buttoned at the neck but with no tie and a *sombrero de ala ancha* (the wide brimmed Andalusian hat). Some also wear *zahones* – leather chaps, often decorated with elaborate tooling, which are worn over the trousers. The important aspect of the costume is that it is equestrian wear and it is based on that which is worn by the landowner and his senior employees when they work from horseback. Álvaro Domecq, the bull breeder and *rejoneador*, emphasizes this aspect of the relationship with the countryside when he writes: 'The *rejoneador* represents the country in the *plaza*...and his dress ought to recapture the seriousness and sobriety of our countryside'(1969; 376). He goes on to say that the *rejoneador* should give 'the impression that he has dressed many times in country clothes and that it isn't merely fancy dress' (p. 376). All of which suggests that the *rejoneador* should not be a mere public performer got up in a costume, but should be someone who has real links with, or rather a real existence in, the country. What the event comes down to for Domecq is this: '*Ser señor del campo en el ruedo*' ('To be a country gentleman in the arena') (p. 375).

This event, then, relates to an essentially aristocratic tradition based on skills of horsemanship valued by members of that class. Even though all *rejoneadores* today may not come from aristocratic families (although many do), they usually come from a class of rich landowners, which allows them the finance and facilities to own and train a string of horses to be able to perform in this event. The horsemanship and the style of dress is an obvious link with a rural elite. This is further emphasized by the fact that a *rejoneador* is often announced as *Don* (a courtesy title – see Pitt-Rivers 1971: 72–3) on the posters advertizing the event, and a nickname or a familiar name would certainly never be used, as it often is in the case of *matadores*. The social distance between the performers and the majority of the audience contributes to the fact that *rejoneadores* do not become popular figures or excite interest in the way that *matadores* do, and I found no example of *aficionados* who followed a particular *rejoneador* – as is common with famous *matadores*.

Although the *corrida de rejoneo* is always well attended during the *Feria de Abril* in Seville, the composition of the audience is essentially different from that attending the regular *corridas*. The numbers are swollen by those who are not so much *aficionados* of *toreo* but rather *aficionados* of horsemanship, and many regular *aficionados* who attend all the other *corridas* do not attend this. Most friends and acquaintances of mine who had season tickets for all the events were not interested in attending and lent their tickets out on this day. *Aficionados* who did not attend referred to the event as *bonita* (pretty) and regarded it as a pleasant spectacle, in contrast to the *corrida* which they regarded as being serious and having an emotional depth which was lacking in *rejoneo*. In many ways it was regarded as a highly suitable event for women to watch, and season tickets were often loaned out by *aficionados* to female members of their families for this event. In the *plaza* I was struck by the vastly increased number of women attending compared with the number who attend regular *corridas de toros*.

Festivales

Festivales (literally, 'festivals') are closely akin in form to a normal *corrida*, but there are important differences. They originally always took place outside the season of the normal *corridas*, and although this is still largely true the slightly more flexible modern season (that is to say, *corridas* are now held before Easter Sunday, the traditional start of the season) does mean that some *festivales* take place when *corridas* are being held. *Fesitvales* originated as charity events and the modern event still retains its connection with charity. The breeders give the bulls for nothing (usually a breeder gives one animal, which means that six ranches are represented), the *matadores* do not charge for their performance and only their assistants receive payment. All the profits are then given to whatever charity the *festival* is held for. The animals for this event are *novillos* (full *toros* are never used) and they must have the tips of their horns trimmed flat. Usually the animals are of inferior quality and a breeder is certainly not expected to send a prime animal; he gains no dishonour from sending an ill-formed animal, as he would if he sent a similar animal for a *corrida* or *novillada*. For this reason there is no very strict examination of the animals by the veterinary surgeons.

Both *matadores* and *novilleros* are able to perform in the same *fesitval*, and it is the only occasion on which a full *matador* is able to take a step down and perform with *novillos* in public. The relatively informal nature of this event is emphasized by the fact that the performers do not wear suits of lights; instead they wear a form of the *traje corto* described above in the section on *rejoneo*. Some wear a refined version of this, in that the trousers may not be the three-quarter length equestrian style but the full-length style as worn by *flamenco* performers, and some wear leather shoes instead of boots; they do not, however, wear the ballet style shoes worn with the suit of lights. In the parade they do not have the ornate dress capes described in the section on the *corrida*; instead they carry the outer jacket of the equestrian dress – not the short jacket of the *traje corto*, but the jacket which is worn over it on particularly cold days. This jacket is rolled up in the same way that a rider rolls it to fold over the pummel of his saddle, and is carried by the *matador* over his left shoulder in the procession.

The assistants also wear *traje corto*, but a more basic form of it. They do not wear the wide-brimmed hat, but instead wear caps of the sort worn by those country labourers who do not work from horseback. The *picadores* do not wear the wide-brimmed hats as might be expected, but caps and a rough outer jacket and riding trousers rather than *traje corto*. Although it is a general rule that those who work from horseback on Andalusian ranches, particularly bailiffs and the foremen, wear the wide-brimmed hats whereas those who work on foot wear caps or straw hats, this is not always the case, and there are those who are mounted who prefer caps, something I saw on several ranches. What is never seen is men working on foot using the wide-brimmed hats. Even if he does not wear one on a day-to-day basis on the ranch, the *mayoral* (the foreman) will certainly wear one as part of his full *traje corto* which he wears when he brings the bulls to the *plaza* for a *corrida*.[4] In the *festival* the difference in headgear distinguishes the *matadores* from the assistants; this does not happen in the *corrida*, but there the gold-embroidered suit of the *matador* distinguishes his from the assistant, whose suit is embroidered with silver.

The *festival* is structured in the same way as the *corrida* and the animal goes through the same process. There is a difference, however, in that usually there are six *matadores* performing (instead of the three in a *corrida* or *novillada*), and so each takes one bull according to the order of seniority. The bulls are not selected by lot as they would be in a normal *corrida*, but are sent out in accordance with the date of registration of the ranch, the bull from the oldest ranch first.

Aficionados certainly do not give the same emotional weight or attribute the same seriousness to the *festival* as they do to the *corrida*. *Aficionados* I knew who would normally go to great lengths to attend a *corrida* with good *matadores* performing did not bother to go to a *festival* with the same programme if it was out of their way. The only way they might be motivated to attend is if there had been no *corridas* in the area for some time; but this was regarded very much as filling a gap until a 'real' *corrida* took place.

In a conversation with a group of *aficionados* after a *festival* in a village near Seville, I was told by those who attended that the emotion of the event was not the same as that at a *corrida* and they offered several explanations for this. A major concern was that the animals were of inferior quality and their horns were trimmed, both of which reduced the risk and therefore the emotional impact. Others said that an essential part of the atmosphere was missing because the performers were not dressed in the suit of lights, and that the *traje corto* did not carry the same emotional weight. My informants readily drew out the connection with the *traje corto* as the country gentleman's dress, and I was told that the festival had the atmosphere '*los señoritos divertiendose*' ('gentlemen at play' or 'gentlemen enjoying themselves'). No one would ever refer to *toreros* as '*divertiendose*', and what is emphasized here is the essential seriousness of the *corrida* in contrast to this event.

The *traje corto* is used by the wealthy when they ride through the streets of the town on celebratory occasions; it is also the dress used by bull breeders on the days that they test calves for bravery on their ranches, occasions which are often marked by a small party; and it is the dress for *rejoneo*. All of these are occasions or activities which have a connection with the *corrida*, in that the association is with the countryside and livestock farming, but when combined with the form of the *corrida* bring the wrong sense to it. *Matadores* dressed in a similar way to *rejoneadores* create a wrong impression of what a *torero* should be. He should not be perceived as a member of the landed gentry, and although he has obviously not changed his social class by changing his clothes, his visual presentation is wrong. A final element which should be mentioned is that, as will be argued, the *corrida* is an urban ritual event which involves the triumph of the world of culture over that of nature, of the processes of the urban world over those of the rural, and all the factors in the arena combine to emphasize this. Once again the *traje corto* with its association with the countryside, an association brought with it into the arena, conveys a wrong sense in terms of the cultural significance of what is acted out in the arena. In the arena it should be the bull alone which conveys the sense of the countryside, while the man, dressed in the suit of lights, an exaggeratedly 'cultural' costume, represents a world distanced from this.

It is important to mention that although the word *festival* corresponds to the English word 'festival', a *festival* is not regarded as a suitable event for a celebration as a *corrida* or *novillada* is. It would seem that the reason for this is that it can neither command the same respect nor carry the same cultural significance as the *corrida*. People told me that *festivales* were not used for town or village celebrations, and during my time in Andalusia I never saw a *festival* used in this way. Not only are they out-of-season events with regard to *corridas*, they are also seen as unacceptable substitutes for *corridas* or *novilladas* with regard to town and village celebrations.

Becerradas

Becerradas are events using calves (a '*becerra*' is a calf), usually female calves, in which aspiring *toreros* or *aficionados* perform. If *aficionados* (that is to say, non-professionals) alone perform, the regulations state that there must be a professional *torero* in attendance to direct the event; this is not necessary if the *aspirantes* who are performing are registered with the Syndicate of *Matadores* and *Novilleros*. As with the *festival*, suits of lights are not worn; some performers wear *traje corto*, but if they cannot afford this, some approximation is made with a white shirt and a pair of black trousers. Because the animals are so small there is no need of *picadores* in this event, neither are *banderillas* used. There are therefore only two stages, the first with the cape and the second with the *muleta*, before killing the animal.

Unlike *festivales*, *becerradas* are held as part of town and village celebrations, usually when the town is too poor to stage a *corrida* or *novillada*; but *becerradas* are often held in conjunction with these other events and announced as being held with the intention of encouraging interest in the art of *toreo*, especially among the young. Despite the fact that it might be held during a town fair, there is no sense that a *becerrada* is an acceptable substitute for a professional event; it does not have the same emotional impact as a *corrida* or *novillada* and it is regarded as an enjoyable, lighthearted occasion. From the point of view of this study, one of the interesting aspects of these events is the way that the organizers sometimes try to copy the form of the formal *corridas* in order to create more of a sense of occasion. In the midsummer of 1979, I attended one in a village near Seville which provided a fine example of this attempt.

The *plaza* was set up on the edge of the fairground during the annual celebrations of the village. It was a rudimentary construction consisting of a stout wooden fence around a sandy area; there were no seats and the audience stood around the outer edge of the fence. The presidential 'box' was a ramshackle wooden platform some ten feet above the ground. In a *corrida* there is usually some decorative cloth or tapestry hanging from the presidential balcony, and in this *becerrada*, serving the same purpose, there was a tourist-type teatowel depicting a poster of a famous *matador*. The president was a young local doctor who did not know exactly what to do, but the platform was full of people who were only too willing to advise him. As those in the arena were *aficionados*, there was a professional *torero* in attendance and it was he who called out instructions to the president, who finally became so confused that he gave up signalling anything. There was no band, so the president had control of a small record player with one record of suitable *pasodobles*. The machine actually had so little power that it could hardly be heard on the far side of the *plaza*. There was also one trumpeter, who was rarely able to play the whole trumpet call at the correct moment or without a mistake.

Those performing were a local doctor, a *practicante* (a trained medical assistant) and a working-class lad who desperately wanted to be a *torero*. The doctor and the *practicante* didn't mind making fools of themselves; the other, however, was in deadly serious mood, but largely unsuccessful, and the more frustrated he became the more the audience were amused. In fact the audience spent most of the afternoon howling with laughter at the ineptness of the performers. They had not attended to see the art of *toreo*, they had come to be amused. As the afternoon wore on, all semblance of order broke down, members of the audience asked for a chance to perform, others were volunteered by the audience and pushed over the fence into the arena. At one point someone suggested that it would liven things up if *banderillas* were used (*banderillas* are not normally used in this event), so the professional in attendance (an ex-*banderillero*) took two of the small spiked sticks used in the *muleta* and placed these in one calf. One small boy, probably about nine or ten years old, asked for permission to have a go, and was given a *muleta* by the professional; the crowd were delighted by this and were even more delighted when the lad who should have been performing attempted to push his way back and a fight ensued. The *becerranda* only finished at dusk when the dim light from the single electric bulb strung across the arena did not allow the performers to see from which direction the animal was coming.

I have attended some *becerradas* where there were so many of the audience in the arena that it was almost impossible for the calf to turn around. At one in particular, not all the animals were to be killed and members of the crowd in the arena were able to pack around the quite large calves and carry them out to the pens. *Becerradas*, then, are events where the division between the audience and performers begins to break down and there can be general participation in the arena.

Capeas and toros sueltos

Both of these types of event are included in this section because they have many common features, and it is often difficult to define exactly which category of event one is watching. *Capeas* (capings) are usually held in a town or village square closed off for the occasion, or a roughly constructed *plaza*. One of the traditional ways of making a *plaza* in villages in Spain is to draw farm wagons into a circle; the audience watches from the wagons or from between the wheels. In this event there are no prescribed costumes and anybody is allowed into the arena to attempt to cape the animals. The animals might be bulls or cows and are often beef animals crossed with wild stock. In some areas quite large animals are used, and it would be stretching the definition somewhat to say that they are calves (as in *becerradas*), although it is true that calves are usually used.[5]

The public in the arena may be equipped with capes or *muletas*, with jackets, tablecloths or nothing at all; the atmosphere is one of riotous confusion. It is very much a popular celebration and, like *becerradas*, *capeas* are put on during *ferias* in towns and villages, often in those which cannot afford to hold a *corrida*, and little attempt by those in the arena to establish a performance. The public is not set apart as at a *corrida*, which does not mean to say that there are no spectators; there are obviously many who prefer to watch from behind the barriers, but there is no attempt to restrict the entry of those who wish to enter the arena.

If the animals are to be killed and there is no professional *matador* to do so, the animals are tied up or led away so that a slaughterman can kill them. In these events neither the death of the animal itself, nor the form in which it is killed form an integral part of the event as it does in the *corrida*; it is merely a way of bringing the event to a close.

The name *toros sueltos* (literally, 'loose bulls' – '*suelto*' comes from the verb '*soltar*', which in this context means 'to release or set loose'), is a name which can refer to many events that have certain essential similarities. An animal, or sometimes several animals, is or are turned loose in the street, rather than in a *plaza*, and the streets allocated for the event are sealed off from the rest of the town. Some events of this type use calves with their horns trimmed, some use cows with their horns intact or wild/domestic-cross bulls with their horns trimmed, padded or intact. I attended and participated in two events in Arcos de la Frontera where a halfbreed bull weighing over 650 kg was used; its horns were neither padded nor trimmed. In this event the bull was loose in the streets for nearly two hours and the aim of those in the street was to run in front of it along the prepared route, or, if the animal stopped, to encourage it to follow by moving in close and enticing it to charge. Individuals were much admired for the way they approached the animal, touched it and yet avoided being caught. People waved improvised *muletas* at the animal, but it was impossible to cape it as a *torero* would with a bull in the arena. The end of the event came when the animal was too exhausted to run any more; it was lassoed and tied tight against the axle of a farm wagon, where it was killed without ceremony by the butcher.

In other events, several animals are released at the same time; in some, one animal is released and, when tired, is recaptured and led to a corral to recover. In some, the animal is killed at the end, as in the event described above; in others, the animals are returned to the ranch to be used again. In some villages, notably around Valencia, Teruel and Toledo, there are night events in which the animal has a frame fixed over the horns, and to this are attached burning torches. Grazalema, near Ronda, has a famous event in the summer in which a bull attached to a long rope is run through the streets and teams of men attempt to control it. All of these events are set within the context of a general celebration in the town or village, and although they may be held in conjunction with a *corrida* or *novillada*, this is not usually the case. These events do not seem to have a strong tradition in Andalusia and are more often to be found in the north of Spain, especially in the provinces of Castille, Valladolid, Toledo, Soria, Salamanca, Teruel and Valencia.[6]

3

A historical outline

Rather than attempting to link the history of the *corrida* with economic, political, social and intellectual developments in Spain, this historical sketch aims to give a sense of key developments which gave shape to the professional, formal and highly structured modern *corrida*. Especially important is the change from aristocratic celebration to popular public spectacle; from nobles on horseback lancing bulls to death to the professional performances of *toreros* on foot. From the eighteenth century onwards, it was this latter form of the event that became the most complex and pre-eminent of the various types of celebration based on the man–bull contests. This form eventually enjoyed such immense popularity that it came to be called *la Fiesta Nacional* (the National Celebration), a name by which it is still often known: certainly no Spaniard would think of any other event if *la Fiesta Nacional* were mentioned.[1]

Historians of the *corrida* have long been concerned to define the origin of the event. Some have suggested a possible link with Cretan bull-leaping;[2] others have argued that there were no outside influences and that it was from the religious celebrations of the ancient Iberians that such contests first developed.[3] Those who wish to stress religious celebrations as an origin have attempted to set the *corrida* in the context of the ancient complex of bull-worship in the Near East, North Africa and the Mediterranean.[4] Although not dealing with ancient material, there are those who emphasize the element of the bull as a symbol of fertility which featured in many local rituals and ceremonies, particularly wedding celebrations, and argue that these practices formed the basis of later contests between men and bulls, which developed into the modern *corrida*.[5] Some historians, pointing to the Roman influence in Spain, suggest the animal–human contests held as part of the games in Roman amphitheatres as a probable origin of the *corrida*.[6] A commonly espoused belief is that the aristocratic practice of hunting wild bulls from horseback and lancing them to death was the forerunner of the later event, which involved bringing bulls from the country into the city to be killed by similarly mounted aristocrats.[7] There are those who hold this view but argue that it was the Moors who were instrumental in this shift from hunting bulls in the country to killing them as part of an urban celebration.[8] Finally, there are those who look for the origin much later. They deny the Moorish influence and suggest that killing of bulls in arenas in towns was developed by the Christian aristocracy during the Reconquest (that is to say, in the four hundred years or so leading up to 1492), something they associate with the idea of the growth of some form of 'Spanishness'.[9]

Luis Toro Buiza, in his study of the importance of Seville in the history of *toreo*, succinctly pointed out the faults of many of his colleagues:

> I believe that the majority of our specialist historians incur imprecision and confusion in treating the theme [that of the history of the *corrida*] in a general way without limiting themselves to a clearly demarcated model [that is, of what constitutes a *corrida*]. Various sports and games, with a more or less remote origin, both on foot and on horseback have grown up around the fighting bull in Spain and they cannot be studied in a unitary or synchronic scheme. (1947: 19)

Certainly a fundamental problem on reading many of the historical works which deal with this subject is that the writers have never made clear what sort of event is being referred to by their use of the modern term *corrida*. Quite often any example of men contending with bulls is referred to as a *corrida* – just as in English the word 'bullfight' is used to refer indiscriminately to a variety of events. The result has been that such events are then analysed or interpreted as though they were essentially the same cultural phenomenon in a slightly different guise.

In any historical interpretation, a basic division should be drawn between popular, local celebrations involving bulls – in which members of the community could freely participate – and the more spectacular and ornate celebrations of the nobility. Little is known of the form of the popular events because the chroniclers did not record them in detail. De Cossío refers to them but does not produce any concrete description of their form. He writes: 'The riotous and anarchic playing and killing of bulls and cows in the town squares temporarily arranged for the occasion was without doubt the primitive form of the taurine spectacle. We cannot doubt that when the venerable medieval texts speak of "running the bulls" they refer to spectacles of this type' (vol. 1: 679). Garcia-Baquero et al, suggest a similar atmosphere for these village celebrations: 'when the documents refer to the celebrations in which bulls were run it seems to be clear that they were referring to a tumultuous pursuit in which the villagers took part as a crowd. In such runnings (*"corridas"*) the animals were cut down after having been ferociously wounded with arrows, javelins, with knives and darts' (1980: 26).

From the little evidence that exists, it seems probable that (apart from the severe wounding of the animal) these events were somewhat similar to many modern *capeas* or other events in which bulls are turned loose in the streets and members of the public run in front of them. Extrapolating from contemporary events and those of recent history, it is probable that such events would be held as a part of the local saint's day festivities during the annual village celebration or on another day of local importance which would give rise to celebrations. Such events would be marked by the general and free participation of members of the public rather than by an audience watching an individual performance.[10]

Much more specific and detailed information is available about the occasions for the taurine celebrations of the nobility. From the chroniclers it is known that such events were organized to celebrate such important occasions as meetings of the Cortes, royal or noble births and weddings, visits from foreign monarch or important religious occasions. The earliest existent report on such a noble celebration is from 1080, on the occasion of the wedding between Sancho de Estrada and Doña Urraca Flores in Avila (see Alvarez de Miranda 1962: 99). Once again in Avila, it is recorded that in 1107, at the wedding of Don Velasco Muñoz and Doña Sancha Díaz, both Christian and Moorish nobility alternated in lancing bulls from horseback. In 1124 in Saldaña, in the festivities for the wedding of Alfonso VII, king of Castile, and Doña Berenguela, daughter of the Count of Barcelona, contests against bulls were an important attraction. Throughout the Middle Ages, references to such events abound in the literature. From the material available one is able to construct an idea of the basic form of the event, which consisted of members of the aristocracy, mounted on horseback and aided by foot assistants, lancing bulls in closed arenas, often in the main square of the town, in front of an audience. The performers were not professionals but a social elite whose position was associated with horsemanship and military prowess, who were given to public display, to pomp and to dressing up in order to demonstrate their personal and social status and, in this particular sort of celebration, their skill and bravery.

The aristocratic celebration probably reached its most elaborate and ornate form in the sixteenth century, by which time this public demonstration had come to be a reflection of the prestige of the aristocracy: a homage to the ideals of knighthood and chivalry. The very location of such celebrations, usually in the most important square of a city, emphasized this quality of a celebration of power and prestige. Such celebrations in sixteenth-century Seville, for example, were held in important squares such as San Francisco, a location which emphasized the prestige of the event, bounded as it was by the law courts, the royal prison and the town hall. On days of *corridas* the balconies of the surrounding buildings were occupied by members of the aristocracy and town worthies, and over the railings were hung decorative cloths and tapestries, many of which were embroidered with the insignia of noble families.[11]

Perhaps exemplary of such aristocratic *fiestas* was one held in Valladolid on 28 January 1592, and attended by Philip II. The king sat with his sons on a platform in the doorway of the town hall, the windows of the buildings around the square were occupied by spectators and the balconies were decorated. The noblemen who were to perform in the arena

> made their entrances and exits in order to display their beautiful teams which were led by their footmen; among the noblemen the Duke of Osuna, Don Pedro of Toledo and the Marquis of Villafanca entered most sumptuously attired and accompanied by eighty footmen in their respective liveries, each of whom carried various canes or lances. (Ortiz Cañavate 1934: 404)

The accounts suggest that the general public were able to attend such events but, although they were there as spectators, those in the arena were not directly performing for this audience. It was the recognition and approval of their skills and courage by their peers which they were seeking. At another level, however, the general public was an important audience, for those in the arena, through their display, were also making a dramatic statement of the political power, authority, and status of members of their class. The structure and presentation of these festive events can perhaps be interpreted as designed to convey this sense of dominance. Such events were ritualized contests, as, in a similar way, jousts and other tournaments were, governed by the ideals of an earlier chivalric code which seemed to have directed behaviour and performance in the area and in which the participants could demonstrate their military skills while off the battlefield.

Although it is not known exactly how the early taurine *fiestas* of the nobility proceeded, what descriptions there are suggest them to have been fairly chaotic. What is certain is that they were not like the modern *rejoneo* (the horseback event seen today and described in chapter 2) with one man on a swift, agile horse facing the bull and his few assistants well out of the way. The event does not seem to have been divided into acts as is the modern *corrida*; the performance consisted of an attempt to kill the bull by lancing it in whatever way possible. There were, however, preferred styles of performing and available descriptions suggest that the styles of the spear or lance thrusts reflected military skills. One style which was particularly admired was called *rostro a rostro* (face to face). In this the rider held his horse (which had its eyes covered with a velvet blindfold) quiet while he waited for the bull to charge. When it did, just before it hit the horse, he would thrust the lance deep into the neck or ribs of the bull and at the same time attempt to turn his horse away from the horns (see García-Baquero et al., 1980: 40 for example). If the animal was not killed from horseback the rider could dismount to kill the bull with a sword. Once again, this was not done in the stylish fashion of today when a *rejoneador* dismounts; the assistants would help by cutting the animal's legs with a *media luna* (a large half-moon-shaped sword), knives or hand lances in order to immobilize the animal for the kill.

Certainly by the sixteenth century, though, there was a sense of giving a shape and style to the performance. By the latter part of the century, books such as Pedro Aguilar's *Tratado* (*Treatise*: 1572), Juan Suárez de Peralta's *Tratado de la Caballería de la Gineta y de la Brida* (a treatise on two styles of horsemanship, '*la gineta*' and '*la brida*': 1580), and Argot de Molina's *Discurso Sobre Monteria* (*Discourse on Riding*), a work ordered by Alfonso XI in 1582, were being written to deal with aspects of riding style and performance.[12]

Although little is known about the exact form of the non-aristocratic events, it was certainly not always the case that only members of the community participated in caping bulls, for it is known that from an early date men performing on foot in non-aristocratic celebrations were earning money by killing bulls. For example, in 1385 in Navarre, the king, Charles II, 'ordered fifty librass to be paid to two men from Aragon, one Christian and the other a Moor, whom we had brought from Zaragoza to kill two bulls in our presence in our city of Pamplona' (quoted in de Cossío vol. 4: 815).

Such examples are not found for Castile because of a series of laws in that kingdom. In 1277, Alfonso X published his lawbook *Las Siete Partidas*, in which was an article (VII.Tit.Vi Ley 4) which defined as 'infamous' anyone who earned money from killing wild animals. Such a person would lose all his legal rights, his testimony could not be accepted in a court, his children could be disinherited, he could be excommunicated and, if killed, would be refused burial in consecrated ground. This law was specifically an attack on the local popular events, which were therefore unable to develop the aspect of individual performance by professionals. The law did not apply to the aristocratic event, because those who took part in it and killed bulls from horseback earned no fee for their participation and were thus exempt from the law and its penalties. The existence of such an edict at least provides strong evidence that a class of professional bull killers was already well established by the thirteenth century. According to Alvarez de Miranda (1962: 49) these professionals were responsible for directing, as much as was possible, the development of activity in the arena or the street. Once the public had finished its sport with the bulls the professionals would then kill them. In any case, the law of Alfonso seems to have had effect, allowing the aristocratic event in large areas of Spain while curtailing the popular manifestations directed by itinerant professionals.

Although exact and detailed information is lacking, it seems certain that from the end of the sixteenth century or early years of the seventeenth onwards important changes occurred in the *fiestas taurinas* associated with the nobility, which were to transform the nature of the events. Those performing on horseback had always been accompanied in the arena by servants or assistants using capes, jackets or cloths to attract the bull's attention, monoeuvre it around the arena and, when necessary, withdraw it from the horseman should he be in difficulty. In 1620 Francisco Morevelli, a gentleman from Seville, was writing complaints about assistants who were encouraged by the plebian section of the audience into taking a more active performative role and thus, he said, reducing the quality of the event. García-Baquero et al. give considerable importance to the role of the plebian members of the audience:

> the interventions of the noisy common people...who occupied the stands of the *plaza*, who were dedicated to urging on and encouraging the servants, rascals and rogues who, in their playing of the bull or in their *quites* [a process whereby the bull is removed from the horse] in aid of the mounted gentlemen, began to show attractive moves and postures more often for the emotional and aesthetic satisfaction of the spectators than for the mere fact of service. (1980: 61)

Another sign of what some have called '*la invasión del plebeyismo*' ('the invasion of the common crowd') was the appearance of *ventureros* (adventurers) who went from *plaza* to *plaza* performing. These were teams of men who were willing to risk their lives in order to earn some money. They would get into the arena during a celebration and entertain the crowds with their playing of the bull. Although the aristocratic event continued to be celebrated and to be esteemed, the seventeenth century also saw an increase of popular interest in the performance of those on foot, performers who were certainly not aristocratic.[13] Increasingly, though, there were complaints from members of the higher echelons of society that the event was becoming disorganized, undisciplined and chaotic; a state which was attributed to the increasing role played by non-aristocrats in the arena. Martinez Rueda, commenting on the same period, argued that: 'A fatal blow was dealt to the combat; the art, once practised by knights and gentlemen, degenerated into the vulgar butchery of mecenary bullfighters who contended not for honour but base lucre' (1838: 394). Nestor Luján, a historian, disparagingly characterizes the foot performers in the most graphic terms, as 'hopeless adventurers, dirty and drunk, fleeing from prison and without a place in the movement of wayside banditry, brutalised and insensible indians from our American colonies, peasants of limited intelligence spurred on by hunger and misery, got together in bands and travelled around the villages. Their *toreo* didn't have any order but rather the pace and brutality of a witches' sabbath' (1954: 14).

It was not, however, simply the fact that there was a new set of contenders in the arena which changed the nature of the activity; there is also the suggestion of a decline in the quality of the performance of those on horseback. De Cossío quotes from a letter written by a certain Don Francisco Melchon to a Don Pedro Antonio Pla, in which the former comments on the decline of the prestige of the event which had 'lost its noble prestige at the hands of poorly mounted *rejoneadores* without fit and adequate horses, destitute and poor gentlemen who had to seek not honorific but real and monetary protection' (vol. 4: 844).

Gradually during the seventeenth century the numbers of aristocrats performing in the arena in *fiestas taurinas* declined, and this was accentuated by changes at court at the end of the century. Charles II had no children, and when he died in 1700 it was the Duke of Anjou, a grandson of Louis XIV, who finally came to the throne as Philip V, the first Spanish king of the house of Bourbon. He had been educated at the French court, he had French tastes and, once in Spain, surrounded himself with a French-influenced court. He found the celebrations which involved the killing of bulls distasteful and those members of the aristocracy who wished to keep favour at court withdrew from the plaza

(Pérez 'Villamelon' 1955: 57; Pérez de Ayala 1925: 198). Whereas the previous dynasty had taken an interest in the *fiesta* and defended it, at times even against papal criticism (see Pérez 'Villamelon' 1955: 56, Vincens Vives 1961: Vol. III: 243), the new king refused to take any interest in it and did not attend such events. For example, to mark his visit to Seville in 1729 a *fiesta taurina* was organized, but the king absented himself (Pérez 'Villamelon' 1955: 57).

There are also what might be termed technical or stylistic reasons for the withdrawal of the nobility from the *plazas*. By the eighteenth century, the style of performance in the arena had come to be similar to the modern *rejoneo* in that it involved a riding style that depended on the agile movements of the small and fast Andalusian horse; a riding style called *la jinete*, in contrast to *la brida* in which large, deep-chested and slow-moving horses were used. These latter horses were the breed used for jousting and the early *fiesta* in which bulls were lanced. With the change of monarchy came a change in riding style. Philip favoured the *la brida* style, which was reintroduced from Italy; the aristocracy followed suit; and this further influenced the decline in *rejoneo*, which could not be performed with this style of riding horses as they were unsuitable because of their size and weight.[14]

Although the eighteenth century can be characterized as the period which saw a fundamental transformation of the event from a performance based on the skills of a mounted aristocrat to that based on the skills of professional, non-aristocratic foot performers, aristocrats were occasionally to be seen in the arena. For example, despite the fact that he personally was not favourably disposed to the event, a *corrida* was held to celebrate the entry of the new king, Charles III, into Madrid on 15 July 1760. Officially such events were still prohibited (on this occasion it was noble or courtly *corridas* rather than popular celebrations with bulls which were subject to prohibition) by a decree issued by Philip V in 1754, and they were to be further prohibited by Charles III in 1785 and 1786 (Ortiz Cañavate 1934; 436), but exceptions were made; *corridas* were held to celebrate royal occasions during the reigns of both Philip and Charles. Charles IV seems to have been willing to celebrate special occasions with *corridas* and, for example, on the occasion of the swearing of the loyalty oath by his son Fernando, Prince of Asturias, on 23 September 1798, *corridas* were held in the Plaza Mayor in Madrid. For these two events 133 bulls and 67 horses were purchased. The central performers were five mounted gentlemen who had as their sponsors or patrons the Dukes of Osuna and Arión and the Marquis of Cogollundo. The occasion was obviously regarded as a particularly special one, for among the assistants of the horsemen were three of the most famous foot performers of the day; Pedro Romero, Joaquín Rodríguez Costillares, and Jose Delgado (see Kany 1970; 101ff for an account in English).

Between the period of the withdrawal of the noblemen as performers and the acceptance, from about the mid-eighteenth century, of the performer on foot as the chief character, there was a brief period of importance for the mounted performer known as the *varilarguero* (literally, 'a man with a long lance' – (from '*vara*', 'lance' and '*larga*', 'long').[15] These men did not belong to the same social class as the nobility and instead of performing simply for honour they were doing so for money. Some were modest landowners, some were impoverished gentlemen, and in the south they were often the most senior ranch hands of the cattle ranches on the flatlands of southwestern Andalusia. The horse and the long lance were the principal tools of the trade of those who had to work with the herds of semi-wild cattle, and the skills they learnt in the country they put into practice in the *plaza*. These *varilargueros* did not perform in the *rejoneo* style of the aristocrats, that is to say, lancing bulls and placing *banderillas* or rosettes in them from swiftly moving horses. The *varilarguero* was mounted, held the lance out in front of the horse and, attended by foot assistants, advanced slowly to receive the bull and thrust the lance into it as it attacked. It would appear that rather than developing a definite style of their own they offered a half-hearted harking back to an earlier style; certainly they appear not to have offered such an exciting style of performance that people attended to see them as the principal performers. Although they headed the formal procession into the arena and appeared to have a higher status than those on foot, they were a shortlived phenomenon. By the mid-eighteenth century, the question of status and prestige had been reversed. From that time on, the mounted performers were only assistants of the *toreros* on foot, very much like the modern *picadores*.

Although the first half of the eighteenth century was very much a transitional period in terms of this event, what is certain is that by mid-century not only were those on foot the chief performers, but there is evidence of some ranking and order within the teams. Certainly by 1733 there were well-known *matadores* performing at the heads of teams, and from 1761, the date from which posters advertising *corridas* are preserved, one can follow more easily who was performing and where. In terms of the activity in the arena, whereas previously the task of killing the bull had been a collective one (if it was not killed from horseback the assistants armed with assorted weapons worked as a group to kill it) it was now the responsibility of one man using a sword and, a little later in the century, with a cloth in the other hand to perform this task. By 1750 there had developed a sense of hierarchy among the *matadores*, based on levels of individual manifestations of style. Accordingly, their order of performance and rates of pay began to vary. As certain styles became distinguishable, a knowledgeable section of the public began to express preferences, supporting those performers whose techniques they approved.

It has been suggested that at this time an intimate link was formed between the developing event in the arena and the urban industrial process of meat production; a link which was formed through the slaughterhouse (Toro Buiza 1947: 99ff; Luján 1954: 36 and 49; García-Baquero et al. 1980: 76–7). The slaughterhouse can certainly be seen as a point of contact between the agrarian culture (the producer) and the urban culture (the consumer), in which living products of the country are processed in the city. As will be suggested later, the *corrida*, although essentially an urban process, cannot be understood without reference to the countryside; it is an event which mediates between these two zones. In the eighteenth century, a most obvious aspect of the linkage between the *corrida* and the slaughterhouse was the fact that many of the well-known *toreros* – men such as Joaquin Rodriguez 'Costillares', Jose Delgado 'Pepe-Hillo', Antonio Ruiz, Juan Rodriguez and 'El Sevillano' – were employed or had been employed in a slaughterhouse. Many of the skills learnt in the course of their daily work in the slaughterhouse were put to use in the public arena. Toro Buiza even makes the exaggerated claim that the slaughterhouse was the birthplace of the modern *corrida*.

Documents from Seville from as early as the mid-sixteenth century show that bulls had been caped in the corrals of the slaughterhouse (Toro Buiza 1947; 99–107). Most of the documents are concerned with attempts by the authorities to forbid this practice, but they seem to have been notably unsuccessful. A document dated 22 May 1758 forbids the playing of bulls in the slaughterhouse on the mornings of *fiesta* because the public which attended this then failed to attend Mass. It was also forbidden for such events to take place on workdays, because it was claimed that it resulted in people not attending to their duties. The only time when it was permitted to hold them was on the afternoons of *fiestas*. The practice was so popular that the numbers attending were seen as a potential problem of law and order by the authorities, who then stationed a constable permanently in the slaughterhouse, and at least once it is recorded (in May 1786) that the constable had to have the assistance of soldiers using fixed bayonets to keep out the extraordinarily large crowd which was demanding entrance.

It is not known what form these events took in the slaughterhouse, but it is to be presumed that there were no rules, that the affair was disorderly and that those who took part were probably workers from the establishment making a public performance of their work skills. The animals which were killed here were not fighting bulls but those which had been brought in for slaughter to supply the meat markets of the city. Aspiring or professional *toreros* who were not slaughtermen by trade also seem to have taken part for practice. It is known, for example, that Francisco Romero, a carpenter by trade, from the famous Ronda family of *toreros*, often caped and killed bulls in the slaughterhouse of that city. This sort of improvised caping of bulls also took place in the pastures just outside the city, where the animals were left by the drovers prior to moving them to the slaughterhouse. When the cattle arrived a crowd would gather and people would attempt to isolate the fiercest animals in order to cape them with their cloaks.

Associated with the gradual development of the *corrida* as a popular urban spectacle, there was in the eighteenth century a spate of construction of special *plazas de toros*. It was not a new idea to have special places set aside for these celebrations; indeed, as early as the thirteenth century there were municipal regulations in some parts of the country which prohibited them from being staged within the city except in the special places set aside for the purpose (Vincens Vives 1961; vol. 1: 355). Those places which were set aside, however, do not seem to have been permanent structures, nor indeed was it the norm to hold them in such places, for in most parts of Spain it was the village square or the main town square which served for this purpose. It was not until the seventeenth century that *plazas de toros* of a permanent nature were built. In 1617, Felipe III had his architect, Gómez Mora, commence work on a special *plaza* in Madrid which had seating for more than 50,000. By 1707, Seville had a wooden *plaza* near the river, a structure which was renewed several times before 1761, when the present one was built. In 1743, a *plaza* was built on the outskirts of Madrid in Puerto de Alcalá. Ronda had its *plaza* by 1763, Zaragoza in 1764 and Aranjuéz in 1796. In the first half of the nineteenth century, many permanent stone or brick structures were built, starting with those of Valencia and Cadiz in 1802. It seems that every town or city over 10,000 inhabitants soon had a *plaza*.[16] A significant aspect of the building of *plazas de toros* was that these were sections of urban space given over to a particular event, and as such they were the only structures in Spain, apart from churches and cathedrals, which were built to hold large numbers of people. The existence of such buildings suggests control, ordering and specialization. Rather than taking place in the everyday setting of the town square which was coverted and decorated for the purpose, the *corrida* began to be contained within a space set apart from daily life.

The early eighteenth century *corridas* were fairly chaotic events in which individuals in the arena were mainly concerned with showing themselves off in idiosyncratic, improvised ways rather than through establishing a structured performance. During the century, however, there was a gradual ordering and regulating of the event and the beginnings of a canon of aesthetics. *Matadores* began to operate with definite teams, each member of which had a particular task; and slowly, different and deliberate styles of performance began to develop. The *matador* had unquestionably become the most important figure in the arena, and the public came to see the performance of known individuals.

In 1726, Nicholas Rodrigo Noveli wrote a book entitled *Cartilla de Torear* (*A Primer in the Art of* Toreo), a text which is mainly concerned with styles of performing from horseback, and which Pérez de Ayala has suggested is the last monument to 'noble *toreo*' (1925: 195). However, even this work recognizes contemporary developments and attempts to influence them, for it also gives details about how to perform on foot. More important than this early work was a systematic treatise by a *torero*, Jose Delgado (better known as 'Pepe-Hillo'), called *La Tauromaquia o Arte de Torear*. Published in 1796, the work set out to codify practices in the arena and to instruct both *toreros* and *aficionados* how a *torero* ought to perform. This work had an enormous impact with regard to the ordering of the event, and in the early nineteenth century it was published in several editions. Following this, the next most influential text was *Tauromaquia Completa* by Francisco Montes ('Paquiro'), published in 1836. This laid out and codified what had slowly become accepted practice, the major divisions of the *corrida*, the caping, pic-ing, placing of *banderillas*, performances with the *muleta* and the killing with the sword. Although this work did not have the status of being a set of legally enforceable regulations, it did indeed become the basis of subsequent legislation.

The works referred to above were basically concerned with establishing an internal structure for the *corrida* and with establishing certain norms of performance. They deal with such questions as what to do when the bull takes up a defensive position, how to place *banderillas*, what cape passes to use with particular animals and how to resolve the problems associated with killing (de Cossío vol. 2: 60ff). There were, however, earlier regulations which attempted to deal with the problem of public order during such celebrations. The Council of Castile and later the Council of Mayors of House and Court, for example, were bodies which issued decrees dealing with the control of spectators and law and order in the *plazas*. Unlike today, when the spectators go directly to their seats, it was the custom well into the nineteenth century for them to congregate in the arena, and at an even earlier period to attempt to get into the arena during the event. An order of 1659 covered the problem of spectators who climbed into the arena, who drew weapons and apparently joined in; there are similar orders for 1660, 1671, 1674 and 1675 (de Cossío vol. 1: 804). Particularly important regulations were drawn up in 1770 by the Council of Castile on orders from Charles III. As a result of these regulations, magistrates were to govern what went on in the *plaza*. They had two constables who (with the assistance of mounted troops) were to watch over the proceedings generally and make sure that the arena was cleared of spectators; something they still do, albeit in a ceremonial manner. Provision was made, under these regulations, for medical assistance should it be needed.

It was not until the nineteenth century, however, that unified sets of legislation relating to the organization and control of the event appeared. The first example of this comprehensive legislation, which attempted to draw together in one legal document previous regulations and customs for organizing *corridas*, ordering the nature of the performance in the arena and controlling the spectators, was drawn up in 41 articles by Melchor Ordoñez, a political official in Malaga. It was published in 1847 and used in various cities apart from Malaga, and later became the basis for the first book of regulations for Madrid in 1852. In 1880, there was a new set of legislation and finally, in 1917, the first comprehensive national regulations were approved. The regulations governed every aspect of the *corrida* from the contracting of the *toreros* and bulls, the advertizing of the event and the sale of tickets, to the organization, structure and control of the activity in the arena, the provision of medical services and the keeping of public order in the *plaza*. Even though these were *national* they actually only had to be enforced in Barcelona, Madrid, Seville, San Sebastian, Valencia and Zaragoza; in other capitals the civil governor could opt to use them or not. In 1923 came new regulations, which were legally binding for all *plazas* in Spain; these were revised in 1930 and again in 1962, and these 1962 regulations (with some additions and changes) are those which currently govern the event.[17] The *corrida* therefore became highly regulated and ordered, and the process in the arena was not controlled by the performers but by an official appointed by the state. The regulations defined the order and nature of the stages which the bull had to go through and what was left for the performers was the stylistic freedom of executing the movements considered appropriate to each of the predetermined stages.

By the mid-nineteenth century, the role of the *torero* had become thoroughly professionalized and the solo performance of the individual *matador*, supported by a team whose function was to aid him and to help show off his performance, had become the central focus of the event. The *corridas* were structured and the *matador* had to take the bull through a complex, rule-bound process. It is possible to see the concern with the method and style of killing the bull, which required particular skills on the part of the *matador*, as exemplifying an essential change in the nature of the event from the 'free-form' improvisation of primitive *toreo* to the structured form. In the earlier form of *toreo*, when it came to the killing of the bull it was:

> the death itself which [was] of interest, not the skill in executing it. The opposite is true in the new taurine spectacle which began to assert itself everywhere; the primary end is the demonstration of the *knowledge of how to kill the bull*, that is to say the *skill of killing*. In fact what is being attempted is not simply to kill the bull in any way possible but to do so according to certain rules which demand that it be carried out in a requisite time and by a determined method. (García-Baquero et al. 1980:90 – emphasis in original)

The *corrida* had not only become a highly ordered celebration but, in an important sense, because of the careful attention given to timing and to ordering the details of the processing of the bull, it also became a celebration of order; a theme which will be taken up in greater detail in a later chapter.

By the end of the nineteenth century, the *corrida* definitely had arrived at basically its modern form; it was an urban, highly regulated and structured event, controlled by the state and usually taking place in a specially constructed *plaza de toros*, and it featured paid performers with the principal performer on foot. It was divided into four main sections: a preliminary caping, the section with the *picador*, the section with the *banderilleros*, and finally the performance with the *muleta* and the killing of the bull by the *matador* using a sword. Although there were many changes in the detail of the organization and structure of the event from the nineteenth century to the present day, there has been no essential change in what, in terms of its format, is a *corrida*.

4

Fiesta taurina or *espectáculo taurino?*

Some Spanish commentators have suggested that as the *corrida* became a highly regulated, structured, professionalized event it suffered an essential change in its nature, in that from being a true occasion of celebration, a *fiesta taurina*, (a celebration with bulls) it became an *espectáculo taurino*, a spectacle or show with bulls.[1] This they feel came about because of a divorce from its proper setting in the context of local community *fiestas* or *ferias* (feast days or fair days) as it became an event held on a regular basis in the larger centres of population (in the same way as cinema or theatre), rather than as a part of the festivities of a special day. For those who emphasize the importance of the festive element, the idea of the *fiesta taurina* involves two integral elements: participation and communality. The *fiesta* is either a celebration in which members of the public take an active part as they do in *capeas, toros sueltos* and *becceradas* (see chapter 2), or, in the case of *novilladas* and *corridas* which involve professional performers, they are integrated, as community events, into the local celebrations. Those who lament that the *corrida* has become a spectacle suggest that it has lost its sense of being a community celebration and a celebration of community, and has become little more than a show watched by an audience that is not only non-participating but one which is interested only in the rarefied level of the aesthetics of individual performance. Their concern is that the *corrida* has become little more than an economically exploitable entertainment which is simply a vehicle for individual artistic performance, something which for them implies both sterility and a loss of the cultural significance of the *corrida* in its totality.

As was explained in the previous chapter there certainly was a change in the nature of the event from the late eighteenth century, correlated with the growth of professionalism of the *toreros* and the growing orderliness in terms of the structure of performance. The individual *matadores* came to be the focus of attention as they developed their techniques and styles, alongside which developed ideas on what the *arte de toreo* consisted. The public began to attend *corridas* to see these individuals and their performance in much the same way as one would go to the theatre or concert hall to see or hear a particular performer's interpretation of a work. But despite this process the professional *corrida* did not cease to be an important celebratory event; *corridas* went on being used to celebrate local or national occasions, as they still are, but within the event the nature of the performance slowly came to occupy the centre of attention.

In terms of the present audience, one can make a crude distinction between those who attend for the aesthetic experience of seeing the art of *toreo* and those who are less interested in the aesthetics and technicalities of the event and who attend for the excitement and enjoyment of the total experience of all that is the *corrida*. This is a crude distinction, in that those purist *aficionados* who attend the *corrida* also enjoy the whole atmosphere, pageantry and display of the event. Most of the men with whom I attended *corridas* were of this type, but they still wanted to be outside the *plaza de toros* half an hour before the start, to meet friends, smoke a cigarette, chat, mingle with the crowd and experience the gradual build-up of excitement. On the other hand, those whom I have characterized as attending with less interest in the art of *toreo* still prefer to see good *toreo* than bad.

In a large *plaza* such as that in Seville, there will be in any *corrida* a public with a wide range of tastes and interests. There are those who go along because they have nothing better to do on that particular Sunday and feel like attending a *corrida*. They are not particularly concerned who they are going to see (although they are more likely to go if there is a famous *matador* performing), they are going to enjoy themselves and pass a pleasant afternoon. There will also be those who go every week and who take an active interest in the event. They will know who is performing, the record of the performers and which bulls are being used; they will be interested in the weights of the bulls; they will even know the names and qualities of the assistants; and they will certainly have very strong personal opinions about how the art should be performed. The non-purist *aficionados* tend to comprise a more boisterous group within the *plaza*; they shout, boo and cheer with great alacrity. They are there to enjoy themselves and so anything which is bad is loudly booed and abused, because that is an enjoyable thing to do, and anything which is vaguely good is applauded and cheered because they like to feel that they have seen good *toreo*. The individuals in the other category are less given to such explosive reactions; they are less demonstrative and one gets the sense of quiet consideration and contemplation from them. They do not give their applause readily, but when they do one can be sure that something special is taking place in the arena.

Even within the formal *corrida de toros* outside the context of a *feria*, there still exists an element of popular enjoyment, as well as there being an appreciation of the event as a work of art only properly understood by those versed in its technicalities and associated aesthetics. Two elements often seen or heard in a *corrida* illustrate the two styles of watching and appreciation: these are *espontáneos* and the shout of *olé*.

Espontáneos (spontaneous ones) are youths (at least they are usually young men) who manage to get themselves in the arena during a performance and attempt to make a few passes with a *muleta*, shirt, jacket or whatever they have to hand, before being caught by the assistants and pushed to the safety of the alleyway. There is usually a cheer from a large section of the public when an *espontáneo* manages to get into the arena, especially if the *corrida* has been somewhat tedious. Such youths are not merely applauded for their audacity (although that is part of it) but they provide an interlude of confusion which many find amusing. The *espontáneo* is trying to get near the animal, one group of assistants is trying to keep the bull from him while another is trying to catch him, and at the same time there are policemen and various officials running around the alleyway trying to persuade him or order him out of the arena. Generally there is a great deal of confusion, and many in the audience consider this a bonus to what they paid for and find it highly entertaining. They also seem to delight in booing the policemen who inevitably take the youth away. Although most *toreros* are understandably annoyed by someone who breaks into their performance, if they wish to get the sympathy of the crowd it is best for them to approach the president's box at the moment the police seize the youth and ask for him to be pardoned and released.

Critics claim that this is not the way for aspiring *toreros* to make their mark and they chide the audience for applauding them; after all, was one comment, no one would applaud a young music student who made his way onto the stage during a performance of *Otello*, pushed Plácido Domingo out of the way and began to sing. Antonio García-Ramos y Vazquez, commenting on the regulations relating to *espontáneos*, writes: 'Those who applaud *espontáneos* cannot be described as good *aficionados* since they ought to know that such intruders...are not able to show off their art, even though they might possess it, because of the disorder which is produced in the arena by the racing about of the *espontáneo* and the assistants who want to catch him' (1980: 509). Many comments are of this type and they emphasize that what is going on in the arena is, for many people, the performance of a work of art which should be respected and certainly not interrupted.

Those who do applaud do not have this reverence for the event; they are determined to enjoy themselves and anything which enlivens the event only makes it more enjoyable. Even more then this, the *espontáneo* is someone who, by leaping into the arena, breaks the division between spectators and performers and, in a significant way, challenges the structure of authority controlling the event. Corrochano suggests a considerable identification of the public with *espontáneos* and claims that the *espontáneo*, as an active participant demonstrating what *he* can do, represents something which many members of the audience would like to be:

> The public performs in the *plaza* with gestures and movements and with shouts and applause for what it sees, for what it would like to have seen and for what it believes *toreo* ought to be, all of which sometimes becomes condensed in someone who leaps from the stands into the arena and is called an *espontáneo*. The *espontáneo* is the representation of the public in the arena. Each spectator is an *espontáneo* who does not dare leap. It is for that reason that they become annoyed with the *toreros* who prevent or obstruct the performance of the *espontáneo*. For that reason they defend him with their protests against the authorities who detain him and throw him out of the *plaza*. (1966: 31)

Another example which points to this difference in audience attitudes in the larger *plazas* is the use of *olé*, a cry very much associated in the public mind with the *corrida*. It was claimed earlier that the shout of *olé* was the spontaneous appreciation of something which was just right; it is indeed, but it is also somewhat more complicated, because that which is 'just right' will vary with the person having the experience.

Soon after having established myself as a regular attender at the *Peña Taurina* (Taurine Club) where I did much of my work, I went with a group of club members to see a *corrida* in which Curro Romero (to whom the club was dedicated) was performing, during which he gave one of his very rare great performances. On returning to the club, one of the men who by this time had taken over my education in matters related to the *corrida* asked the others about my response; he particularly wanted to know if I applauded and shouted *olé*, but more than that he wanted to know if I had done so at the right moment. He was trying to discover whether I had a real appreciation for the event, something which would demonstrate that I was moved when confronted by good *toreo* and so shouted *olé* at that which (according to purist *aficionados*) was truly deserving of this reaction. Such a response was expected to come naturally or instinctively, an audible outcome of a welling up of emotion. It would not have been a valid response if I had turned to one of my neighbours to ask, 'Is that a good pass?' and on being told that it was, to shout '*¡Olé!*'. Of course the reaction on my part could not have been truly instinctive because when I arrived in Spain I did not know how to evaluate *toreo*, and I had been taught which passes were better than others and why. What the man in the club wanted to know was whether I would recognize and respond emotionally to good *toreo* when I saw it.

Of course not everybody shouts *olé* for the same passes. Those who shout it for a pass which is not well executed demonstrate that they are not purist *aficionados*. They are excited by the event and thus they shout *olé*. It could be that they shout *olé* because they actually think that the passes are good, or because the word is one traditionally associated with the event and it is known that it is something which is shouted at the end of a series of passes. Leaving aside the matter of what constitutes 'good passes' (it is difficult to deal with this because it is a value-laden matter), what is important is that members of the audience are excited by what is going on and *olé* is a shout of excitement. To have a large crowd of people shouting *olé* in unison adds to the *ambiente*, the atmosphere and excitement of the event, for this is not shouted at the end of a part of the performance but actually accompanies it. Members of the audience will also call on the band to play even if the *matador* is not performing particularly well because, again, it helps to create a more emotional atmosphere. The purists also shout *olé* but for them to be moved to do so the passes have to be very special. They are not interested in adding their vocal contribution to the creation of atmosphere; it is the relationship between the man and bull which should create that.[2]

It is in the *corridas* or more likely the *novilladas*, held during the *ferias* of the smaller towns and villages, that one encounters the full atmosphere of *fiesta* which the commentators referred to earlier claim to have been destroyed with the development of the professional *corrida*. In such events there will be only a minority who attend as purist *aficionados* of the art of *toreo*; the majority attend because that is what is done during *feria*. Those who are performing might well be relatively unknown *toreros* who are trying to make their way in the taurine world, and the bulls are unlikely to be of the highest quality, but none of that really matters. The important thing is that it is *feria*, a time to enjoy oneself, and going to *los toros* is the correct thing to do on the afternoon of a day of *feria*.

In the smaller towns and villages, the majority of the population may be expected to attend the event. Families attend in groups, food and drink may be taken along and the whole atmosphere is very much more like that of a party, a festive occasion, than in most larger plazas in Andalusia. Of course the audience would like to see good *toreo*, but so long as the bulls charge well and the *toreros* attempt to do something they are usually satisfied. The total spectacle, the music, the costumes and the pageantry, is an attraction in itself, but it is the fact that there are men who risk themselves with dangerous animals which gives the event its main interest and emotional impact. The audience certainly does not sit passively; the people are quick either to applaud or to abuse; both of which provide much enjoyment. They do not even seem to mind ineptness on the part of the *toreros* so long as they show a desire to succeed. I have attended village *novilladas* where the *toreros* spent more time in the air or knocked over on the ground than they did on their feet; they had their capes torn from their hands and the trousers of their suits of lights ripped to pieces; and yet the audience would be cheering with delight and shouting encouragement to the *toreros* to get back on their feet to have another go, and applauding them when they did. If the *toreros* were cowardly or unwilling to attempt to fulfil their obligations, then they would be vociferously abused. In these events it is true that there is a division and distinction between the audience and the performers (although the public does have an essential role to play, as will be discussed later), but one could not claim that the atmosphere of celebration, of *fiesta*, was lacking.

Each of the major *plazas de toros* in Spain mounts a series of *corridas* during *feria*, and at these times the audience will be swollen by those who attend few *corridas* during the year but who do attend during the *feria* because that is when the most famous *matadores* perform, and because going to a *corrida* at this time constitutes an important aspect of taking part in the total celebrations. In some *plazas*, the most famous perhaps being Bilbao and Pamplona, the atmosphere of *fiesta* is more exaggerated than in the more sedate *plazas* of Seville, Barcelona or Madrid. In Bilbao and Pamplona the dancing, singing, and drinking which go on night and day in the streets are carried into the *plaza* for the two hours of the *corrida*, and those making merry and incidentally enjoying the event in the arena probably outweigh the number of reserved purist *aficionados*.

While engaged on a project in another part of Spain, I attended such a *corrida* in Teruel, when the greater part of the audience seemed to be completely drunk. There were six or seven brass bands (apart from the official band for the event) accompanying each of the clubs present in the *plaza*, all of which played as loudly as possible and at the same time throughout the *corrida*. In addition to this, most of the members of the clubs sang, danced, and drank for the entire two hours of the *corrida*. What with the bands playing, the people singing, shouting abuse at the two famous *matadores* who were performing badly, and roaring approval at the attempts of the third *matador* who was from Teruel and therefore attempting to perform well in front of the home crowd, there was not a quiet moment during the whole event. As soon as it was over the party spilled back into the street and the singing, dancing, and drinking continued as before.

All the discussion above has dealt with the notions of *fiesta* and spectacle within the context of the formal, professional *corrida* or *novillada*, but there are other celebrations featuring bulls which have not been superceded by the professional event and have long existed beside them. These are the various events mentioned in chapter 2) in which bulls or cows are turned loose in the closed-off public square, or less often in a *plaza de toros*, and members of the public are allowed to remain safely behind the barriers or to enter the *plaza* and risk themselves running with the animals. In such events there are no professional performers; indeed those who run with the animals and who finally dive for the safety of the barriers when the situation becomes too dangerous can hardly be said to be performing at all (see Marvin 1982 and Mira 1976). Such events usually take place during a larger celebration within the town or villages and are generally accompanied with singing, drinking, and dancing. With these events one is dealing with the sense of 'the community at play characterised by the *fiesta* in the public square' (Romero de Solis 1978: 21) – in other words, with the participation and community celebration which some claim to have been destroyed by the growth of the professional *corrida*.

The *corrida de toros* exists in Spain, particularly in the *plazas* of larger towns and cities (where there is a large potential audience), out of *feria* time as an event which many of the audience attend because they wish to see the art of *toreo*. They are *aficionados* who take a particular interest in this form of artistic expression and attend regularly, as other people might attend concerts or the theatre, or as still others might seek the excitement of a professional football match. The *corrida* also continues to exist as a traditional and popular entertainment intimately connected with local celebrations, and in fact still constitutes an essential part of such celebrations in very many towns and villages in Andalusia. The two aspects of the *corrida* as spectacle and celebration are not mutually exclusive but are rather intermingled. The 'spectacle' element is always present, even in small village *novilladas*, and the celebratory' element is always present in the *corridas* held out of the context of *feria*. One might see superb *toreo* from an unknown performer in a village event, just as a *corrida* with a prestigious *matador* or with prestigious bulls can be a celebration, a part of *feria*.

Members of the audience attend for different reasons and have different levels of appreciation. Although there is also a difference, in terms of the elaboration of presentation, between the events held in the villages and those held in important *plazas* such as that in Seville, from the point of view of the basic structure and the meaning of the *corrida* in the context of Andalusian culture there is no essential difference between these events. It is the nature of the structure of the *corrida* and the associated structure of meaning which will be focused on and interpreted in the rest of this book. But first, although the question of the relationship between the *corrida* and the village or town celebrations has been touched on here, this needs further consideration in order to understand the cultural significance which is carried by the *corrida*.

5

The setting

As the *corrida* became regulated and structured and rules for style and types of performance were laid down from the eighteenth century onwards, it slowly gained a rich and complex aesthetic element, but unlike many systems of aesthetics the understanding and appreciation of the artistry within the *corrida* was easily accessible to the majority of the public. Great numbers of people became interested in the *corrida* as an exciting artistic event, with the result that in the larger centres of population in Spain there came to be enough people to form a regular audience for the event outside the context of it forming a part of some wider celebration; the *corrida* came to stand as an event and a special occasion in its own right. Despite its independence in the urban context, the *corrida* was never a mundane event; the fact that a *corrida* was to be held on a particular day would produce a good deal of excited anticipation which would mark out that day as special. Bartolomé Bennaser, writing about the perception of time in early modern Spain, suggested that: 'the quality of the time during which an act was performed could easily modify its meaning' (1979: 29); and the folklorist Ben-Amos has noted that: 'the time and locality in which [an] action happens may have symbolic implications' (quoted in Bouissac 1973: 127). This chapter will therefore consider the social quality of the time at which the *corrida* is held and how this relates to the meaning of the event. The *corrida* will be considered both in the context of its being a regular, usually weekly, event in the larger towns, and in its traditional setting of *feria* (the secular fair) and *fiesta* (religious holiday).

The season

Corridas take place during a season which usually extends from Easter Sunday to late September or October; the final date actually depends on whether there is good enough weather to stage the event, although the Feria de San Miguel (29 September) marks the end of the season in Seville, and traditionally Saragossa's Feria de Pilar in the first week in October marks that for Spain as a whole. Easter Sunday is traditionally the date on which the *temporada* (the season) begins, a date still adhered to in Seville, but as Easter is a movable feast and sometimes falls quite late in the spring, the season begins later in some years than others. In such years a *novillada* or a *festival* may be held before this date in Seville, but no *corrida* ever takes place before Easter. In Spain as a whole this tradition of no *corridas* during Lent has been broken with the fair of Las Fallas in Valencia, a fair with several *corridas* taking place before Easter. Most *aficionados*, at least in Seville, still feel that Easter is the real beginning of the *temporada*; the Easter Sunday *corrida* in Seville is looked forward to with great interest, and the impresario there tries to contract especially good performers and bulls for this occasion. As was seen in chapter 2, the months before and after the season, between October and early April, are the time for *festivales*, the more informal charity performances of lesser importance. *Novilladas* used to be regarded as out-of-season events, but since the first decades of the twentieth century they have followed the same season as the full *corridas*.

'At five o'clock in the afternoon
It was exactly five o'clock in the afternoon'

Corridas and *novilladas* are always held in the afternoon,[1] and are usually held on a Sunday unless they are part of a large fair, in which case there are likely to be *corridas* on several days in the week. The general point can still be made, though, that they are held on a day set aside for recreation and relaxation. Sunday is the day *par excellence* for not working, and in a largely agricultural society (as Spain was when the *corrida* developed) Sunday would be the only day, apart from *feria* days, when everybody would be free to attend a public entertainment. Since the *corrida* does not have a restricted audience it continues to take place (with rare exceptions) on the days when the majority of the public are free to attend, and not only that, but at a particular time during those days. One can contrast this with the cinema, for example, which is a public entertainment which can go on all week because, not depending on natural conditions such as daylight, it can begin late in the evening when those who have been working during the day are able to attend. Even football can now take place in the evening because of artificial illumination whereas, as will be mentioned below, this would be unacceptable for a *corrida*. Football matches are usually held on Saturday and Sunday afternoons because that is when most people, because of the usual organization of the working week and the pattern of weekend relaxation, are able to watch them. However, the suggestion that a football match be held on a Sunday morning, or even on a Friday morning, would not provoke a feeling of inappropriate timing from football fans in the way that a similar suggestion would in the case of a *corrida*. When talking to both *aficionados* and non-*aficionados* about the timing of *corridas*, I was struck by their strong sense of the inappropriateness, rather than a sense of inconvenience, of anything other than an afternoon *corrida*. There was something about the idea of a morning, lunchtime or night-time *corrida* which was instinctively felt to be 'wrong' – something which was out of place and which jarred with the concept '*corrida de toros*' itself.

Even during *feria*, when people do little or no work, *corridas* are still held in the late afternoon, although from the practical point of view people could attend in the morning.[2] Very briefly (for the significance of *feria* will be considered more fully later in this chapter), in terms of the organization of the traditional Andalusian *feria*, the stock fair takes place in the morning (as do any religious events, including processions; on days of *fiesta*, cockfights also take place between midday and early afternoon), and at this time people are involved in the round of socializing in the streets, in the bars and, if there is an area set aside for it, in the *feria* grounds. After lunch there is usually a *siesta*, followed by a *corrida* in the late afternoon. In the early evening, people stroll in the streets and go to bars to meet friends and for drinks and snacks. In the late evening, after dinner, the socializing, the dancing, drinking and merrymaking really begins. A factor contributing to the strict adherence to the late afternoon as the appropriate time for those *corridas* not held in the context of *feria* is that there is still a firm association of the event with its traditional setting in a wider celebration, and in that setting, where there is a strong sense of social activities appropriate to particular parts of the day, *corridas* are afternoon events.

The general image of the *corrida* as an afternoon event is emphasized by the contrast with the case of the night *corridas* held in some *plazas de toros* which have good artificial illumination. Such a *corrida* is held annually sometime in the midsummer in Puerto de Santa Maria in southwest Andalusia. The *corrida* begins at 11 p.m. and makes use of a *plaza* with the best illumination of any in Spain. I once went to this *corrida* because the programme promised to be good. Despite the fact that Curro Romero was the senior performer, I was surprised that the majority of the *aficionados* whom I would have expected to attend did not bother to do so. This was certainly not because Puerto de Santa Maria is too far from Seville, for I made the journey on many Sunday afternoons when Curro was performing, and on the occasion of this evening performance there was even the promise of free tickets. Members of the club told me that they were not going because the 'atmosphere' was 'different', and that they did not consider it worth attending; and, when pushed further, said that sunshine or at least sunlight is an important aspect of the *corrida*, and without it something vital is missing.

I tackled many friends and informants about this but none of them could be more explicit about why the sun is so important. Some offered 'technical' reasons for not liking the night *corridas*; they told me that the bulls need sun to be able to perform well and also that the floodlights of the *plaza* pick up the metal embroidery of the suit of lights and make it sparkle, thus causing the bull to take notice of the man rather than the cape. Finally, however, their comments came down to such phrases as '*No hay ambiente*' ('There is no atmosphere'), '*El ambiente es diferente*' ('The atmosphere is different') or simply '*¿No sé? pero no es lo mismo*' ('I don't know, but it's not the same').

Most critics are scornful of or at least regard such events as not being worthy of the same consideration as 'true' *corridas*. Some are particularly severe in their criticism; de Cossío, for example, in his four volume encyclopedia, gives less than a page to them, considers that 'they do not deserve special consideration' (Vol. 1: 671) and assigns them to 'the lowest realm, from the taurine point of view' (Vol. 1: 671). Lozano Rey is even more scathing than de Cossío, and writes: 'if the inventiveness of the impresarios has created nocturnal *corridas* it is certain that it is nothing to do with serious *corridas*, but rather, when not repugnant pantomimes, with grotesque events, which are attended not by the true lovers of *corridas* but only by the lower levels of the *afición*' (1931: 10).

This last comment from Lozano Rey points to a highly significant element – the fact that night *corridas* are seen as 'entertainments' – which takes us back to a comment made earlier with regard to the relationship of appropriateness between certain activities and the time of day at which they should occur. In terms of the way that a day of *feria* is constructed, the central feature of the night is intensive socializing, drinking, singing, dancing and the noise and bustle of people in the street. It is a time of light-hearted, merrymaking entertainment, and the serious drama of the *corrida* is not a *diversion*, an entertainment, in the sense that we would understand the term. Although it is to be enjoyed, the *corrida* should therefore not be held at this time, and if it is, it tends to be interpreted as an event which has changed its essential quality, almost as though it had absorbed or become subject to the prevailing spirit of the night.

There are other aspects which contribute to the feeling that a *corrida* held at night is not a 'proper' *corrida*. The first of these is that one of the signs of the progression of the event, the increasing shadow moving across the arena caused by the setting sun, is missing in the night event, when the whole arena is perfectly and uniformly illuminated throughout the entire event. The intense electric lighting also reduces the naturalness of the event and increases the sense of the theatrical; under such lighting the arena looks very much like a stage. Anything which conveys a sense of unreality and fiction is an entirely inappropriate setting for the drama of real life and real death which is the essence of the *corrida*. A final aspect is that because it starts after dinner and finishes around 1 a.m., the entire pattern of social activity, particularly that of meeting and chatting with friends in bars and outside the arena before the *corrida* and then retiring to bars afterwards, is disturbed. Many people also commented that they found it strange and somehow wrong to leave their house at night to go to the *plaza de toros*.

To pursue the comment about 'atmosphere', most newspaper reports of *corridas* begin with a short comment about the weather. Fine weather is not only important for the *corrida* to take place but also to add to the atmosphere; the ideal weather for the *corrida* is bright sunshine with no wind (the latter being important because wind moves the capes in an unpredictable way, and is thus a nuisance and a potential danger). Rafael de Paula, one of the great artistic *toreros* from southern Andalusia, commented, after a rather uninspired performance on a chilly and overcast day in Madrid, that he found it difficult to perform on such days because he was '*un torero de sol y moscas*' (a *torero* of sun and flies'). It is a comment which very much fits with the general sense that the *corrida* should not only take place in bright, warm sunshine but also that it is a 'hot' event, a quality strongly associated with idea that it should be conducted in a spirit of passion and should evoke a passionate response from the audience.

In attempting to get more definite comments about the importance of the weather I suggested to many *aficionados* that a roof on the *plaza de toros* would solve the problem about bad weather, and it would mean that *corridas* could be held all year round. This idea was condemned as even more unacceptable than the night *corridas*. Although to put a roof on the *plaza* guarantees no problems with the weather or with the wind, and although those who attend the *corridas* do not want any problems with the weather, they want this to occur as a natural process. Once again, the concern seems to be to retain certain natural elements in the construction of the *corrida* – to put a roof on the *plaza* to turn it into an *indoor* event brings it closer to being a theatrical show and thus an essentially different event. Certainly one hopes for fine weather, for a *corrida* held in the rain is a miserable affair, but I think that the word 'hope' is a clue here. *Aficionados* go to the *plaza* with the hope that the bulls will be good, with the hope that the *matadores* will be inspired and with the hope that the weather will be fine and that all will go well, all of which are important topics of conversation before the *corrida*. People even wish each other '*suerte*' ('good luck') as the groups of friends outside the *plaza* break up and they make their way to their seats. '*Vamos a ver si tenemos suerte hoy*' ('Let's see if we have good luck today') is a phrase which is heard time and time again. Although *aficionados* go with the hope of seeing a great performance, they know that this is not possible every day; the variables are too great. There is a popular refrain which says, '*Cuando hay toros no hay toreros y cuando hay toreros no hay toros*' ('When there are bulls there are no *toreros* and when there are *toreros* there are no bulls'), meaning that things are unlikely ever to come out perfectly. This is an important aspect of the *corrida*; it cannot be perfect on every occasion, and yet any individual *corrida* could be the one where everything gels and a magnificent afternoon is the result. It is this 'maybe today' which gives a special spark of interest to the event. In this sense, going to a *corrida* is unlike going to a concert to hear Horowitz or to the opera to hear Plácido Domingo, because although neither might be especially inspired on that particular night one can be fairly certain of hearing a good performance, and certainly the artists will not be fumbling to remember the music or words. At a concert or opera one can be sure that the orchestra will not be playing one concerto and the soloist another, and that Plácido Domingo will not be trying to sing *Otello* while everyone else is singing *Rigoletto*, but such is the closest analogy with a bad *corrida*.

If it could be guaranteed that a *corrida* would turn out perfectly every time, it would lose much of its emotional impact, an impact which comes from a struggle on the part of the human performers against both the difficulties of the situation and human imperfections. *Aficionados* would lose interest in guaranteed perfection because it would smack of an event which was mechanical, ordered and pre-set. It is the existence of the difficulties and obstacles to a great performance, and yet the ever-present possibility of seeing a great performance, something which would signal that the difficulties had been overcome, which keeps their interest.

The basic variables are the bulls and the *matadores*. The bulls might have been bought from the most prestigious ranch in Spain and yet may be defensive, slow, and refuse to charge. The *matadores* might be the most famous in Spain, but they may be uninspired or completely unnerved and not be able to perform. If it is difficult to see a great performance by one man, it is almost impossible to see a great *corrida*; there the variables include the weather, especially the question of the wind, the temperament of six bulls and the temperament and skill of three *matadores*, nine *banderilleros* and six *picadores*. It is because the obstacles are so great that the emotion generated when things go well is so great.

The setting in *Feria*

Feria in Andalusia is a complex, multidimensional event which celebrates many of the aspects of what it means to be human in this culture, and it will be argued later that the *corrida* is an event which within itself presents in a highly dramatic form important aspects of the theme of being human. Exactly what it celebrates and how it celebrates it will need a chapter in itself; here the intention is to give no more than a brief account of the *corrida* in its traditional setting of *feria*.

A town's or village's patron saint's day is a time for celebrations, such a day often being linked with the secular *feria*, and a *corrida* or *novillada* is a customary part of the general celebrations. Andalusian *ferias* are, or at least were, usually associated with an agricultural stock fair when farmers, gypsies and others with animals for sale bring them to a site on the outskirts of the village or town, and trading takes place on the morning of the *feria*. The Spanish anthropologist Alfredo Jimenez Nuñez, working in Villamanrique, a village near Seville, was told by his informant that:

> Formerly the *feria* was one of stock and a little diversion for the people. Mares, horses and donkeys were traded but there were no cattle or pigs. Families of gypsies came, each bringing six, eight or ten animals and the deal could be 'to exchange' or 'to sell'. During the negotiations drinks were

consumed under the sunshades. There was flamenco dancing and singing, but the girls did not dress in flamenco dress as they do now. (1978: 156)

The connection with the stock fair is even to be found in Seville, where the Feria de Abril has now become an important and internationally known event and a major tourist attraction. Indeed, this *feria* was set up in the mid-nineteenth century as a stock fair with a livestock exhibition in order to stimulate what was seen as a declining agriculture. From the earliest of the *ferias*, however, there was some aspect of celebration and enjoyment for the public, in that there were *corridas* held during the days of the *feria* and food and drink stalls were set up near the stock fair itself, and there was dancing in the evening. This aspect of the *feria* soon became very important; concerts were held, there were theatrical performances and more stalls serving food and drinks were set up in the fairground itself. The authorities tried to emphasize that the most important factor was the stock fair and they tried to limit the *fiesta* element to 'those hours which were not suitable for trading' (Collantes de Teran Delorme 1981: 35). Although the stock fair continued to be important into the twentieth century, it was the public celebration which gained ascendancy as the most important aspect of the *feria*.

In the modern Feria de Abril the buying and selling of stock is not particularly important, although this does still take place in another part of the city on the mornings of *feria*. The mornings, however, do emphasize the connection between the *feria* and the country, in that those with horses, or horses and carriages, parade on or in them around the streets of the fairground. Even those who do not actually own horses can still ride, because the animals can be rented for a halfday, day or week during the *feria*, so those who might actually have no link with the country can dress and ride as though they had. The men wear *traje corto*, the country equestrian wear described in the section on *rejoneo* (see chapter 2), and women, if they are riding on their own, wear the female equivalent of *traje corto* which features a skirt rather than trousers. Women who are riding on the same horse as a man usually wear the traditional *traje gitana* or *traje flamenco* (gypsy flamenco dress). The important aspect of all this is to *lucirse*, to display oneself or show oneself off. One displays oneself simply by dressing in the traditional style and riding a horse (both of which are extremely expensive things to be able to do) and by parading around the fairground, stopping at the private *casetas* (small 'houses' set up in the fairground) to have a drink with friends or relatives. The ability to be welcomed at many *casetas* shows that a person has a wide circle of friends among the most important people in Seville.

Antonio, in the quotation above from Jimenez Nuñez, mentions that as well as the stock fair in his village the *feria* also consisted of a 'little diversion or entertainment for the people'. In most towns and villages in Andalusia, this consists of the establishment of a fairground just outside the town where both a funfair and rows of *casetas* are set up. '*Caseta*' means 'little house', and it can take several forms. The smaller ones are rectangular rooms formed by canvas fixed over a scaffolding frame, the interior of which is decorated and has a bar and a small dance floor. The largest can accommodate tables and chairs where the patrons can eat, an extensive dance floor and maybe a stage for a *flamenco* group. In some *ferias* there are public *casetas* which are open to all, but this is a recent addition, and it seems that originally there would be only one *caseta* which belonged to the town hall and was open to selected guests. In the smaller towns there are few *casetas*, but in Seville there are several hundred set up along ten streets (each of which is named after a famous *matador*), so that the fairground seems to be a city set up just outside the city, and on any of the key nights of *feria* there will be over a million people there. The *casetas* belong to groups of individual friends or families, organizations, clubs or professional associations, and in them members and their invited guests can drink, eat snacks, dance and sing.

It will be emphasized in a later chapter that, in terms of Andalusian culture, there is a highly significant distinction between the *casa* (house) and *calle* (street); they are perceived as different types of space with different forms of behaviour associated with each. The contrast is between private residence with restricted access and an area open to view and associated with public life. The *feria* ground (especially the larger ones such as those in Seville), in that it has streets lined with pavements and houses, can be regarded as a 'town' on the outskirts of the town. These *casetas* are not exactly like normal houses, for they are more open, access to them is less restricted, even those to whom access is not allowed are still able to look into them to see what is going on, and within them there is a freer than normal expression of human feeling, especially in the dancing and drinking.

The *feria* can be interpreted as an exaggeration of Andalusian street life. Andalusians judge a place and its suitability as a place to live (for a more detailed interpretation of this aspect of Andalusian culture see chapter 8) by the quality of *vida* ('life', and in this context 'liveliness, social activity') which it has. The city has this quality more than a village or the country, and the centre of the city has more *vida* than the outskirts. *Vida* is epitomized by the *feria* where there is noise, music, singing, dancing, bustle, lights, drinking, throngs of people and generally that concentration of human activity and liveliness which is *vida*.

Whether in the *casetas* or in the streets of the fairground, the late evening and the whole night is the time for drinking and for singing and dancing *flamenco*. In the evening the men who have worn *traje corto* during the afternoon change into suits or informal jackets and trousers, and most women, especially the younger ones, wear *flamenco* dress, the dress associated with gypsies. The riding of horses and the use of *traje corto* emphasizes the connection with the country, whereas the gypsy dress is associated with a world that lies beyond the countryside.

Gypsies are 'wild' people, they have no fixed abode and thus live outside the moral community of the town or village. Because of their life style they are regarded, as a group, as *sin vergüenza* (without shame) and amoral, and thus the use, by non-gypsies, of the dress associated with gypsies emphasized the relaxation of the normal rules of conduct that is associated with this part of the *feria*. Gypsies are also associated with music-making and dancing (*flamenco* being the form especially associated with them) and thus with gaiety – something which is very important in the *feria*. Pitt-Rivers puts the points of gaiety and lack of *vergüenza* together in his analysis of *feria*:

> the gypsy has become the symbol of merry-making, not only because of the grace and wit of gypsy women but because of their accepted shamelessness. By donning the *traje de lunares*, the gypsy dress, for the fair, *romeria*, or flamenco party the young girl or woman of good family can feel free of the excessive *vergüenza* which might make it impossible for her to enjoy herself. Through the pretence of disguising herself as a gypsy of whom shame is not expected, she can permit some of her habitual reserve to lapse, while at the same time she would never be taken seriously for a gypsy. Through the cult of gypsies, people can participate in the realm of behaviour where they are not thwarted by the sanctions of a society which demands attitudes of shame and respect – the trammels of the social structure. (1971: 187–8)

It must be emphasized, however, that although in *feria* there is a relaxation of norms, and sensuality, for example, is publicly demonstrated in *flamenco* dance, there is no *complete* abandonment of the norms of behaviour – no complete letting go.

In summary, then, the *feria* should be understood as an urban event, and yet it is closely linked with the country. It brings together many of the themes of the relationship between the country and city, between nature and culture, and generally the relationship between the natural and cultural aspects of being human, as viewed in terms of Andalusian culture. The stock fair brings domestic animals from the country to the outskirts of the city where they are bought and sold; activities here centre on the contest between two men as each tries to achieve the best deal from the other. The morning and very early afternoon parade of horses brings nature right into the cultural realm, but although the horses in one sense belong to the realm of nature, they are also tamed and controlled by man, and in that sense they come closer to the realm of culture (an important point which will be dealt with much more fully in chapter 8). The *corrida* in the afternoon brings nature, the wild bull, into the cultural realm; not only is it a contest between man and bull, although that is important, but it is also a celebration of the exercise of man's control of himself, and thus of his control and domination of nature, here represented by the bull – an argument which will form a central theme of the analysis of the processes in the arena (see chapter 10). The evening, which involves eating and a lot of drinking and dancing, expresses the sensual side of being human and many of the normal rules of behaviour are relaxed. *Flamenco* is an essential part of the evening celebrations and *flamenco* dance is both sensual and sexual; it celebrates the animal passion aspect of the human being, an aspect which is usually rigidly controlled, both by men and women, in public. In *flamenco* this animal element threatens to rise to the surface and engulf and dominate both the men and women involved in it, but the sensuality and the provocativeness are contained by the movements and structure of the dance, and thus the dancer remains in control.

Feria is a period of celebration in this culture which encapsulates key aspects of the relationship between human beings and the world in which they live. The *corrida* which is symbolically linked to all the elements which constitute *feria* is itself based on and explores such themes as man and his relationship with the world of nature, his place in the natural order of things, public display, sensuality and control, all of which are worked out in the context of a ritual performance. The *corrida* itself is a celebration, and the main emphasis of the chapters which follow will be an interpretation of the nature of this celebration.

6

The fighting bull

In order to understand the *corrida* or the art of *toreo*, it is essential to understand the animal which is at the centre of it. The way in which Spaniards refer to the event emphasizes that the central focus is the bull. The most common way to refer to it is simply as *los toros* (the bulls) or *la corrida* (literally, 'the running'), which is merely a shorthand way of saying *la corrida de toros* (the running of the bulls). If asked where he is going on a Sunday afternoon, a Spaniard who is on his way to the *plaza* will probably reply '*Voy a los toros*' (literally, 'I am going to the bulls') or '*Voy a la corrida*' (literally, 'I am going to the running'), both being terms which emphasize the bull. The very name of the place where the event is held, *la plaza de toros* (the place of the bulls), emphasizes the animal rather than the human performers. Of course most people do go to see particular *toreros* rather than particular bulls (although it must be said that there are people who are primarily *aficionados* of the bulls rather than having a particular interest in the *toreros*), but one never hears, '*Voy a los toreros*' ('I am going to the *toreros*') or even '*Voy a ver los toreros*' ('I am going to see the *toreros*'). One can ask, '*¿Hay toros hoy?*' (literally, 'Are there bulls today?', meaning 'Is there a *corrida*?') or '*¿Hay una corrida hoy?*' ('Is there a *corrida* today?'), but one would never ask '*¿Hay toreros hoy?*' (literally, 'Are there *toreros* today?'), a question which would actually imply, 'Are the *toreros* performing today any good?'. The page in a newspaper devoted to this event also emphasizes the animal, in that it is often headed *Los Toros*, and the television programme devoted to the *corrida* is called *La Revista de Toros* (The Review of the Bulls). Even though it takes both a man and a bull to make a performance there is a sense in which the bull is the essential basis of the event.

Although the name *corrida de toros* emphasizes that bulls are run, with no mention of human performers, they are only important animals in this culture because of that performance. There is interest in *toros bravos* as animals because, through their interaction with them in this particular event, men assert and demonstrate certain culturally valued qualities about themselves as human beings. Not only that, but it is this interaction which allows the bulls to reveal most completely their true bull nature, a quality which is greatly admired by the audience. Most people are only interested in the bull when it is in the arena of the *plaza de toros* being engaged by men. Few are interested in it simply as a fine zoological specimen and few travel to the countryside to see it in its natural habitat, because the bull on its own is not important; in the fields with other bulls it merely represents the bull it will become in the arena.

Breeders, ranch workers, and some *toreros* and *aficionados* will talk lyrically of the joy of seeing fighting bulls in the countryside, and there exists a rich poetic literature which deals with the pleasure of seeing such powerful and noble creatures tranquil in the countryside. But in order to understand the sets of images and impressions created, one must understand that the emotional response does not come simply from the immediacy of the experience (it is not a naturalist's experience), but rather depends on imaginatively placing the animals in the arena of the city where they will end their lives. If they lived out their lives in the countryside, these animals would not stimulate the imagination and the emotions as they undoubtedly do. It is what they represent and what they will become which is important; they are animals waiting to reveal their character. Although they are originally animals from the country and live out all but their last few days there, that life is private and known only by a few. The place where each bull is known and its character judged is in the public arena in the city, where it should gloriously reveal its true nature. As will be argued later, in one sense the fighting bull is out of place in the centre of the city; wild animals should not be allowed to run through public places where they can threaten humans; but on the other hand this *is* where this particular animal should be. It is not destined to remain in the country – it is a creature of the country which only fully expresses its nature (and thus acquires its cultural significance) in the city. What is of primary importance in the *corrida* is the qualities of both man and bull revealed by their interrelationship in the arena. Be that as it may, it is not possible to understand that relationship unless one understands something of how the *toro bravo* is perceived.

It is important at the outset to correct a common misconception among non-Spaniards and to explain that the bulls used in the *corrida* are not domestic animals which have been ill-treated to make them angry and thus aggressive and willing to attack. Although now raised on specialist ranches, the fighting bull is regarded by Spaniards as a wild animal (although, as will be seen later in this chapter, it is in fact a 'modified' wild animal)p the name *toro bravo* means 'wild bull' and not 'brave bull' as it is usually mistranslated in English books dealing with the *corrida*.[1]

The modern fighting bull appears to have an ancestry traceable to animals introduced into the Iberian peninsula from North Africa, particularly from Egypt, in Carthaginian times. These animals bred with the aurochs, or primitive bison, which already existed on the peninsula, and they were husbanded in a semi-wild state in the south and centre of Spain. This form of wild cattle continued to exist in Spain long after it had died out in other parts of Europe, for the reason that sports (particularly hunting) and celebrations which were based on the very wildness of the animals became so popular that the animal, as a type, was preserved.[2]

According to zoological classification, the *toro bravo* is a degenerated auroch of incomplete domestication of the species *Bos taurus Ibericus*, race *Bos taurus Africanus*.[3] Although the ancestry of the *toro bravo* can be traced to wild cattle, it is also known that such cattle were kept for domestic consumption. Unfortunately it is difficult to find information detailing how these animals were husbanded prior to the mid-eighteenth century, although it is presumed that they were kept in herds in a semi-wild state (see de Cossío vol. 1: 243ff; Vera 1951: 9ff).

Although the animal is now specially bred for the *corrida*, this has not always been the case. For the earliest recorded celebrations using bulls, the most suitably fierce animals were selected from those sent for slaughter for domestic consumption. When the organizers of celebrations which were to feature bulls needed the animals, they simply contacted the local butchers and asked them to supply however many were needed. It was the great increase in the number of *corridas* from the latter part of the eighteenth century onwards which gave the stimulus for the commercial production of an animal especially for the event. As was mentioned in a previous chapter, the nobility withdrew from the arena as performers during the eighteenth century, but at the same time as they did so many entered it in the new role of producers of fighting bulls. Instead of relying on finding bulls with the necessary characteristics in a herd, these ranchers attempted to breed a regular supply of bulls which were suitable for the *corrida*. Sanz Egaña, one of the most important Spanish writers on this topic, comments on the similarity between the work of men such as Robert Bakewell in England in the mid-eighteenth century and that of the new fighting bull breeders: 'the Spanish ranchers...formed the fighting bull with the same zootechnical methods followed by the famous English farmers and with the same results; the meat bull, the sheep for wool...just like the fighting bull they are true specialities of animal husbandry' (1947: 21).

In the case of livestock farming, the farmers are generally breeding for qualities such as powerful shoulders on a draught animal, thick wool from sheep, or milk or meat from cows. These are measurable, they are quantifiable. Although the breeders of fighting bulls are also attempting to breed good physical specimens, they want to preserve the very qualities of wildness and resistance to manageability which other livestock producers wish to eradicate; they wish to avoid domestication.

The fact that there is selective breeding may appear to contradict the earlier statement that the fighting bull is a *toro bravo*, a wild bull, for wild animals are usually found rather than created, and this needs some explanation. Tim Ingold, in a recent study dealing with aspects of domestication, breeding, pastoralism and ranching, has shown that the terms 'domestic stock' and 'wild stock' need to be reconsidered because there is actually considerable imprecision in their use. He suggests that:

> tame animals may be domestic in the sense of incorporation as members of human households, but need not be morphologically 'domesticated'. Conversely, selectively bred animals may run wild, as in emergent ranching systems, while the herds need be neither 'domestic' nor 'domesticated'. It will not do to refer to such combinations as states of 'semi-domestication' for the implication that they are in a process of evolution towards full domestication is not always warranted. (1980, 1982)

This is certainly true of the *toro bravo*, for although the animal is selectively bred it is certainly not tamed.[4] The system of raising fighting bulls is best described as a ranching system, and as Ingold has pointed out, the 'morphologically domesticated stock of ranchers' is not tame.

In the cultural context of Spain in general and certainly within the context of the *corrida* itself, the *toro bravo* is not perceived as or referred to as a domestic animal in the sense that, for example, beef cattle are. Some people will comment that it is a wild animal in the sense that elephants or lions are wild animals, while others are not so definite and argue that it is a special creature which cannot be easily compared with any other because of its special behavioural characteristics. It is certainly the behaviour rather than the morphology of the animal which commands attention. Zoologists working within another frame of reference might argue about the location of this animal in terms of a distinction between 'domestic' and 'wild' (see Paños Marti 1969); what is important for this study, however, is the perception of the animal by those who breed them, those involved in the *corrida*, those who attend it and the Spanish general public who do not attend.

Edmund Leach (1972) has produced a classification for English animals which has pets, farm animals, field or game animals and wild animals as the major categories. As part of his analysis of the social significance of each of these categories, Leach considers the observances with regard to the consumption or non-consumption of these animals as food. Pets are not eaten, farm animals are usually edible but only if female or, if male, then immature or castrated, and wild animals are regarded as inedible and usually only suitable as trophies.[5] A similar division can be made with regard to Andalusian animal categories, a division which throws light on the position of the *toro bravo* in terms of the classification of animals and concepts associated with the division of space. Leach's 'game' category is particularly illuminating in this context. He writes 'game animals live under human protection but they are not tame. They are edible in sexually intact form, but are killed only at set seasons of the year in accordance with set hunting rituals' (1972: 54). Game animals are therefore neither wild animals nor domestic animals and yet they have aspects of both. They are raised directly under human guardianship – humans protect them from predators, leave food for them if necessary, and protect and regulate their environment. Despite all this, the animals should behave like wild animals; the most important characteristic being that when confronted by a human they should attempt to fight or flee.

The 'game' category comes between that of 'domestic', where the animals are completely under human control, and that of 'wild' where people exercise no control over the animal. It is not claimed here that the *toro bravo* is a 'game' animal; indeed, there is no term in Spanish which exactly translates the English term 'game',[6] and it must be emphasized throughout that most Spaniards perceive the *toro bravo* as a wild animal. There is an ambiguity, though, in that this 'wild' animal is raised by humans, and the comparison with the English 'game' category is made because it helps to bring out the difference between a fully wild animal and a fully domestic animal. The *toro bravo* is an animal which is raised by humans and yet it is not a domestic animal, neither is it tame. It is eaten as a sexually intact mature male and it is killed in a set ritual which can be compared in many of its aspects to the hunt, the other event in this culture in which wild animals are killed; a comparison which will be made in a later chapter and which indicates essential qualities of the two events.

There is a fundamental ambiguity about the *toro bravo* which should not be ignored. It is not simply an animal captured from the wild, it has been created by humans; human will and control have been exercised to create this 'wild' animal; it has been shaped for human purposes. People have selectively bred the animals for this quality of 'wildness' and thus have actually created something which is regarded as natural, given by nature; the *toro bravo* is culturally rather than naturally wild.

There is a fine point, though, to be considered about the nature of the breeding and selection of this animal. Although each ranch owner employs carefully controlled selective breeding to produce the best possible animal, there is a point past which human control is felt to be inoperative. Although it is relatively easy to breed for the physical type of animal it is very difficult to select for *bravura* (the behavioural quality of wildness), a quality which is essential for a good bull and yet is something which is not fully revealed until the animal is actually in the arena. It is the uncertainty which gives a significant part of the interest to the *corrida*; each bull is very different and will react differently, thus causing the *torero* different problems to resolve on each occasion. *Aficionados* would complain if each bull came into the arena with the same predictable qualities, something which would suggest artificiality, or something mechanical, whereas unpredictability emphasizes naturalness. There are certain qualities, for example, strength, aggressiveness and willingness to charge repeatedly even when suffering pain, which are looked for in all bulls, but *aficionados* know that not all bulls can be the same, that some are stronger and fiercer than others, that some will attack whereas others will flee. The product of this breeding should not be readily predictable or easy to manage – qualities associated with domestic animals – but unpredictable and difficult and dangerous to manage, and thus conform to an idea of the bull's being a wild animal.

At the entrance to most ranches which raise such animals there is usually a warning sign to the effect that there are dangerous animals on the land. The term used is '*ganado bravo*'. 'wild stock', a term only used for fighting bulls. The opposite of *ganado bravo* is *ganado manso*, this being a term which is used for cattle raised for meat or milk. The actual terminology is significant, in that whereas *bravo* in this context means wild and by implication unmanageable and uncontrolled, *manso* means tame and by implication meek and controlled and in this context domesticated. On the ranches where fighting bulls are raised, those who work with the bulls actually make use of oxen (castrated males) to herd the fighting bulls. Their exercise of control over these docile, denatured animals allows them to control the difficult and dangerous fighting stock.

Manso also has the implication, when referring to male animals, of castrated, such animals being regarded as more manageable than sexually intact ones. Domestic cattle, if male, are castrated (except for those necessary for stud purposes) to make them more manageable, whereas *toros bravos* are kept sexually intact and are therefore less manageable and more aggressive; qualities which are important for the *corrida*.

As will be shown in the section dealing with the construction of male identity, there is a highly elaborate set of imagery concerned with being a true male and the possession of testicles. Such a relation is not only expressed in the everyday conversations of men when talking about themselves or about bulls, but can also be found in technical works dealing with the fighting bull. Sanz Egaña, a veterinary surgeon, in an address to a veterinary conference, had the following to say about the character of this animal: 'From time immemorial the presence or absence of testicles has been considered to have a marked influence on animal temperament' (1958: 125). He goes on to quote with approval the work of another veterinary surgeon, Sanchez Belda, who characterized the fighting bull as an animal 'with a marked hypergenital character' (p. 125) and continues to make the comparison between the fighting bull and domestic cattle in terms of character being altered by castration:

> The fighting bull must be a complete (i.e. uncastrated) animal, castration causes profound cellular changes of the pituitary gland with an influence on psychological activity; castration is practised on many animals precisely in order to make them more manageable; the ox displays a calm, tranquil and definitely peaceful temperament, lacking in aggressiveness, with slow reactions, submissive and easily scared. (p. 125)

So important is the image of its being the possession of testicles making the fighting bull the creature that it is, that doubt may be thrown on the quality of an animal if it is seen to have only one properly formed testicle. After a *corrida* in the fair in Seville in which one of the bulls performed badly I remember a complex discussion between breeders, *toreros*, veterinary surgeons and *aficionados* which centred on the fact that the bull was *chiclan*, a term meaning having one testicle, and this reason was advanced as a possible explanation of why it did not perform well.

The word *manso* can also be applied to describe a man who is meek, unassertive, retiring, not seen much in public places – the realm of men – and who spends too much time at home – the domestic realm, the realm of women. This insult may be pushed further to claim '*el no tiene cojones*' ('he has no balls' – *cojones* being an essential quality of maleness and masculinity) because he is not behaving as a true man. In this sense the notions of tameness, meekness and domesticity are linked. One can therefore discern a set of related distinctions: *bravo/manso*; *cojones/sin* (without(*cojones*; aggressive/meek; uncontrolled/controlled. These points will be taken up in more detail in a later section.

Testing and selection

It has been mentioned that fighting bulls are raised on ranches and it must be emphasized that the breeding and raising of such animals is a specialist activity. The animals are pedigree creatures and the sorts of control which are required and records which are kept for other pedigree animals are also involved in this activity.[7]

Perhaps surprisingly, given that it is the males which are used in the public arena, it is the young females which are tested to see if they have the necessary qualities for producing fighting bulls. The males' test comes at the end of their lives in the arena and until then they must be kept in ignorance of any experience similar to that which they will encounter then. The central feature of the selective breeding of high quality fighting bulls is for the owner to decide which females will be allowed to mate with the stud bulls, and the first part of this process is to remove unsuitable stock. When they are between one year and eighteen months old the male and female calves are separated, a separation that lasts for the rest of their lives, for there must be no indiscriminate breeding. Certain cows are mated with certain stud bulls and a careful record is thus kept of the pedigree of all the animals. Although sexually intact, the majority of the bulls do not and cannot make use of their sexuality because they are kept apart from cows.[8] Fighting bulls are thus sexually intact males which have been forced into a life of virginity.

Each year all the two-year-old females are tested to see if they possess the necessary qualities for breeding, and if not they are either marked down for early slaughter or perhaps for sale to another ranch which does not have such exacting standards.[9] The testing is called a *tentadero* (from the verb '*tentar*', 'to test or try out') and takes place in the small *plaza de tienta* (testing arena) to be found on each ranch. This is similar to a small *plaza de toros*, but without the seating for an audience. Although on many ranches a small party with a few invited guests might well be held at the time of the *tentadero* to make more of an occasion of it, the event is essentially a working occasion and certainly not a performance for the public.

In the arena, a man mounted on a horse takes up a position opposite the gate through which the calf will be released. He has the protective leggings of the *picador*, but he wears no special costume (although if it is being treated as a social event many of those participating will wear *traje corto*, the Andalusian country dress described in an earlier chapter). The horse, however, does have all the padding and the eye band of its counterpart in the public *plaza*. Around the *plaza* are various ranch hands who act as assistants to the one or two *matadores* whom the owner has invited to carry out the testing. It is important to understand that the event is not like a *corrida*; it is a serious but not a formal affair. The *matador* is not there to perform; he is there to work for the owner who controls the whole affair.

The owner calls for the first calf to be released and the *picador* waits for it on the far side of the arena. What the owner is looking for is a calf which will charge the horse from a great distance with little provocation. The very best calves are those which charge immediately and which do not stand and think first. As the calf charges, the *picador* pushes the point of his pike (similar to the one used in a *corrida* but with a much reduced spike) into the neck muscle of the animal. When the owner has seen how the calf reacts, particularly whether it is willing to continue pushing into the horse despite the pain of the spike in its neck, he will instruct the *matador* to lead the animal away with his cape and to line it up for a further charge. This will be repeated several times until the owner is satisfied that he has a clear idea of the quality of the animal. Most professionals in the world agree that the testing of the calf against the horse is the most important aspect of the *tentadero*, for it is believed that it is here that the *essential* spirit of what makes a fighting bull a fighting bull is revealed.

The *matador* then works the calf backwards and forwards with the *muleta* again following instructions from the owner. This section is not incidental to the testing but an integral part of it, for it is necessary to see how the animal responds to both the cape and the *muleta*, and a calf which has revealed good qualities in the previous part of the trial may well react badly – by shying away, for example – at this stage. Such an animal would have to be rejected because it reveales an unacceptable trait which might well be passed on to the offspring, with disasterous results in a *corrida*. Once the owner is satisfied that he has enough information on which to base a judgement about keeping the animal or not,[10] the calf is caught and pinned to the ground, its horns are cut flat so that it is unable to injure other animals in the herd, the spike wounds are treated with disinfectant and quite often an injection of vitamins and various antibiotics are given before the animal is turned loose.

As well as looking for qualities of fierceness, willingness to charge, a good attacking style and endurance, the owner is also interested in the physical charactristics of the animals. He does not want to select an animal for breeding which will pass on unsatisfactory characteristics. Each ranch tends to have a 'type' which it breeds for and which knowledgeable *aficionados* are able to recognize. Some breed large and heavy bulls; others smaller, more streamlined animals; others a certain type of horn shape or even colour characteristic. There is an extensive and complex vocabulary to describe the physical characteristics of a bull. There are, for example, at least fifty-nine descriptive terms to refer to the coloration of the animal. Horns are obviously very important, for it is here that the whole danger for the man resides; in a major sense they are the emotional focus of the whole event, and their significance is attested to by the fact that there are some forty-two terms with which to describe their shape and colour.

It is rarely nowadays that young bulls are tested, but if they are the method is different from that used for female calves. It is claimed that a bull is an intelligent animal, quick to learn and with a good memory. The whole basis of *toreo* is that the bull does not know the difference between the moving cape and the unmoving man: if it did the man would be caught every time. It is therefore important that prior to entering the arena the bull has never confronted a man on foot, and certainly not a man with a cape. If young bulls are tested it must be done from horseback.

The young bulls to be tested are kept in one field, where they form a herd, and it is therefore necessary for those doing the testing to isolate one animal at a time. Working in as a pair, the riders chase the isolated animal and while at the gallop attempt to turn it over by the use of long poles tipped with a small spike. These are the *garroches* or work lances used by the mounted ranch hands who work in the fields with the bulls. One of the riders attempts to place his spike in the neck and the other on the rump of the animal, and once it has been tipped over, the owner waits to see whether it gets up to attack – a good sign – or to flee – a bad sign. A *picador* is also used in this form of testing; the animal is lured towards the *picador*, who waits some way off from the herd. The theory is that the bull has a natural tendency to go to the herd where it feels secure and comfortable, so a bull which is willing to charge away from the herd is exhibiting the quality of assertiveness and aggressiveness which is required. Again, the same sorts of qualities as have been referred to before are looked for when the bull attacks the *picador*.

There is one other form of testing which is much more rigorous and complex; the testing for selecting a *semental* (stud bull), an animal which never appears in public and is used solely for breeding. A ranch may have up to seven or eight stud bulls, the actual number depending on the size of the breeding herd and the form of the breeding used. These animals must be replaced every few years, and so the owner will always be looking for a possible new stud bull in his stock. Over the years the owner and his foreman keep a watch on a young bull which looks as though it might have the physical and psychological qualities necessary for a stud bull. It is watched to see how it develops physically and whether it possesses the necessary form which the owner wishes to perpetuate in his animals. Its behaviour in the fields with the other bulls is observed, and it might be tested for aggressiveness a couple of times in its youth; but the time must come when the owner has to decide whether to sell it as a fighting bull or to test it for a *semental* and keep it on the ranch.

The testing takes place in the *plaza de tienta* on the ranch, and is usually an irreversible process; if the bull fails to show the necessary qualities at this point it will have to be killed, having had too much experience to be used in a *corrida*. Some owners have the bull 'caped' with leafy branches, so that if it fails at the *picador* stage it can still be used for a public performance, but this is rare. An associated reason why the selection of such a bull is an important decision is that many owners trim off the points of the bull's horns, so that there is less danger for the *matador* who is to test the bull and who is then willing to work much closer to the animal and thus reveal its qualities more effectively; once it has had its horns trimmed it certainly cannot be used in a *corrida*. Some breeders and *toreros* suggested to me that it was not necessarily a good practice to have a highly skilled *matador* to do the testing, because with his experience and skill of working difficult bulls he can make it appear that the bull being tested is better than it really is. Such skill is important for the *matador* in the arena but here what is wanted is knowledge of the true characteristics of the animal, not a demonstration of the ability of the man. The testing is similar to but more rigorous than that of testing the female calves. The spike of the lance is longer and thus the punishment inflicted is greater; *banderillas* are also often placed during a testing; and in fact the bull goes through similar experiences to those of the bull in the public arena, except that the testing lasts much longer and of course the animal is not intended to be killed at the end.

Naming

If it has been accepted for breeding, the calf will now be given a personal name and marked down in the pedigree book as part of the breeding stock. All *toros bravos* and *vacas bravas* (wild cows) have individual names, the young bull always taking the masculine form of the mother's name; hence the male calf of *Engañadora* (Deceiver) will be *Engañador*. Unlike the male, which takes its name at birth, the young female does not have a personal name until the testing. Until that time she is called by her mother's name or is referred to as 'the daughter of *Engañadora*', or whatever the mother might be called. Interestingly, the name of the stud bull is not perpetuated in its offspring, and the bull which performs in the arena, when it is out in public as it were, carries its mother's name. On being selected as part of the breeding stock, the young female will be given an individual name. This name might be semantically linked to the mother's name or it might receive a totally different one; this really depends on the tradition of the ranch.[11] The names are always simple (that is, not composite) single names, and are thus not like those given to pedigree show dogs and race horses, which incorporate several names of the pedigree. Indeed, the name does not need to refer to a pedigree of great depth, for the individual bull is not a link in a complex ongoing genealogy. All the male offspring of the stud bull–cow mating die; they have no heirs because they do not breed, and hence there are no 'families' of fighting bulls and no genealogies in the normal sense of the term.

Unfortunately it has not been possible to trace the origin of, or the earliest dates for, the naming of bulls. De Cossío, in his history of famous bulls (Vol. 1: 325–401), has as his earliest reference the bull *Barbero* in 1801; it should be emphasized, though, that this history is *only* of bulls which have become famous. Although there are few mentioned in the early part of that century, by the mid-nineteenth century there are dozens of examples of named bulls.

The fact that animals which are perceived as wild are yet given individual names again points to the ambiguous status of fighting bulls. Wild animals are attributed what might be termed a 'species personality', any individual of that species being supposed to have the same character as any other member. They are distanced from humans and are therefore not individuated according to their particular character, and individual names are not given to them unless a particular human being has developed a special relationship with an individual wild animal. Zoo keepers and the animals in their charge might be an example of this,[12] or, for example an animal might be rescued from the wild, taken into the home and treated as a pet. Giving an individual name implies incorporation into the human, cultural world, although the extent of this incorporation and the type of name given will vary (see Lévi-Strauss 1966: 204–8).

The names given to fighting bulls and cows are never the same as those given to humans in this culture; one does not find names such as Pilar, Maria, Carmen, Juan, Antonio or Diego used. As was mentioned before, each ranch has its own tradition of naming, and the range of this process is well summarized by the breeder Álvaro Domecq y Díez in his recent encyclopaedic text on the raising of fighting bulls (1986: 163–7). He suggests that most names fall into one of eight categories: first, occupations, such as *Cigarrero* (Cigarette Maker/Seller), *Cocinero* (Cook), *Colmenero* (Beekeeper); then birds or animals, such as *Cisne* (Swan) *Tejón* (Badger), *Ruiseñor* (Nightingale); then plants or trees, such as *Chaparro* (Dwarf Oak), *Toronjito* (Little Grapefruit Tree), *Sauce* (Willow); then the region or province of birth, such as *Malagueño* (The Malagan), *Salamanquino* (The Salamancan); then some particular physical character- istic, such as *Chato* (Snubnosed), *Ojinegro* (Blackeyed), *Zurdo* (Left- handed); then the colour of its hide, such as *Retinto* (Very Dark), *Castañero* (Chestnut One); then names with reference to character, such *Serenito* (Little Serene One), *Furioso* (Furious), *Lozano* (Lively); then names which refer to some occurrence in their life, such as *Rompecapas* (Cape Ripper), *Rompelindes* (Boundary Breaker), *Viudito* (Little Widower). There is also a final category that includes names which are not easily explicable but which Domecq sees as suggestive of the country, names such as *Manano* (coming from the verb '*manar*', meaning 'to gush forth', 'to spring from' or 'to be plentiful') and *Duende* (either an elf-like creature of the spirit of inspiration). I would add a further category of names which appear to be descriptive, though it is difficult to see how they would apply to characteristics of actual bulls; *Sisón* (Lightfingered), *Mentiroso* (Liar), *Idealista* (Idealist). Bull breeders do not operate with such a classification in mind; they choose according to their own particular tastes. As Lévi-Strauss has said of naming racehorses, 'Their creation is entirely unrestricted so long as they satisfy the requirement of unambiguous indivduation' (1966: 206).

In my experience, the only people who knew the names of individual bulls and cows were the *mayoral* (the ranch foreman) and sometimes the other employees who worked regularly in the fields with the bulls. The ranch owner might or might not know the names; this would depend on the amount of interest he took in the herd. Some, for example, take a daily tour through the fields with the foreman, while others who live away from the ranch may only visit rarely and leave the day-to-day care of the stock to the administrator and the foreman. It is on the ranch, though, that the bulls are most fully known as individuals. The foreman recognizes all the animals on the ranch; he often addresses them by name as he rides through the herd on his inspection trips, and he is able to give the personal history and character of each of the animals in his charge.

The significance of their individualism declines when they leave the ranch and go to the *plaza*. There they are only referred to by their ranch number.[13] Once in the *plaza*, and more particularly once in the arena, each bull is merely a fighting bull, a representative of its type. Although a small notice with details of the ranch number, name, weight and order in which bull will be used is usually pinned near the main doors of the major *plazas de toros*, and many people go to look at it, they only ever comment on the weight of the animal, and if they note down anything it is only the weights.

Press reports and the critics' evaluations of the *corrida* might include the names of the bulls as a matter of information, but in the text of the report the bulls are almost always referred to as number 1, 2, 3, etc. according to their order in the *corrida*. The individual names are very rarely used to personalize/individualize the bull, and reports do not, except on very rare occasions describe '*Engañador* doing this' or '*Engañador* doing that'. An example of such a rare occasion did occur in Seville, in a *corrida* during my fieldwork in which there was a particularly good bull. The animal was called *Fulero*, a term which means 'something useless, a sham, something of poor quality': an obvious misnomer for this bull which, without being encouraged, charged from a great distance at the *picador* and kept charging, without hesitation, at whatever cape was offered it. The critics picked up on the anomaly between the bull's name and its performance and made great play with it.

Those watching the event are not interested in the name of each animal; they are only interested in whether it is good, bad or indifferent (judgements which are made in terms of how they think a fighting bull should look and perform). It is once the bull is in the arena that the importance of it being a 'true' wild animal is greatest and where anything which suggests the cultural aspect of the bull, as opposed to its naturalness, is inappropriate. It is not important that the bull in the arena is called *Medroso*, that its mother had a difficult time giving birth and was reluctant to allow it to suckle, that it always stood apart from the other calves when they were separated from their mothers and that it always shied away from the horses when the ranch hands went into the fields; information which *is* important to the owner and the foreman. Such information would be inappropriate for members of the audience or for the performers; it makes the animal too much of an individual, and they have not come to see *Medroso* killed in the arena. They have come to see six anonymous bulls, animals with which they do not in any way identify, performed with and killed. To make the bull in the arena a particular individual would be to create an ambiguity at a most inappropriate time.

There is a further peculiarity about the fighting bull, in that it is a pedigree animal which is very carefully bred and raised for an event in which it will be used only once. Those who go to horse races need to know the name and past form of the horses which will be racing because this helps them to predict what will happen in the race they are attending. The bull, however, is used only once, there is no past form and no matter how good it is during the *corrida* it will never be allowed in the arena again. Members of the audience are therefore only interested in the animal for a short time. They are concerned with its behaviour for the time it is in the arena and thus they do not need to individuate it; it is merely a good, bad or indifferent representative of a type – *toro bravo*. Interestingly, although performers and *aficionados* may remember the performance of a particular bull in a particular *corrida*, it seems that only those bulls which have killed famous *matadores* are remembered by name. De Cossío's history of famous bulls (Vol. 1: 325–401) contains details of bulls which have been particularly impressive in the arena (in the nineteenth and early twentieth centuries, it was usually for the number of spikes they received or for the number of horses they killed) but few know anything about them. People remember, however, that it was *Bailador* which killed Joselito, *Islero* which killed Manolete and, more recently, *Avispado* which killed Paquirri. It is not that these are thought of as 'bad' bulls, but rather that they are somewhat special because they have inverted the normal relationship between man and animal and, more than that, they have been able to do so with a particularly skilled *matador*.

The qualities of the *toro bravo*

The bulls selected for stud purposes are mated with a certain number of different females and a record is kept of the various offspring, so that the owner has a note of the different combinations of qualities exhibited by the offspring of each pairing. The performance of a bull in a *corrida* will be recorded by the owner's representative and a note of this will be added to the records. If a cow is found to be producing poor quality animals she may be removed from the breeding stock. Alternatively it might be felt that the stud bull is at fault; if several females mated with it regularly produce substandard animals, it might be replaced by a younger bull.

The qualities of an adult female are never shown publicly because cows do not appear in the arena: it is only her male offspring which reveal the quality of good animals. As Arauz de Robles puts it: 'the female is considered only as a vehicle for transmission, she is simply a matrix' (1979: 179). Many people made similar comments to me. It was said that the female passed on qualities which her male offspring then revealed in public. Cows of *ganado bravo* will attack as quickly as will a bull, are equally dangerous in terms of ferocity, and yet are never used in *corridas*.[14] It is always emphasized that the *corrida* involves and *must* involve the meeting of two males; the idea of using cows for the event would be inconceivable. The significance of this confrontation between two males will be examined in chapters 8 and 9. To a certain extent, the division between the private realm of the ranch and the public realm of the *plaza de toros* parallels what happens on the human level in this culture, for, as will be shown later, there is a strong distinction made between private and public realms; the former is traditionally associated with women and the latter very definitely associated with men. It is men who have an active public role whereas the traditional female role (except where domestic female duties take women into public) is largely contained in the private, domestic domain. Although, to continue the parallel, cows are not used in the *plazas de toros* and it is only bulls which have a public role, one must not be tempted to push a symbolic analogy between women and cows and men and bulls too far; whereas men are primarily associated with the public and women with the private/domestic, both move back and forth between the two realms. In the world of *ganado bravo*, however, cows always remain in the private realm (the ranch) and bulls move from private to public (the arena), but this is a one-way passage. Once they have embarked on it they are unlikely to return except under very special circumstances.[15]

The owner must decide each year which animals are to be set aside for *corridas* and which for *novilladas*. He does this on the basis of how the animals develop. Those which fill out particularly well, have well-developed horns, and generally have the necessary presence, will be kept for selling as full *toros de lidia* (a more technical term for 'fighting bull' –

see appendix for full discussion of the term *lidia*) between four and six years old. He will further decide whether certain bulls ought to be kept for certain *plazas*, for there are certain regional variations in the tastes of *aficionados*. In Bilbao or Pamplona, for example, the preference is for large bulls with wide horns, whereas in Seville the preference is for smaller, slimmer and generally more finely proportioned bulls. The decisions of the owner will also be based on whether he is asked to supply bulls to a range of *plazas*, which he will be if his ranch has a good reputation nationally, whereas at the opposite end of the scale a ranch which is small and with no particular reputation may only be asked to supply *novillos* for small village celebrations. Such a rancher would not keep bulls until they reach the age of full *toros de lidia*, because he would be unlikely to sell them and once they have passed this age they are unusable.

Bulls prepared for *novilladas* can be sold at three to four years old, and it is also possible, as already mentioned, to supply bulls with slight defects, something which is not possible for a full *corrida*. *Novillos* with deformed horns or which are blind in one eye may be used in *novilladas* but on the posters they must be announced as *desecho de tienta* (rejected from the testing). This does not mean that all bulls in *novilladas* are deformed or substandard, and even with those announced as *desecho de tienta* it is often difficult for the untrained eye to see why.

The examination of the bulls for the *corrida* by the veterinary surgeons has already been mentioned, but it is necessary to elaborate a little more on this. According to the regulations the bulls for a *corrida* must be perfect physical specimens and should not be deformed in any way. The horns in particular should be well formed and undamaged; the bulls should show no sign of lameness and should be in good physical condition, a state judged by the sleekness of the hide and clearness of the eyes; and they should meet the age and weight requirements of the *plaza*. The veterinary surgeons also have to judge the *trapío* of the animals, rejecting them if they do not have this quality. *Trapío* is the general form, presence and bearing of the animal and it is a notoriously difficult term to come to agreement about with *aficionados*; Domecq has commented (1986: 181), it is not something which can be defined by the regulations of weight, age or lack of deformities. Some told me that *trapío* was *presencia* (bearing), others that it was *un toro muy bien hecho* (a well-formed bull). It certainly relates to physical qualities; for example, a bull with small, inturned horns would not be said to have *trapío*, neither would a bull with a large or long body and a small head and neck. Generally what is being looked for is a harmonious and attractive conjunction of shape and volume combined with a majestic presence. Gilpérez García and Fraile Sanz also insist that the apparent character traits of the bull must be taken into account. They suggest that what should immediately stand out with a true fighting bull is: 'a lively, bright, penetrating and fierce look, which gives the obvious sensation that the animal is always and at whatever moment prepared, without pausing for a moment to consider the consequences, to rush forward in an irate and bold attack against whatever person or object dares to invade its territory' (1972: 6). The problem is further complicated by the fact that there might be an accepted sense or concept of *trapío* for a particular *plaza*; for example, bulls which are acceptable in Marbella might not be acceptable in Bilbao or Seville. For veterinary surgeons to reject an animal for *falta de trapío* (lacking *trapío*) does not mean that they are unfit for use in another *plaza*. I have recorded many examples of bulls which were rejected for lacking *trapío* in important *plazas* which were later used in other *plazas* on the south coast where the standards are different.

It is only once it is in the arena that a full judgement can be made of the quality of the bull; here it is necessary to return to the term *bravo*. Earlier in this chapter, *bravo* was used to define the bull as a wild animal in contrast to a domestic animal; but the word *bravo* is closely associated with the term *bravura* (wildness or ferocity) which is used to describe the *quality* of a good fighting bull. A bull with *bravura* should demonstrate it in the arena by charging repeatedly at whatever moves and by the ability and willingness to continue charging even when suffering pain. Dr Zumel, at one time president of the Taurine Federation, when asked to describe the basis of the power of the fighting bull, replies '*La bravura no gobernable*' ('Ungovernable wildness/fierceness). The idea of *ungovernable* wildness or fierceness is most important, in that it emphasizes that these are natural qualities, that the animal is not trained to charge, that it should not think but rather that it is responding to natural urges.

The other important psychological characteristic which the bull should possess is *nobleza*. *Nobleza* is a difficult term to define in this context and there seem to be as many definitions of it as there are *aficionados*. Basically, though, in this context, it refers to a quality of nobility and honesty in behaviour but it also signifies that the animal is not treacherous, and in these senses it is also used to refer to horses. When applied to bulls it means those which attack smoothly and do not suddenly hook to one side with their horns or deliberately seek the body of the *torero*. All the breeders, *aficionados* and *toreros* with whom I spoke said that a bull with *nobleza* was one which was *suave* (smooth), that did not have any *trampas* (nasty tricks) and, connected with this, that it was one '*que no mueve los dos cuernos*' (that doesn't move its horns') and '*que los cuernos no sirven pa' na*" ('that its horns aren't used for anything'). Both of these comments indicated that the bull should not be looking for an opportunity to gore the *torero*, for the implication drawn from such behaviour is that the animal is deliberately trying to kill the man. It is morally unacceptable for a man to want to kill another man, but is thought even more unacceptable for such a desire to come from an animal, and in the context of this event it is a very wrong cultural association.[16]

This is not to imply that the bull should pose no threat to the *torero*; any fighting bull with its horns intact constitutes a very real danger to the man confronting it, for he risks serious injury if he does not have the nerve to stand his ground and the technical skill to control the animal. While it is perfectly acceptable for the man to take the decision to bring his body ever closer to the bull, it is totally unacceptable to see the bull apparently deciding to bring itself closer to the man, and there is never any pleasure expressed in seeing a bull threatening the man by twisting its head towards the man's body. Domecq (1986: 251ff) in his detailed discussion of *nobleza*, has suggested that a bull with this quality is one which allows the *torero* to be relaxed when confronting it. Needless to say the notion of being 'relaxed' is relative to this context, for only a skilled performer would be relaxed when standing in the path of a 500 kg fighting bull, however smoothly it charged, but it implies that the *torero* should have no more difficulties to face than that charge.

What is expected of the bull in the arena is that it attack anything which moves and that it should do so unhesitatingly. The bull which paws the ground before charging, a standard Hollywood image to suggest a dangerous animal, is not a good bull in the context of this event, for it indicates that the animal is hesitant; it is threatening but is not sure enough of itself to attack and, according to most *aficionados*, it has cowardly qualities. A bull which waits before it charges, which looks from the cape to the body of the man and then back again, is not a bull with *nobleza* but rather it is one with *sentido* (sense or judgement); it appears to be weighing up how to attack. A bull with *sentido* is difficult to perform with, because the *torero* cannot be certain what the animal is going to do. The whole basis of *toreo* (see appendix), which is that the man deceives the bull, breaks down if the bull attempts to deceive the man as well. A bull with *sentido* is not a good bull because it implies decision and judgement on the part of the animal; qualities which should only apply to men. The animal should attack without hesitation, without thinking. In terms of the arguments advanced earlier this is important, because *sentido* is regarded as a learned rather than a natural quality, and thus a bull which exhibits *sentido* is ipso facto less 'natural', less of a wild animal. There is a term which, as it were, describes a state beyond the mere possession of *sentido*. A bull that wants to attack the man, which shows no interest in the cape or *muleta*, is described as one which '*sabe latín*' ('it knows Latin'), that is to say, it is 'educated' or 'wise', and this implies the opposite of being natural. In one *corrida* I attended, the bull had no interest in following the cape, so much so that one man commented '*Él sabe latin*', to which his neighbour replied '*¡Sí, y griego tambien!*' ('Yes, and Greek as well!'). At one level the basic contest between man and bull is that between intelligence and animal force; if the bull has *both* of these qualities it constitutes a very wrong sort of challenge.

It is important, however, that the bull does constitute a real challenge to the man. If a bull shows itself to be excessively *manso* (meek or tame and, in this context, by implication cowardly), by not attacking or by shying away from the capes or the horse, then *aficionados* will deny that it is a fighting bull at all. It is felt that there are certain qualities of behaviour expected of a fighting bull, and if it does not demonstrate that it possess these then it is not worthy of the name *toro bravo*. An animal which does not have the qualities of a *toro bravo* does not have the power to generate emotion in the public, and thus a vital and essential element of the atmosphere of the *corrida* is missing. At a *corrida* in Seville, in which the *matador* was struggling to extract some sort of performance from a bull which would not charge, my neighbour yelled out '*¡El toro se fue! ¡No tienes toro, matalo ya!*' (literally, 'The bull has gone, you don't have a bull anymore, kill it!). By this he meant that the essential quality of 'bull-ness' had gone and that the animal was not worth bothering with. On the other hand, in the *plaza* one can hear the comment '*¡Es más toro!*' ('It is more of a bull!'), meaning that a much more acceptable animal is in the arena. Gines Serran Pagan, writing about a celebration in Grazalema where the bull is run through the streets, makes a very important point about this loss of quality of the animal, and it is worth quoting a passage in both Spanish and English to get across the point that a change in behaviour or character is seen as a change in the essence of the animal:

Sin bravura, el toro dejaba de ser toro para convertirse en un animal manso, y entonces es cuando acaba la fiesta.

Without wildness/ferocity the bull ceases to be a bull [that is, a fighting bull] and becomes a tame animal, and that is when the celebration finishes. *(1979: 127)*

In general conversation in Spain, one can assume that in the majority of cases when the word *toro* is used the speaker is referring to a *toro bravo* and not just any male of the bovine species. The quotation above further emphasis that *toro* does not simply refer to the male of the bovine species nor even to the *toro bravo*, but also to the qualities that such an animal is expected to possess. Once the wildness or ferocity of the animal has gone it is no more than a tame animal; it still has the physical form of the fighting bull but it is now much closer to a domestic animal, and is therefore unfit for the celebration. Exactly the same thing occurs in the formal *corrida*; the *toro bravo* beginning as a wild animal is symbolically transformed and converted into a tame or domestic animal and as such it is killed and subsequently eaten. The analysis of this process will be undertaken in chapter 8.

7

The *matador de toros*

The career of a *matador* has traditionally been seen by many young men in Spain as a possible means of economic and social advancement. The literature of fiction and biography in Spanish abounds with examples of accounts in which poor would-be *matadores* gain a glimpse of the apparently easily gained riches of a successful *matador* and the wealth of the ranches which they have seen while attending *tentaderos* (the testing sessions, described earlier), and vow to risk all to escape their disadvantaged economic and social situation. This attitude is perhaps summed up in the famous sentence of El Cordobés who told his sister, who brought him up, that he was going to be a *matador* and that, 'Either I'll buy you a house or I'll dress you in mourning' (Collins and Lapierre 1970: 278).

The matador until quite recently has been regarded by many as 'an exceptional person who broke a general rule of acceptance [that is, of his station in life], of submission, a national hero, a man who has gone beyond his circumstances, who was splendidly out of tune with his class' (Arauz de Robles 1979: 90). Brandes, writing about the young men of Monteros, a town in eastern Andalusia, who carry the large, heavy statue of El Señor de Consuelo during the town's religious celebration, suggests that: 'their personal sense of prestige and power emanates from community recognition of the supposedly remarkable physical feat in which they are engaged' (1980: 208). In a similar way, the *torero*, traditionally a young man with a poor educational background and with a low socio-economic status, is able to gain public recognition and prestige by being able to perform what is culturally accepted to be a difficult and dangerous task; the role of *torero* being certainly a male Spanish ideal. Applause, attention and prestige are the immediate rewards if he performs well on a particular occasion, but if he goes on to perform well on many occasions and to become a successful *matador* he will gain much wider public recognition, prestige and wealth, and will be able to rise out of his disadvantaged socioeconomic background.

Toreros have rarely come from the middle or upper classes, where there has always been the possibility for economic and social advancement; they have come from the rural labouring class or urban working class where opportunities are more limited. Araúz de Robles points out that most *toreros* have come from either Andalusia or Castile, but especially Andalusia, both of which have particularly inflexible social structures so that upward mobility is extremely difficult for the lower classes. He refers to the *torero* as:

> the prototype of the hero of great ignorance from an inhospital and tough social background. He knows nothing and is not interested in anything other than his own struggle for glory which is at the same time a struggle for existence for without success life for him is so miserable...that it is not worth living: 'To be rich, to have the newspapers talk of him and people greet him even though it were at the cost of his life'. (1979: 95 – the quotation within a quotation is from Blasco Ibanez)

As was mentioned before (see the section on *rejoneo* in chapter two) members of the upper-middle and upper classes do perform in *corridas*, but they do so as mounted *rejoneadores* (a style of performing which is much more in keeping with their status) rather than as foot *toreros*. The exception to the general rule that *toreros* come from the lower classes would be those who are the sons or nephews (and there are many examples of both) of successful and wealthy *toreros*. Such young men do have other opportunities open to them, and yet they have opted for this career because they have inherited their father's or uncle's interest (an interest which is possibly coupled with desire for fame, public recognition, wealth, and excitement) in the event.

The fact that *toreros* can escape their social backgrounds is illustrated in this century by the way in which, although from the lower classes, individuals of the stature of Joselito El Gallo, Sanchez Mijias, Juan Belmonte, Manolete, Pepe Luis Vazquez and Antonio Ordoñez (to name but the most famous) have been sought after and lauded by intellectuals and high society. Most recently, in the 1960s Manuel Benitez, 'El Cordobés', became an international celebrity and national hero. Araúz de Robles suggests that 'the *torero* who emerges from nothing [is] the synthesis of the people, a born leader, an example of self-sufficiency. Without a doubt El Cordobés has travelled on this convenient street-car to popularity' (1979: 162). In fact, during this time El Cordobés was promoted as an example of what a young Spaniard could do with his life; his was a classic 'rags to riches' story (see Collins and Lapierre 1970). In an interview, Manolo Arruza, a *matador*, made the point that the career of the *matador* represents the image of the possibility of escape for young men with few opportunities open to them: 'The *torero* was formerly the symbol of something in which the people needed to believe, the possibility of avoiding a grey future. The opportunity to emerge from nothing to fame and fortune. Knowing that someone could escape the misery meant that miracles were possible' (*El Mundo de los Toros* 4 April 1978, 644: 23).

Although the role of *matador* was for long a symbol of social and economic escape, Araúz de Robles has pointed out that the *matador* is a rebel, not a reformer. He sees economic injustice and has often been on the unpleasant side of it but he does not want to change the system, only to change his relation with it. To quote again from Araúz de Robles:

> their apparent rebellion, that rebellion of El Cordobés for example, is nothing other than an individual thing. They don't attempt to change the status quo nor do they seek a greater social fluidity, but rather to occupy one of the highest places on the social scale. The *matador* is not a reformer: things will remain the same after he has achieved his glory. (1979: 96)

Successful *matadores* tend to invest their money in land, especially in agricultural land, and many buy herds of fighting bulls. In this way they are able to identify themselves with the rural elite, for owning land and stock gives a more solid status than that of simply being a *torero*. Araúz de Robles suggests that this desire to own land, to become a rancher, has an aspect of revenge about it. The *matador* 'wants to get his teeth into the cause of the social injustices in his region, not in order to remedy them but to benefit from them himself in a spirit of revenge' (1979: 96).

A general spirit of revenge was certainly noticeable among many of the young *toreros* with whom I spoke, especially of course among those who were not yet successful and were in the position of submitting to various economic abuses, of having to go to impresarios to beg the opportunity to perform, and generally of being manipulated by others. A particularly close friend always told me that he would put up with these indignities now but that once established he would be looking forward to teaching a lesson to those who had treated him badly.

Toreros wish to change their disadvantaged economic and social position, and the successful ones have demonstrated to the others that the restraining social system is not as closed as it might appear. Even though they might become wealthy men, they are not expected to make themselves aloof from those of the social stratum from which they came. The literature has many examples of *matadores* losing the sympathy of the public and incurring its hostility in the *plaza* if it is felt that he is attempting to deny his humble origins and associating exclusively with high society. Whether a *torero* is to be found in the bars where members of the taurine world meet depends on the individual. Some of the most famous have such a heavy programme of performances during the season that they have little time for social events, and some do not like to go out and about in public. There is still the expectation, however, that they should be accessible and in public; certainly there are several bars in Seville where one would have a good chance of meeting on any one day a cross-section of the taurine world. I was particularly struck by the easy familiarity with which even famous *matadores* are treated, and their hotel rooms before a *corrida* might well be full of people who have dropped in to wish them luck.

The familiarity is emphasized in the way that people use the familiar *tú* when addressing *toreros*. They also use Christian names, diminutives and nicknames. Pitt-Rivers has shown (1971: 160) that nicknames are not usually used in Andalusia as terms of address, but this is not so with *toreros* (as he notes), especially because the nickname is often used as a performing name and can hardly be kept a secret. The first time I was on my way to be introduced to Curro Romero, a *matador de toros* of legendary fame in Spain (Curro, incidentally, being a diminutive of Francisco), I asked those with me how I should address him. I wanted to know whether I should address him as Sr Romero and use the formal *usted* as one would expect to do when addressing someone older more senior and unknown. I was immediately told that this was a ridiculous suggestion, that he was Curro and should be addressed as *tú*.

This easy familiarity does not exist with *rejoneadores*. There is no expectation that *rejoneadores* should be as accessible to the public as *toreros*. *Rejoneadores* are not drawn from the same social class as *toreros*, the fact that they must own a string of horses plus all the equipment shows that they must be wealthy, and they are thus isolated from the public to start with. Although such possessions can be acquired by a successful *torero* the point is that in terms of general public awareness these are *ascribed* to a *rejoneador* by virtue of his birth into the landed gentry; whether this is actually true or not is another matter.

The horse and horsemanship are associated with the nobility and with wealthy landowning classes; the word *caballero*, gentleman, literally means 'horseman'. The *rejoneador* is perceived as a representative of his class and Vincente Zabala sums up the general opinion of *rejoneadores* thus: 'The general idea is that a *rejoneador* comes to be a type of little lord, landowner and latifundist, who mounts a horse in order to show himself off' *Aplausos* 31 August 1981, No. 205). Although Vincente Zabala in his article goes on to attack this view, claiming that *rejoneadores* are all committed artists, this comment *does* reflect a generally held view. Despite the fact that the best *rejoneadores*, such as Alvaro Domecq, Joao Mora, Angel and Rafael Peralta, Manuel Vidrie and Antonio Vargas, are well-known names to the *aficionados* and their skill is admired, *rejoneadores* have never captured the public imagination in the same way the *matadores* have. The general public cannot form an intimate relationship with members of this class, they have never become idealized figures and *rejoneo* has remained of secondary importance to the style of *toreo* on foot.

The career of a *matador*

An aspiring *matador* must have a great *afición* for and dedication to the event (without full time commitment to being a *matador* he stands little chance of becoming one), and an enormous confidence in his own ability to be a good *matador*, in order to sustain himself through the difficult years of absolute and relative poverty he is likely to suffer as he attempts to establish himself. He knows that few are lucky enough to become famous and wealthy; some make a living wage, most fail. A *novillero* friend of mine who was in his mid-twenties lamented the fact that he had been trying to get established during the last thirteen years, and yet his life was extremely precarious. He added that not only was he not earning money but that he had to train hard every day, he couldn't drink or smoke and he had to be careful what he ate in order to remain fit. If he had opted for a different career, he said, he would now be established and have a good income and a comfortable life, instead of living on a meagre income, supplemented by what he could come by illegally.

An important factor in the path to success is to obtain a good patron who is willing to commit himself to considerable financial support. Such financial support allows the *torero* to spend all day concentrating on becoming a *matador*. If he does not have to worry about having to earn enough to live, he can train during the day and go to the bars where people in the taurine world meet. There he will obtain information about contracts which are being made and of *tentaderos* being held on the ranches. If he does not have to go out to work he will be able to leave for these testings at very short notice, and so have a greater chance of bringing himself to the attention of someone who might be able to help advance his career.

Better than a patron is an official *apoderado* (literally, 'a supporter', but in this case 'an agent or manager') who has good contacts and is willing to invest the time and money necessary to secure contracts for his protégé. Of course an aspiring *matador* must first bring himself to the attention of such an *apoderado*, which he can only do by showing his qualities at a *tentadero*, or by using his own money to buy his way on to a programme and thus perform in public. He can only do the latter when he has had enough practice in *tentaderos*.

Aspiring *matadores* have to practise without bulls, and the sports ground of the swimming pool in Seville is a regular meeting place for all sorts of *toreros*. Here they have a wooden mock-up of a bull with which they practise the sword thrusts necessary to kill a real bull. They also have a set of horns mounted on wheels, which one person operates in imitation of the bull whilst another person uses the cape. The assistants also make use of the same contraption for practising placing *banderillas*. All of these activities are accompanied by a great deal of discussion between the young men on the efficacy and the aesthetic merit of the various passes.

At the swimming pool they also play *frontón*, a game which consists of hitting a small rubber ball with a small wooden bat against a high wall. The game requires fast movement and good concentration and it strengthens the wrists; it is therefore felt to be an ideal exercise. Many of the *toreros*, for these games and exercises, dress in an old suit of lights or something similarly heavy, over which they wear a track suit. All of this is extremely hot and heavy and helps them to get used to the discomfort and weight of the suit when they come to perform in the *plaza*.

As mentioned in the previous chapter, bull breeders must test their stock in order to keep a high quality, and this is done by testing the young cows for fierceness before they are accepted as part of the breeding stock. Apart from being important occasions for the breeder, these *tentaderos* are important for aspiring *matadores* because they offer them the opportunity to practice their capework with live animals.

The owner will invite one or two *matadores* to do the testing for him, and various ranch hands will act as assistants. Traditionally any *aficionados* or aspiring *matadores* who show up at the ranch are never turned away on these occasions, and for that reason the owners attempt to keep the dates of *tentaderos* as secret as possible because they don't want to be flooded with aspiring *matadores*. It is an accepted custom that if someone arrives with a *muleta* the owner will allow him to make a few passes with a calf after it has been tested. Once the owner has seen enough of the qualities of a particular calf and the invited *matador* has finished, one of the visitors will be invited into the arena. Each is given the opportunity of spending a few moments in the arena at some point in the *tentadero*. Those who have come along with the hope of practising (as opposed to those who are there merely to watch) draw straws among themselves, to decide the order they will take when they are invited into the arena.

An illegal form of getting a chance to practise is for the youths to go into the fields of the bull ranches at night and cape the animals. As the *corrida* relies on the fact that the bull has never faced a man on foot with a cape before it enters the arena, this illegal night practice can cause serious problems later. Some of those who do go to the fields at night, even though they are acting illegally, act responsibly and only practise with cows. As several of them pointed out to me, they never know whether it will be they who have to face a bull in the arena which has had the experience of night caping.

Although aspiring *matadores* can get themselves physically fit with exercises and can get the feel of cape movements using the mock bull, what is most important is to be able to get into the arena to work actual bulls and learn by experience how to kill them. Bulls are expensive, so unless a young *matador* has contracts to perform in a *plaza*, it is no easy matter to gain this experience. It was quite common until a few years ago (it certainly now seems to be in decline) for *matadores* to go to slaughterhouses in order to practise the use of the *descabello* (the sword-like instrument used to finish off a bull – see description in chapter 1). Because of the way slaughterhouses are organized they are unable to run the animals around and are thus unable to use the sword with which the *matador* first attempts to kill the bull in the arena, although I did hear stories of youths who attempted to sneak into the stock yard at night and to cape the animals ready for slaughter. A number of my friends would go to considerable lengths to get the money to buy a bull which for one reason or another had been rejected for public performance by the ranch owner. One of them, who was a good-looking fellow, set himself up as something of a gigolo and had a string of wealthy women friends from whom he would try to extract money to buy such reject bulls. Having purchased such an animal he would then either practise with it in the *plaza* on the ranch, or in some other private *plaza*, and would thus have the opportunity of practice with the cape and *muleta* and finally would be able to kill it; something which of course is not possible in a *tentadero*.

Aspiring *matadores* can also attend *capeas* which are open to all but few actually do so. These affairs tend to be extremely chaotic and it is actually rare for an individual to be able to execute more than a couple of passes before the animal is distracted by someone else. Some *capeas* do make use of professional *toreros* if the animals to be played are more than calves, but these occasions do not afford much chance for practice either. Such animals are rarely killed and have often been played before. This means that they immediately know the difference between the man and the cape and are not easily deceived into following the cape. It is because of these factors that many commentators have argued that there have never been great *matadores* who have had to rely on these events for their practice.

If the young *matador* is lucky enough to find a manager with genuine interest in him and who is willing to pay to get him contracts, he will begin his career in the *novilladas sin picadores* (*novilladas* without *picadores*), will be registered with the *matadores'* union as a *matador de novillos* (killer of young bulls), and will be referred to in general usage as a *novillero*. The first *novilladas* for which he is likely to be contracted will probably be in villages and small towns and are likely to do little for his reputation, but they will give him an invaluable foundation of experience. From these he will move on to *novilladas con picadores* (*novilladas* with *picadores*), which are again likely to be in villages and small towns. This is where a good manager is essential, because in order to be contracted for a *novillada* it is necessary to spend money. There are far fewer *novilladas* than there are *novilleros* who are willing to perform in them, and it is thus often necessary to buy oneself onto a programme, or at least to accept little or no money for the afternoon. Even if he does receive the official rate of pay, as he is more likely to do in the larger towns, the *novillero* still has to pay for his team of assistants and the travelling and hotel expenses; the manager takes his share and the press must be paid (see below). Even in the larger towns it is often necessary to pay the impresario in order to get him to purchase good quality bulls, rather than the poor quality animals which would probably be used if the *novilleros* are as yet unimportant, and unlikely to draw a large crowd.

This movement from *novilladas sin picadores* through *novilladas con picadores* in unimportant *plazas* to *novilladas* in important *plazas* is the ideal, but it often does not work that way. Some fairly unscrupulous managers are not willing to spend the necessary money and prefer to get their protégé on to a programme in a major *plaza* because it does not cost them so much. In Seville, for example, there is a *novillada* virtually every Sunday in the season and so there are opportunities for many *novilleros* to perform, and if the *novillero* succeeds the contracts are likely to come more quickly because he has performed in front of people with important contacts. Of course it is a temptation on the part of *novilleros* to accept such a contract, because it is prestigious to perform in a major *plaza*; but, as many of them pointed out to me, it is a risky thing to do because they are not usually prepared for such a *plaza*, not yet having enough experience to rely on. If they only perform once or twice a year and then perform in Seville, for example, they are more likely to fail than to succeed, and thus seriously damage their chances of getting contracts anywhere else.

Those involved in the taurine world were reluctant to be specific with me about double dealing, secrecy and illegal activity, although rumours about malpractices flourish. However, the *novilleros* and *matadores* who were close friends of mine gave accounts of some of their personal experiences and they verified the rumours I heard on other occasions and from other sources.[2] The manipulation necessary to be able to perform in public can go to such extremes that for a friend of mine to perform in a *festival* (the out of season charity event), where the *matadores* take part without a fee, he had to pay so many different people that it cost him a considerable amount of money to be able to give his services free!

In whatever *novillada* or *corrida* he is performing, it is important for the *matador* to have *preparado la prensa* (literally, 'prepared the press', meaning to have paid a certain amount of money to the reporters and photographers who will cover the event), because the reports of a performance can have a considerable influence on the chances of further contracts. If not sufficiently 'prepared', the press can damn a good performance with faint praise or can concentrate on the odd bad moments rather than on the overall performance. If well 'prepared' they can do exactly the reverse, and can find good things to say even though the *matador* might have been booed from the *plaza*. The same *novillero* who had the problem with the festival performed extremely well on two afternoons in a series of *novilladas* in a town near Valencia. He paid as much as he could to the local newspaper critic, who was also a correspondent for a national magazine dedicated to the *corrida*. The amount paid was obviously not enough, and he received a few cursory lines in the report. Other *novilleros* who had not done as well but who had obviously given more money received much more coverage, including several flattering photographs.

The roles of impresario (of the *plaza de toros*) and manager were originally distinct, but in recent years impresarios have become managers of the most important *matadores* and *novilleros*. As they have slowly increased their influence as managers, they naturally include the *toreros*

A group of *toros bravos* (wild bulls or 'fighting bulls') on a ranch where they are specially bred. These animals, of the same age, have been selected for a *corrida*.

Matadores practising with the *capote* (left) and *muleta* (right) [note the stick and sword used to hold the *muleta* open]. Learning to execute the passes requires considerable skill and grace but the real difficulty comes when they are attempted with the partner missing here – the bull.

The hotel room which the *matador* has just left; the desk
becomes a temporary 'altar', where he has spent a few
moments in silent prayer, and a candle is left burning until he
returns. The remains of a cigarette and the empty coffee cup
indicate his other human needs.

(*Left*) Dressed for the *corrida*; the *mozo de espadas* (right)
makes a final adjustment to the costume. Note how the 'suit of
lights' sets the *matador* apart from ordinary men.

Here the *matador* performs the first *lance* to bring the erratically charging bull into his orbit and under his control.

A *picador* at work; here the spike is being placed a little too far back, it should be more centrally in the neck muscle. Note metal leggings of the *picador* and the heavy padding on the horse which protects it from the bull's attack. The men in the arena are not *toreros* but *monosabios* (literally 'wise monkeys'), employed by the impresario to assist the *picador*.

A *matador* placing his own *banderillas*, all of which have been well-placed in the neck muscle. The *matador* is so dangerously close to the bull that his assistants have already started to leave the *burladero* to protect him.

This *matador* with his *montera* (hat) raised in his right hand and his *muleta* in the left is offering a *brindis* (a dedication) to someone in the audience before the final part of his performance.

A *pase* with the *muleta* during the last part of the performance. The bull is brought gracefully close past the body of the *matador* who is calm and perfectly in control.

A perfect kill. The *matador* takes his final controlled risk to lean over the horns and kill the bull.

(*Overleaf*) The appropriate relation between bull and *matador*. The bull is dead on the sand and the *matador* is standing and triumphant. Note the *banderillero* asking the president if he should cut the ear as an award for a fine performance.

(*Left*) The ever-present risk has become reality; the *matador* is caught on the horns. Here the proper relationship has been reversed, with the bull controlling the man. On this occasion, as the *matador* leaned over the horns to plunge the sword in, the bull turned its horns upwards into the man's stomach.

The *matador* has already placed the sword extremely well in this bull but he has decided to use the *descabello* to sever the medulla. He uses his *muleta* and the assistant his *capote* to encourage the bull to lower its head so that he can stab between the cervical vertebrae; the bull should fall immediately.

they manage on the programmes in the *plazas de toros* which they also manage. A small group of men (about six or seven) control a very large number of *plazas* in Spain, including all the major ones. It is clearly important for a *novillero* to have a manager who has links with members of this select group if he wishes to appear in the major *plazas*. Impresario-managers will take on promising *novilleros*, who obviously benefit from the increased opportunity to perform in many *plazas*. Even small-scale impresarios can be extremely important in a *novillero*'s career. For example, an impresario who rents some half a dozen *plazas* in southern Andalusia has a son who has become a very good full *matador de toros* at an early age, due at least partly to the fact that he had been aided by the opportunities to perform in his father's *plazas* and in those of other impresarios with whom his father associates, whilst other *novilleros* who started at the same time as him and seemed to have an equal ability have been left well behind.

Most aspiring *matadores* try not to take on any other paid employment because they see this as a sign of defeat, a sign that they are not going to succeed. Those who really do have very few contracts – and some of my friends only performed once or twice a year – are forced to take some part-time job in order to survive, but they regard this situation as temporary. A *novillero* can usually only take a part-time job because he needs to train daily and he wants to be able to leave at short notice for *tentaderos*.

Novilleros, and even full *matadores* who have only just begun in their career, usually have very little money, and yet they must not be seen to be poor. It is a matter of considerable personal honour to be well groomed, neatly dressed and to have enough to buy drinks for their friends, admirers and associates. A *novillero* I knew well had few contracts and no apparent income, and yet was always very well dressed and always had enough money. He told me that he lived by shoplifting (something at which he was excellent; he would even take orders for things such as clothes from major department stores) which he regarded as less degrading than working for wages. It also had the advantage of leaving all the day free for training and if necessary for going to the country to the ranches.

From *novillero* to *matador de toros*

At some point, if he wishes to continue in the profession, a *novillero* must decide that it is time for him to take the graduation ceremony which will make him a full *matador de toros*. His decision will be made in conjunction with his manager and is influenced by a combination of factors. It is important that he feels that he has had enough experience in playing and killing *novillos*, because the older and heavier bulls used in the *corrida* are more difficult to perform with, partly because of their size and weight but also because they are psychologically more mature, and a young *matador* without adequate experience as a *novillero* can ruin his career by making this move too soon. Another important factor in the decision is whether he is likely to get contracts as a *matador*, because once he has graduated to the status of full *matador* he is unable (except in very special circumstances) to return to performing in *novilladas*.[2]

In recent years there has been a decline in the number of *novilladas* held throughout Spain. This is due to the high costs of staging them and to the fact that, as the costs of attending both *corridas* and *novilladas* are considerable, many people become less willing to pay a lot of money to see relatively unknown performers in *novilladas* – they want to see well known *matadores* performing with larger bulls and they thus prefer to attend *corridas*. This decline is lamented by critics, *aficionados* and *toreros*, for in their opinion this gives fewer opportunities for *toreros* to learn their craft. As a consequence, many *novilleros* take the graduation ceremony far too early, in terms of experience which they actually have, in the hope of earning more contracts as a *matador*. Unfortunately they often find that when they begin to perform as *matadores* it is extremely difficult to work with the bulls. Consequently they give poor performances and thus it becomes even more difficult to get contracts.

As the graduation ceremony takes place during a *corrida*, a *novillero* who has made the decision to become a *matador* must find an impresario who will include him in a programme for a *corrida*. The main part of the actual ceremony takes place during the caping of the first bull and is called the *alternativa* (from the verb '*alternar*', meaning 'to alternate or take turns'). The first bull of the afternoon should be caped and killed by the senior *matador* but he cedes this bull to the *novillero*, thus 'alternating' the order of their appearance during the afternoon. The *novillero* capes the first bull and later, when he should pick up the sword and *muleta*, he waits in the arena close to the barrier with his cape. The senior *matador* and the other join him in the arena. The senior *matador* now acts as *padrino* (sponsor) and actually confers the graduation, while the other *matador* acts as the *testigo* (witness). All are bareheaded as the *padrino* hands to the *novillero* the latter's sword and *muleta*, and receives his cape. The two embrace, as do the witness and the new *matador*, and the sponsor says a few words of advice or congratulation to the junior, who now continues with the performance. With the second bull, which now belongs to the senior performer, at the point when he should pick up the sword and *muleta* the three meet in the arena; the latter receives his cape from the senior and they all embrace. The fact that he has now graduated to the status of *matador de toros* is registered with the controlling union.[3]

Although the term *padrino*, which often means godfather, seems to be taken from the language of ritual kinship, it does not carry the responsibilities normally associated with this role, and there is no corresponding term for the *novillero* during the ceremony. The relationship between the *padrino* and the new *matador* is not an enduring one. The *padrino* does not attempt to obtain contracts for the newly created *matador*, nor does he have any other responsibilities for his career, although the latter may gain some prestige and attention in the press if he receives the *alternativa* from a famous *matador* in an important *plaza*. A manager will therefore attempt to get the *novillero* who wants to take his *alternativa* contracted for a high quality *corrida*; his ability to do this will largely depend on how well the *novillero* has been performing and/or how much influence the manager has.

The ex-*novillero* has achieved the rank of *matador de toros* but he still must *confirmar* (confirm) this. The *alternativa* can take place in any *plaza de toros* in Spain, but according to the regulations it can only be confirmed in Madrid or Mexico City, these being the two most important *plazas* in Spain and South America respectively. It has already been mentioned that this is a state controlled event, and this need to confirm his status in the capital of the country emphasizes the relationship between *la Fiesta Nacional* and the status of the national capital, indicating yet another authoritarian aspect of the event. If the *matador* is not particularly successful, it might be years before he is able to confirm his *alternativa*; some never do. If he is successful, then he is likely to be contracted to perform in Madrid in the same season. The confirmation ceremony has the same form as the original, but the *padrino* and *testigo* are unlikely to be the same. The fact that the *padrino* at the *confirmación* need not be (indeed is most unlikely to be) the same as in the *alternativa* suggests that the relationship between the new *matador* and the *padrino* is not particularly important.

Once he has become a *matador de toros* the young man has more opportunities open to him, and he hopes to perform well enough to come to the attention of the important impresarios, and to be included in the programmes of the prestigious *ferias* such as those of Valencia, Seville, Madrid, Pamplona, Bilbao and Saragossa. He will also hope to perform in *corridas* in many other towns during the season, and possibly to go to South America during the winter. If he can obtain a contract with one of the important impresarios and has ability, he is likely to do well because of the opportunities to perform regularly. The most important and influential *matadores* are associated with the most important impresarios, and start the season with a certain number of *corridas* already contracted. Many people complain that this was a bad development because it cut down competition. Prior to the rise of these important impresario-managers a *torero* would not have a whole series of *corridas* contracted; if he did well in one then he would be likely to get another; and it is felt that this encouraged *matadores* to perform well simply because if they did not then they would not be contracted. A *matador* today, with a fixed number of *corridas*, can afford to have a few bad days or not try on some afternoons without its affecting his income. Of course, if he is consistently bad then he is unlikely to win as many contracts in the following year. New *matadores* will not have this security and must regularly try hard and perform well if they wish to be successful.

There are far fewer opportunities to perform than there are *matadores* who wish to perform, which means that many are unsuccessful. The super stars may perform in between fifty and eighty *corridas* in a season, some many more, whereas very unsuccessful ones may secure only one or two. There are also those who claim to be *matadores* who do not perform at all. Many *matadores* and *novilleros* are forced to give up completely because they are unable to support themselves. Some become *banderilleros* because they prefer the steady income of paid assistant rather than taking the risks of being a sole performer. In the nineteenth and early twentieth century, to be a *banderillero* was almost like serving an apprenticeship before becoming a *matador*; today this is not so, and most *banderilleros* are those who have taken a step down rather than acquiring the experience to step up.

The image of the *torero*

Since the mid-eighteenth century, when individual *torero* began to become famous, there has been a popular image of the *torero* as a rake and a libertine. As a result of his continual travelling, the *torero* was less bound by the morals and restrictions of the village or the town where he was known. He was continually on the move and was reputed to keep disreputable company, and was thus categorized as *sin vergüenza* (without shame, a shameless character) along with the beggars, gypsies, bandits and flamenco singers, all of whom lived on the margins of society and with whom he traditionally associated.

There was also a sense in which the *torero* certainly until he was successful but still to an extent afterwards, was regarded as shameless because he did not work, his performance in the arena not being perceived as work: in fact he rejected the sort of work which would normally be available to him. As Martinez-Alier noted of the Andalusian attitude towards work: 'if one does not want to work one is behaving like a gypsy' (1971: 211), and thus by association one is shameless.

The historian Nestor Luján gives several graphic accounts of the lives or *torero* in the eighteenth and nineteenth centuries, and the following extracts illustrate the comments made above. Of Pepe-Hillo he writes:

> His success was that of a great drunken spree: he took part in the pleasures and entertainments of the people of the town, serving as judge in the cockfights, taking part in the wild duck hunts in the corrals on the outskirts of the town, and there was no baptism nor dance in the outlying districts where Pepe-Hillo was not given a formal invitation to come and, by his presence and personality, to add spirit to the uproarious parties of the traditional folk of Madrid and Seville. (1954: 72)

Of Juan Leon in the nineteenth century, Luján writes: 'He had to go about surrounded by a pestering rabble of rascals and folk who enjoyed making a shindy; guitarists, rakes, pimps and layabouts and all the most accomplished low-lifers to come out of Andalusia' (1954: 108). The *torero* has largely lost this low-life image, although it has not completely gone, and El Viti, a recently retired *matador*, can remember a neighbour coming to his house when he was young and asking: 'Why do you want to be a *torero*, my boy? To make yourself shameless like the rest of them?' (*Blanco 7 Negro* 6–13 June 1979, No. 3501).

To some extent the image of the *torero* as a rake having a riotous life does still continue. They are certainly still glamorous figures, and the general interest/gossip magazines carry photographs of famous *matadores* at discotheques, on the beach or at important parties. The history of their romances and marriage problems are also reported, and the latest doings of El Cordobés, Paquirri, or Espartáco become front page news for such magazines. *Toreos* have long represented the epitome of masculine qualities (a theme which will be taken up in much greater detail later) and still have the reputation of being great womanizers and lovers. The Spanish edition of *PlayLady* (June 1978, No. 83) ran a long article about the sexuality of *toreros* as though it was something special, and many *toreros* are often asked about their sex lives in general magazine interviews. Of course this image of the rake does not fit with the actual lives of many *toreros*, who live quiet family lives. The image, however, remains.

Many commentators have suggested that the *torero* as a character has become rather bland compared with the devil-may-care adventurer personality they put forward as that of the 'true' *torero*. They suggest that many of them are now little more than actors who put on a costume, perform for two hours and then change back to being an 'ordinary' person again. The difference between an actor and a 'true' *torero* can perhaps be summed up in two photos and a caption which the noted critic Luis Bollain has in his book *El Toreo*. One of the photos is of Joselito El Gallo (a very famous *matador* in the 1920s) is *traje corto*, smoking a cigar, and the other is of El Cordobés in a suit of lights with his hair all dishevelled, receiving a bouquet of flowers on a lap of honour in a *plaza de toros*. Under the photo of Joselito the caption reads, '*Ser torero...*' ('To be a *torero...*'), and it continues under that of El Cordobés, '*...o estar en traje de luces*' (...or to be in a suit of lights'). Although this is meant to imply a total rejection of El Cordobés as a *torero*, for Bollain regards him as a circus performer dressed in a suit of lights rather than as a *torero*, it also implies that Joselito was more of a *torero* in ordinary clothes than El Cordobés is even when dressed as a *torero*. The general point being made involves the distinction of having the unmistakable qualities of a *torero* something which is bound up with one's whole being, and the mere wearing of a costume and playing a part.

Those with whom I spoke expected that the *torero* should be a *torero* both in and out of the *plaza*. It was expected that one should 'be' a *torero* rather than just 'do' the job of a *torero*, and there was a style of comportment and behaviour associated with this. *Toreros* should be seen out and about in public, especially at the meeting points of *aficionados* and *toreros*. They should not be seen to be poor, even if they are, and they should be well dressed and groomed by Spanish standards – one never sees *toreros* with long unkempt hair, nor do they ever have beards or moustaches.

In the early years of the twentieth century, *toreros*, when out of the *plaza*, used to wear the tight-fitting high-waisted trousers, white shirt, short jacket and wide-brimmed hat which makes up the *traje corto*. Hartley Gasquoine, for example, writing of his visit to Seville in the early years of this century, described the *toreros* he saw there: 'in their faultless tight *majo* costumes and frilled shirts, fastened with diamond studs and diamond rings on their fingers of their faultless hands and with the pigtail upon their head' (1911: 45). 'The pigtail' refers to the fact that *toreros* used to wear their hair long at the back and had it twisted into a pigtail which was then pinned up on the top of the head, the distinguishing mark of a *torero*. Today *toreros* do not wear their hair long but they wear an artificial pigtail when they are performing: this is called the *coleta* (little tail) and is pinned onto the hair at the pack of the head.

The dress described above as *traje corto* was the formal dress of the rural elite and emphasized the connection between the *torero* and the rural world. Today this connection is less emphasized, a point reflected in the dress of present day *toreros* out of the arena. Although it is not expected that they dress as before, they are still expected to dress conservatively, a point made by the Madrid critic Vincente Zabala in a newspaper report on a *corrida*: 'It grieves one today to see young *matadores* so badly dressed both in the arena and in the street. Those absurd blouses and that air of discotheque-goers detract from the former and traditional standing of the *torero' ABC*, 10 July 1979).

Commentators have complained that a *torero* out of the *plaza* is now just like any other man on the street, whereas previously, even twenty years ago, he was a distinctive figure, recognized and respected by a wider public than today. One *aficionado* told me that the *torero* used to be a '*superhombre, más que el hombre en la calle*' ('a superman, more than the man in the street'). He was a *superhombre* and yet still close enough to ordinary men to represent what every man could, potentially, become. A noted critic told me that the *torero* ought to be better than the average man, but that nowadays he is not recognized as a *torero* when he is not actually performing; the *torero* has lost his style, he complained to me, and although he might have personality in the arena he no longer carries this with him into the street.

This change is seen as part of a more general change associated with *toreros*, and can perhaps be linked with the development of the *corrida* as a spectacle which is the province of the trained performer rather than the dedicated artist. Nicholás Salas has written:

> Unfortunately today the Gypsy school [style of *toreo*] cannot exist nor does the Sevillian nor the Ronda school because today *toreo* has been converted into a job like that of bricklayers, the only thing which interests them is that they cut ears on the basis of whatever sort of sweep of the cape past the belly. Today the personality of *toreo* has been destroyed in order to make uncommitted and contemptuous passes. (1973: 372)

I was often told that one of the reasons why the modern art of *toreo* was so monotonous was that *toreros* were becoming mere performers or, even worse, like well-trained athletes. They trained hard but in so doing they were losing the necessary spark of inspiration. Young *toreros* did complain to me that it was a difficult life being a *torero*, because they had to take good care of themselves, they could not just go out and enjoy themselves, they could not smoke or drink and they had to train hard every day. It was interesting that among the young *novilleros* whom I knew, a particular friend of mine had a somewhat bad reputation because he used to spend a lot of time in the bars and discotheques in Marbella and along the south coast, where he would go to meet women and generally have a good time. It was felt by many others that he was not taking the business of being a *torero* seriously because he did not train as much as them. In fact he was living in a way which reminded me of the many stories I had heard about the riotous life which many *toreros* used to lead. An ex *matador*, now in his seventies, told me that when he was a young *torero* he and his friends, more than the *toreros* today, lived within the atmosphere of the *feria* and participated whole-heartedly in it. They were not mere performers who passed through a town at fair time, who took great care of themselves and separated themselves off from the rest. They would go out all night drinking, dancing and womanizing. He proudly told me that in many *ferias* he did not take his shoes off for days – he would sleep when he could not drink and dance any more and as soon as he woke up he would continue.

One critic complained to me that *toreros* today over-train and are concerned with being physically fit rather than being great artists, and that this has withdrawn much of the spirit and spontaneity of *toreo*. In his youth, said the critic, some forty years ago, he remembered that *toreros* would go to the country to practise in *tentaderos*: they would get their exercise from walking in the country; they smoked and drank in the bars and generally they did not change their life style very much. Of course some *toreros* were more careful about what they did, whereas others led a completely free and easy life, and today this is still true to some extent. The same critic, Rafael Rios Mozo, when asked what it was that the *toreros* of today were lacking, wrote: 'I believe that they have too much training and what they are lacking is that slow stroll through the streets of Seville during which we have a few glasses of wine – not in excess of course – and greet everyone' (1979: 115). In other words he feels there is a lack of traditional atmosphere and hence inspiration in the lives of modern *toreros*.

One of the best presentations of this in fictional literature dealing with the *corrida* is to be found in Marguerite Steen's novel *The Bulls of Parral* (1956). The second half of the novel deals with a rivalry between two *matadores* who have been friends from childhood, Paco, El Niño de

Maderas, married the daughter of a rich landowner who raises fighting bulls, and who on the death of her father continues to be a rancher. The other, Ildefonso, married a girl from the village. Both have become famous but both have very different styles. Paco is consistently good from the technical point of view and he is extremely dairing, a style based on being at the peak of physical fitness, itself due to a strict training programme and a controlled life. Ildefonso, on the other hand, is renowned for his dissolute living, a life similar to that of the *toreros* of the eighteenth and nineteenth century mentioned earlier. He is a physical wreck and is often booed from the arena for his awful performances, but when he is good he produces a performance with a special quality which Paco, for all his training and expertise, is unable to achieve.

> Paco's unpopularity with the fancy, the reluctance to award him his very great dues, was not based on a critical depreciation of his work, or even of jealousy – though the latter might enter into it. There was something wanting; something for which there is no name; something that slides down into the heart like a sword and tears at the entrails. They call it emotion, but the word is too loosely and generally applied. (p. 339)

> Paco [was] puzzled, furious, resentful as, fight after fight, he delivered the goods impeccably and never received the award he hoped for. (p. 339)

> They might tear strips off Ildefonso; they might load him with abuse for which bullfight journalism is infamous; but somewhere among the murderous lines would appear the brief statement that proclaimed Ildefonso forever 'the maestro'. (p. 259)

(The following is a quotation within a quotation, a supposed journalist's column.)

> A cold and impeccable artist with the cape, a brilliant *banderillero*, and a master of the sword, Niño de Maderas has a reputation for filling plazas. But, in his innumerable and excellent performances, which have been accepted as a model by the rising generation of bullfighters, there has been, up to now, no flash of genius. In his recent failures, one may detect possibilities to arouse new hopes in the devotees of the *fiesta brava*. Niño de Maderas, who for so long has presented himself as a machine-made killer of bulls, may yet cross the borderline between efficiency and inspiration (p. 375)

The novelist exactly captures the qualities *aficionados* expect from a *matador*. He must be essentially human, there must be that possibility of failure and that sense of struggling to overcome his limitations. Although I quoted an *aficionado* earlier as saying that the *torero* should be a *superhombre*, he must still be human; he is not like the Superman of comics and movies who achieves great things but who is not really a man, and who can actually only achieve great things because he is not human. The *torero* is like the men who come to watch him, and yet he is that bit better than them because he has taken a step, particularly in terms of daring and personal bravery, which they are unable to take; but it is still a step which they understand for he is still human. Many great *toreros* have perfected their art to such a high degree that they have been able to resolve any problem which the bulls have presented without there appearing to be a problem, and they have been able to perform with apparent ease. In such cases the general audience in the *corrida* has often turned against them, feeling that if they can perform so well there must be wrong with the bulls, that they must be too docile or that the *toreros* are doing nothing special. The great *torero* Juan Belmonte at one point even withdrew from performing when he reached this state, because the audience became hostile to him. This is why Paco, in the novel, is unpopular: because he appears to be 'machine-made' instead of a struggling human.

A *matador* who is technically excellent, or who has a particularly emotional or aesthetic style is much admired, and such a performance is expected on every occasion. Much emotion is also produced if the *matador* can be seen to be overcoming difficulties, technical limitations or lack of bravery to produce a performance of a particular emotional depth, a performance which cannot always be repeated, for example, during several seasons in Spain I associated with a group of *aficionados* who followed Curro Romero, and I went with them to see very many *corridas* in Andalusia in which he was performing. They all knew that he would probably be awful, and that we would have spent a lot of money for nothing, but they were willing to risk this because they were waiting for the day when the conditions would be just right and he would give that sublime performance of which they knew from past experience that he was capable.

Henry Higgins, an English *matador* writing about his experiences in Spain, makes an interesting comment about the difference between a technically excellent and an inspired performance, and he puts it in a wider context. He is writing about García Lorca and the concept of *duende*, a quality often attributed to *toreros* as well as singers, dancers and poets.[4] *Duende* is a difficult word to translate exactly; it means an imp or a goblin, but to have *duende* means to have a special inspiration. Although one *has* this spirit within, one is actually possessed by it; one is not able to control it. Higgins writes:

to have 'duende' meant that one played, sang, lived, or fought bulls 'with feeling'. This did not mean that all the artists or Andalucians had duende. There was a sense of irony that surrounded those who had it. Their performance tended to be either wonderful or awful, and more often the latter. What was important was that these men and women seemed to represent the whole range of human experience and possibilities. People who had duende were splendidly imperfect. (1972: 153)

Curro Romero is a *torero* who is felt perhaps more than any other in Spain to have this quality of *duende*.

The *matador* therefore reveals his essential human nature; the possibility of failure is high because the circumstances are difficult; and so he creates drama as he struggles to achieve success. A *matador* who fails to give a satisfactory performance will be criticized and abused by the audience, but people will still go to see him if they feel that he has some ability to work with and that he is actually attempting to do something at every performance.

When I asked about their feelings on arriving at the *plaza* many *toreros* told me that rather than being frightened by the idea that they were about to put themselves in front of a dangerous animal, they were much more nervous because of the responsibility they felt in front of the audience which was waiting for them. Of course this is linked to the fact that they are going to confront a wild animal which poses a threat to them, and the only reason for not acquiting themselves well in public would be if they succumbed to physical fear, became unable to risk themselves and thus unable to perform well. The public has paid to see the *matador* perform with the bull, and the least expected of him is that he dominate his fear, get close to the bull and have enough technical competence to control it, dominate it and kill it well. If he fails to do so he fails to fulfill the minimum obligations of his role.

The term generally used in Spain to describe the fulfilment of any obligation is *cumplir*. In the context of work as an activity, Martinez-Alier has defined *cunplir* as 'fulfilling the obligation to do one's job with the required degree of diligence' (1972: 174) and also to 'perform work according to well established standards of quality and effort, because this is normally felt by labourers as being morally obligatory' (p. 177). The moral comment carried in the use of *cumplir* has been described by John and Marie Corbin as relating to the person's sense of himself as a decent human being, in that 'A person who does his duty in a sense "accomplishes" himself for if he failed to do so his own integrity would be threatened' (1984: 16). People who fail to *cumplir* are defective because they lack shame, 'a sensitivity to the moral judgements of others'

(p. 16). A *matador* who refuses to get close to the bull and who shows absolutely no desire to perform, who refuses to risk himself and in general attempts to avoid his responsibilities as a *matador*, will be reviled in the *plaza* with shouts of '*¡Sin vergüenza!*' ('Shameless one!'). There is a sense in which the *matador* who is performing badly in failing to *cumplir*, and who continues to do so despite the criticism of the audience, is lacking in *vergüenza* because he is showing that he is not sensitive to public opinion. He doubles his crime if he does not correct his behaviour because, as Pitt-Rivers has said of *vergüenza* in general; '*vergüenza* is the regard for the moral values of society...for the opinion which others have of one...True *vergüenza* is a mode of feeling which makes one sensitive to one's reputation and thereby causes one to accept the sanctions of public opinion (1971: 113).

Curro Romero provides an excellent example of this relationship between *cumplir* and *vergüenza*; he has long been the idol of the public in Seville and in the prestigious April Fair he performs on more afternoons than any other *matador*, and these *corridas* are certain to be sold out. The general public opinion of him is that he obviously knows that the *feria* is built around him, that they, the public, are prepared to pay a lot of money to see him, and they also know that when he is inspired and can control himself he is a magnificent performer. This is why shouts of '*¡Sin vergüenza!*' are particularly vicious when he does badly, because given all these factors his lack of responsibility to the public is that much greater. As the afternoons go by in the fair and he does not improve – in fact, he often gets worse – the insults increase, because it is felt that he is doing nothing to change the situation in the face of these criticisms; something which someone with *vergüenza* would do. I have seen the public in Seville so angry at his apparent disregard of their criticism and his lack of responsibility both to himself as a great artist and to them that they have insulted, jeered and booed him from the moment he started to walk across the arena on the parade of his third or fourth *corrida*, that is, even before he showed whether he was going to do anything worthwhile or not.[5]

Also of relevance here is a story I heard from a *matador* who had performed very badly one day in a *corrida* in Mexico City, and left the *plaza* in a storm of abuse and shouts of '*¡Sin vergüenza!*' He was due to perform the following day in the same arena, and as he started the procession the audience continued with the abuse of the day before. He recounted how he did not know what to do to convince the audience of his good faith, because he fully intended to perform well. What he actually did was to take out his handkerchief and, as he walked across the arena in the procession, he bowed his head and made the motion of wiping his eyes. He thus showed that he accepted the audience's criticism and was repentant, something they certainly understood, because by the time he reached the barrier at the other side of the *plaza* the abuse had changed to applause.

To sum up: a *matador* will be excused lack of inspiration, but one who goes into the arena with no intention of fulfilling his duties honourably is demonstrating a lack of responsibility to the public. A *torero* who is unable to produce a great performance, but who fulfils the obligation of being a *torero* and does so in the face of adversity and difficulty, is much admired. A member of the town council in Seville, a person who admitted that he was not an *aficionado*, had this to say of a *matador* after a fine performance: 'He has demonstrated once more that he is a noble exponent of responsible *toreo*. He has given an authentic lesson of honour and honesty and I think he must be a man who conducts himself in life with the same honesty' (*Sur Oeste*, 22 April 1979).

This chapter has dealt both with the career of the *matador* and with certain of the images of and qualities expected of a *matador*, but the picture presented here is not yet complete. The role of the *torero* is a male one dependent on qualities associated with being a 'true' man, and the *torero* has traditionally been perceived as a person who both embodies and demonstrates these qualities. In order to understand the role of the *torero* more fully, a major concern of the next three chapters will be that of an examination of the values and qualities associated with masculinity in this culture, and the assertion and demonstration of these in the context of the *corrida*.

8

On being human

Corbin and Corbin in their aptly entitled *Urbane Thought* (1987),[1] a study of systems of Andalusian cultural meanings based on research in the city of Ronda, have suggested that Andalusian culture can be interpreted as a statement of what it means to be civilized and that the people who live within the terms of this culture are fundamentally concerned with the expression of this quality. The central argument in this chapter is that the cultural significance of the *corrida* can be best understood if it is interpreted as an event which both encapsulates and succinctly and dramatically summarizes the important structural oppositions of nature and culture which underlie the idea of what it means to be civilized or truly human as expressed in terms of Andalusian thought. It is essential to discuss the meaning of the terms of this distinction, and how the *corrida* involves a dramatic representation of them, in order to show that the *corrida* is an event which makes a statement not only about what it means to be human, but more specifically about what it means to be a human male in this culture.

To understand the *corrida* in these terms it is first necessary to appreciate that Andalusians make a fundamental distinction between 'urban' and 'rural'. 'Urban' can refer to both a *ciudad* (city) and a *pueblo* (a small town or village) for, as the Corbins write, urbanity 'is a matter of density of dwellings, not the size of settlement' (1987: 22). The notion of 'density' is most important here because the density of buildings, particularly human dwellings, gives rise to the intense social activity and close human contact so highly valued by Andalusians as constituents of proper human life. Those who live in the country, away from human settlements, are felt to be isolated and therefore unable to partake of a full social life.

The central focus of this clustering is the main *plaza* or *plazas* (town squares). These key points of social gathering are described by Lopez Casero as 'the centre for relaxation, the centre of criticism and the centre of information' (1972: 123). The *plaza* is where men gather in the morning if they are not working, where people meet friends, where people stroll in the evening – it is the location for a concentration of social activity. In smaller towns and villages, where there is only one important *plaza*, the church, the town hall and other important buildings will be found around it. Not only is the *plaza* a place to meet, it is also prestigious to live in a house on it, or at least close to it, and the desirability of residence decreases the further one moves from the centre. As Gilmore points out, the wealthy live around the important *plazas*, for: 'To live on them implies not only wealth and social position but also a close connection to the community's cosmopolitan institutions and nearness to the pulse of life' (1977: 442). It is felt that as one moves further from the centre, so the quality of life gradually diminishes, because at the far limits of the town there are few bars, shops and *plazas* where people gather, all of which are, as Gilmore comments 'highly valued for lending *ambiente* (spirit or atmosphere) and *vida* to a residential district' (p. 441). It is the mingling of many people which gives a place *ambiente*, which in turn is the social basis for the claim of urbanity.[2]

The importance of being close to the centres of social activity and the importance of the urban ethos in this culture is succinctly illustrated in a recent study by Henk Driessen of a small town near Cordoba. A new quarter was built on the edge of town; one of the streets was said to have more *ambiente* than the others, and consequently most of the houses there were occupied whereas in other streets houses were vacant. The street with *ambiente* was one of the inner streets, with houses on both sides, where most of the social traffic between neighbours took place. Two of the outer streets faced the Cordoba plains, and in order to get people to live in those houses members of the cooperative had to draw lots. As Driessen comments, one might have thought that people would have wanted these houses because of the view they commanded, but that was exactly what the people did *not* want; they wanted the close presence of neighbours and the feeling of sociability they offered. As one of them said to him, 'We see enough of the country. When at home, we want to see neighbours' (1981: 27). Driessen draws an important observation from this example:

> In general, proximity to the social centre determines the desirability of houses and the *ambiente* of streets. This kind of distance is obviously

cultural and has little to do with geography. The people who are living in the new *barrio* complain of 'the great distance to the *pueblo*' although it is only five to ten minutes' walk. (p. 27)

In Andalusian terms, urban space is human space; it is created by humans and is an environment of order, controlled and sustained by human will. In contrast the *campo* (the countryside) is perceived as subhuman space, the realm of plants and animals and subject to the control of the forces of nature.[3] The life of those who earn their living in the country is felt to be a continual struggle against nature, something which is felt to be more powerful than people. Here humans attempt to control, to impose order, to impose their will, but they are not always successful. A farmer might plough, weed, plant and fertilize his land and do all in his power to ensure a good crop, but the rain might not come at the right time; he might have built up a good stock of animals, but some might not breed, or they might be struck by a disease. In terms of the perception of those living in the urban centres, country dwellers cannot be fully civilized because their lives are too bound up with the processes of the natural world and with elements which they cannot easily control.[4]

This notion of human control and where, how and when it is exercised is a fundamental concern in this culture. To be fully civilized is to be in control of one's self, in control of one's life and in control of one's environment. This control is a function of will which people put into operation to overcome, on the personal level, their own human animal nature and, more generally, the world around them. Control is thus the domain of culture; lack of it signals the domain of nature. To be fully civilized is to be fully removed from nature, especially to be removed from the effects of its unpredictable elements. To be civilized is demonstrated by living in the urban realm with fellow human beings, by emphasizing that which is distinctively human (as opposed to animal) in terms of behaviour – for, as the Corbins note, 'animality is particularly the quality humanity seeks to transcend' (1987: 18) – and by the successful demonstration of human will and control.[5] The general point which Sherry Ortner makes about culture, that it 'at some level of awareness asserts itself to be not only distinct from, but superior to nature, and that some sense of distinctiveness and superiority rests precisely on the ability to transform – to 'socialise' and 'culturalise' – nature' (1974: 73), is certainly true for the Andalusian context.

Nowhere is this subordination and 'culturizing' of nature, in Andalusian terms, more dramatically demonstrated than in the *corrida*. It is an urban event intimately linked with the country, which brings together, in the centre of human habitation, an uncontrolled wild bull, an item from the realm of nature, and a man who represents the epitome of culture in that, more than any ordinary man, he is able to exercise control over his 'natural' fear (the fear felt by the human animal), an essential prerequisite if he is to control the wild animal. In terms of this culture there is a strong demarcation between humans and animals, and the entirely appropriate relationship of the subordination of animal will to human will is indicated by the fact that people are able to control and make use of animals for their own ends. Normally this relationship is completely unproblematic, but in the *corrida* it is explored and expressed in a dramatic context. The event is constructed in such a way that the imposition of human will is extremely uncertain because of the difficult circumstances; a situation which in turn generates tension, emotion and dramatic interest.

It is significant that the *corrida* takes place in urban space, where it is expected that people should exercise control, and it is interesting to contrast it for a moment with aspects of the hunt, another event in which people also attempt to kill wild animals in difficult circumstances, but in which they do so in rural space. An essential contrast in terms of processes is that of the passage between these two spaces. In the *corrida* the animal is brought out of its natural habitat to be acted on by a man in *his* natural habitat, whereas in the hunt it is the human who moves, attempting to locate, pursue and kill a wild animal in the country. The human being enters the realm of nature and attempts to impose human will there, but this is an attempt fraught with difficulties because the animal is in control of its own will and can escape. The hunter must pit human skill against it in order to defeat it.[6] At one level both the *torero* and the hunter are attempting something similar; to resolve a challenge presented by a wild animal, to impose their will successfully, to dominate their opponent and thus demonstrate their superiority.

The relationship between the *torero* and the bull is actually much closer than that between the hunter and the animal hunted, in that, in being brought from the country and released into an enclosed space in the city, the bull is unable to exercise a fundamental aspect of its will. It is physically contained, it is unable to escape – something it might well want to do – and it is therefore forced to defend itself – something it does by attacking those who attempt to engage it. Apart from the fact that this confrontation in the form of an attack rarely happens in most hunting in Spain, because, except in the case of wild boar, the animals are not the sort which could effectively attack a human being, the event is structured so that the animals can avoid any engagement. The creature which is pursued avoids engagement either by effectively concealing itself or by fleeing from any approach, and at the last moment, if the hunter is a poor shot and is unable to kill the animal, it will still be able to escape. The hunt is a balance between the animal having the ability to use its instinct and physical ability to escape and the human being attempting, by skill and intelligence, to prevent this happening. It is this balance which is the essence of the hunt, for if there were no escape for the animal there would be no sport for the human.

Hunters must also voluntarily reduce or set limits to their ability to kill the animal. The efficiency of modern weapons have improved the odds so much in favour of the hunters that, were they not to operate within these limiting conditions, the balance between the human skill and the animal's ability to escape would be destroyed, and the hunt would be no longer a matter of chance and skill but a simple matter of mechanical slaughter and destruction. Like the hunter, the *matador* must have limits set to his ability to kill the bull. It is easy to kill a bull with a gun from the safety of the barrier; it would also be easy to kill the bull if those in the arena were allowed to carry a variety of weapons with which they could attack it; but if this were done it would not be a *corrida* but simply a piece of unpleasant butchery. In both cases it is not simply the fact that the man triumphs over the animal by killing it; the real triumph comes from the way in which it is killed.

Viewed from the perspective of patterns of the Andalusian cultural model, the domestication of animals involves the subjection of their will to that of human will. People decide how the animals live, what food they may eat, when they may breed and when they must die. In dealing with female animals, domestication usually involves no special process except that of physical control, although sows are sometimes castrated if they are only going to be used for food. It might be argued that females do go through a special process, artificial insemination, but this is unlike castration in that it does not involve a permanent alteration of the nature of the animal. In the case of male animals (except for those used for breeding), their domestication involves castration. Maleness in this culture is equated with wilfulness (which in turn is associated with sexuality), a condition which is undesirable in domestic animals. Castration is the removal of sexual potency and potential, and results in an animal which is *manso* (meek, tame). Such an animal is passive; it has lost its will and is easily controlled. It is interesting to note, as has already been mentioned, that the word *manso* is also used of a man who is unassertive and retiring and therefore by analogy somewhat like a castrated male animal; he is not acting like a true man. (This is something which will be more fully explored in the next chapter.) The ideas of masculinity, sexual potency, willfulness, assertiveness and independence are all closely associated in this culture, as are those of femininity, passivity (in the sense of lack of sexual assertiveness), lack of competitive assertiveness and controllability, which are their opposites. It is argued below that human males must not only be assertive and control others, but must also exercise *self-control*, something which male animals and to some extent human females are not thought to be able to do.

Most domesticated animals are controlled in this culture simply by enclosing them, or (in the case of sheep, goats and cattle) by herding them in pastures, but apart from that people have little contact with them and they are certainly not usually responded to as individuals. Animals are not anthropomorphized, and pet keeping is not popular. There is, however, one animal which is most important in this culture, and with which humans have a more complex relationship, and that is the horse. Horses are not herded (except maybe when they are very young) but used individually, and thus the exercise of control by the rider over the mount is elaborate and ongoing. It is important to consider the process and the vocabulary of the breaking and taming of horses because the bull in the *plaza* passes through a similar process, although, because of the concentrated nature of that process, it is less immediately obvious.

Unbroken horses are not referred to as *bravo* and are not thought of as wild animals in the sense that bulls are. The only equivalent word I ever heard used with regard to horses was *cerrero* or *cerril* (a *cerro* is a hill and *cerril* refers to rough or mountainous terrain; both, therefore, are images of the countryside), which means 'unbroken' or 'untamed' when referring to an animal, and 'uncouth, ill-behaved and rough' when referring to a person. Even so this word, like *bravo*, points towards the realm out of human control, the realm of nature. In the case of the horse it refers to that aspect of it which humans have yet to control, and in the case of a person it points to someone who is closer to the natual rather than the cultural realm, in that the baser animal nature is allowed to dominate over the truly human which should be dominant.

The actual breaking of a horse is called *desbravando* (literally, 'de-wilding') which nicely points up the previous discussion (see chapter 6) about the translation of the word *bravo* as 'wild'. *Desbravando* involves bringing the animal under control, making it manageable and subjecting its will to that of humanity. Once that stage has been reached it still has to be taken through a further process, for it must be trained to accept a saddle and to respond to the will of the rider, a process called *domar* ('to train' or, figuratively, 'to control, master or repress'). Most male horses are castrated as part of the initial process of bringing them under control, but some are left sexually intact, and stallions are used both for breeding and riding. The stallion is regarded as an extremely wilful animal, a condition which is thought to be associated with its sexual potency. In fact, there is some ambiguity about the breaking of the stallion because it is not castrated, and thus its behaviour is liable to move back towards that of its unbroken state and make it a difficult animal to manage. It seemed, in my conversations with those closely associated with horses, that by association this wilfulness confers increased masculinity (for it was usually only men who rode stallions) on the man who is masterful enough to subject this animal to his will, for an aspect of masculinity is the proven ability to dominate and control others. The more difficult and dangerous these 'others' are to control, the greater the reputation and prestige which is gained. As will be shown later, the prestige a *torero* gains and the esteem in which he is held arise precisely because of his willingness to challenge an extremely difficult and dangerous 'other'.

In terms of the conceptual scheme under discussion, the bull is the quintessential wild animal and the quintessential male animal, its aggressive male qualities once again being associated with great sexual potency. But none of these qualities are significant when it is living in the country; they are not qualities with which man has to deal. The challenge which the bull offers to man only comes about because it is transposed from one environment to another. The *corrida* is, as it were, a problem which man sets for himself. The bull is forced into the position of being 'out of place'; the situation is a contrived anomaly, which man then attempts to resolve in order to emphasize dramatically the correct relationship between man an animal, between civilization and the natural world. When the bull is in the country it is in its proper domain, *bravo* and *campo* being associated concepts. In the *plaza*, however, the bull is out of its proper domain. It is deliberately put there to inject an inappropriate element, wild untamed nature, into the city, the site *par excellence* of culture. The city is not the proper place for animals and if they do pass through it, they should be controlled. In fact, horses are often ridden through the city, and even in a city as large as Seville, one sometimes finds animals being herded through the outskirts.[7] Wild animals (except for vermin and some birds, most of which people attempt to remove) are certainly not found in cities, except perhaps in the exceptional case of zoos, where the animals are strictly separated and controlled, in the crude sense that they are physically restrained by being caged and are dependent on humans for food.

In the *corrida* the contrived meeting between the bull and the man is a confrontation between nature and culture, which is worked out in a controlled environment in a stylized and regulated way. That this is a cultural event is emphasized by the fact that it *is* a contrived meeting – contrived by man – and subject to regulations and controls invented by man; by its urban setting (significantly, *corridas* never take place in the country); and by its being held on a holiday or a special day. It usually takes place, moreover, in a building constructed especially for this purpose, a location which closely parallels the main town square in the sense that it is a public place (one must pay to enter the *plaza de toros* but there is no restricted access; anyone who cares to buy a ticket may enter), a place to meet with friends, to enjoy oneself, and to criticize and comment about what is going on. López Casero's comment about the town *plaza* as a place where 'one goes to meet all the village' (1972: 125) is particularly appropriate for the way the *plaza de toros* is used in Andalusian villages during the *corrida* or *novillada* held as part of the *feria*. Other factors which emphasize the cultural nature of the event are the music, the pageantry and the costumes of the *toreros*. The suit of lights, with its bright colours and floral and geometric designs picked out in elaborate gold and silver embroidery, emphasizes, by exaggeration, the cultural status of the *torero*. The significance of the suit of lights is actually more complex than this and will be discussed in greater detail in the following chapter, when it will be considered in the context of masculinity and male attire.

As was suggested earlier in this section, the city in Andalusian culture is perceived as a place of order and control, a place from which nature has been expelled: and yet the *corrida*, which involves the injection of chaos and disorder in the form of wild uncontrolled nature, takes place in a public arena in the city which is consciously made dangerous and unfit for ordinary humans. This aspect is even more dramatically demonstrated when the *corrida* takes place in a sealed-off public square in a town which does not have a proper *plaza de toros*. The *plaza* is then closed off by sealing the streets leading into it with barriers made from wooden poles, farm carts and trailers, and generally with whatever is available. For example, in Algaba, a village near Seville, this tradition of using old wooden farm wagons is still preserved. They are drawn into a three-quarter circle, the other quarter being formed by a set of specially constructed banked seats. Those who do not have a seat sit in the wagons and between the wheels to watch the event.

The key to understanding the cultural significance of the *corrida* is in recognizing that, in terms of the Andalusian conceptual scheme, it can be interpreted as a resolution of the culturally created anomalous situation of a wild animal in the centre of a city threatening humans and attempting to dominate an urban space. The starting point of the event is chaos and danger, and it is for the man to impose order progressively. By organizing the activity in the arena, by establishing regularity and patterns where there had been chaos, and by controlling the bull, the man publicly demonstrates his separation from and his domination of nature, and thus asserts his humanness. This is not to claim that this is the only way that man demonstrates his humanness in this culture, but it is certainly the most dramatic.

When the bull first comes into the arena it usually charges powerfully and erratically, and is extremely difficult to control. Slowly the *matador* forces it to charge the way he wants it to charge and where he wants it to charge; he bends its will to his will. The great critic Antonio Díaz Cáñabate said that the basis of the performance should be that the man is able 'to make the bull go where it doesn't want to go' (1980: 40). If the *matador* is unable to control the animal he will have failed in his task, for the minimum expected of him is that he control the bull. The creation of an artistic performance is secondary to this and dependent on this basic level of control (see appendix, notes on *torear* and *lidiar*). If the man is unable to control the bull, the meaning of the event collapses, for then it is the bull which is imposing its will on the man. As Gregorio Corrochano comments, 'To *torear* is to command the bull, to do what one wants with the bull, to have *toreo* in the palm of one's hand; if one does not command the bull, if the bull does not go where the *torero* wants it to go, the *torero* is not *toreando*, it is the bull who is *toreando*' (1966: 219).

Toreros, *aficionados* and commentators alike emphasize the fundamental importance of human intelligence in *toreo*; however brave the *torero*, he must have intelligence and understanding to direct that bravery if he is to survive. He must also have intelligence to be able to work through the problems created by the bull if he is to dominate and control the animal. The great *matador* Paco Camino was called 'El Niño Sabio' ('The Wise Child') when he was younger because of his extraordinary ability to make the bull do exactly what he wanted it to do, and his first precept for *toreros* was '*Que tenga mucha cabeza en la plaza*' (literally, 'That one has "much head" in the plaza') (McCormick and Mascareñas 1967: 244), meaning that in order to *torear* it is essential to be able to use one's head, to be intelligent. The highly successful present day *matador* Niño de la Capea (Pedro Gutierrez Moya) also emphasized the importance or intelligence as a necessary quality for a *torero*, a quality without which he is unable to survive the confrontation with the greater physical power of the bull:

> The exact nature of the superiority of the man, of the *torero*, consists in putting his intelligence to the test with that of the bull and thus arriving at the point that the animal, being less intelligent, does what the man wants. The superior intelligence in this case is always that of the man. There can be no doubt that the animal has a lot more power but when it becomes aware that its intelligence has been overcome by the *torero* it gives up. (*El Mundo de los Toros* 22 August 1978, No. 664: 6)

This is not a confrontation of force by force. As mentioned in the quotation above, the bull is obviously more powerful than the man. It is a confrontation of force by intelligence. The man uses his intelligence and his ability to control himself, to plan ahead, to react with logic rather than instinct, or more precisely with a logic which has become instinct, to deceive the bull and by the successful use of deceit to survive. (This is in contrast to the bull which is not expected to exert control but to obey its natural instincts.) The bull charges at that which moves and the *torero* must learn to direct that charge. His deception is basic and consists of keeping his body still and moving the cape or *muleta* in order to persuade the bull to follow that rather than attack his body. This is why it is of such importance to have a bull which has never had the experience of a man and a cape before it comes into the ring: a bull which has had that experience will ignore the cape and will attack the man's body. Deceit is fundamental to *toreo*; indeed, the *muleta* is often called an *engaño*, literally, a 'deceit' (from the verb '*engañar*', 'to deceive'). Yet although deceit is an essential and acknowledged part of *toreo*, there are some forms which are unacceptable and forbidden, and this can be seen as constituting a limitation on the means available to the *torero*. For example, assistants sometimes stand close to the *burladero* (the wooden protection barrier) and incite the bull to charge, so that when the cape is moved the animal crashes into the barrier, thus dazing and damaging itself. A *matador* may also *dobla* (double) the bull by cutting a pass short, an action which forces the bull to turn sharply on itself, a movement which severely weakens and thus tires it. These sorts of actions are likely to bring censure from the public.

To return for a moment to the points made about breaking horses, an important aspect of *desbravando* is that of tiring it so much that its will is weakened and thus it is made easier for people to impose their will on it. This is usually carried out by putting a bridle attached to a long rope on the horse; a man then holds the rope and runs the horse around him in a circle. Once the horse is tired he is able to start to put the saddle and other parts of the harness on it. This tiring of an animal to bring it under control is an important aspect of the *corrida*, but it must be managed extremely carefully (indeed, it is part of the skill of the *torero* to know how to pace the process), because if the bull is tired too quickly it will not charge and the *torero* will not be able to perform well – that is, artistically – with it.

The strength of the bull is slowly reduced by the skilled capework of the *matador* and his assistants and by the pike work of the *picador*. The placing of *banderillas* is also important for achieving a balance between reducing the strength of the bull and yet at the same time keeping it lively. It is usually argued that the amount of running which the bull has to do in this act helps to liven it up a little after the sluggishness which comes as a result of the act with the *picadores*. Although some people argue that the *banderillas* themselves have some physical effect in terms of further weakening the bull, in fact the harpoon points do very little damage. What is most obvious about the sticks is the bright coloured paper in which they are wrapped, a marked contrast to the naked wooden pole of the *picador*. The significant aspect of this act is that the bull is decorated or adorned, a sign of the imposition of culture on nature and a further sign of the gradual denaturing of the bull. The reducing of the bull's strength and the process of bringing it under control constitute, in conceptual terms, its domestication; but this use of 'domestication' needs some qualification.

It is not a domestication in the morphological sense. The exhausted bull which is killed by the *matador* has not gone through a domestication process in the sense that agriculturalists or zoologists would use the term (see chapter 6 and Ingold 1980: 82), but in terms of the perception of members of the audience, based on the interpretation of the behaviour of the bull, it is brought closer to those animals normally classed as domestic. The removal of the will of the animal or the domination of the will of the animal by that of the man is indicated by the behaviour of the latter – by its behaviour being controlled by man. A similar process occurs in the breaking of a horse; once it responds to the human will it passes into the realm of domestic animals. The important thing is that behaviourally and conceptually the bull is no longer a wild animal when it is killed; it has been tamed. This taming of a wild animal, though, is not as simple as, for example, in the context of wild animals in a circus. In a circus lions are 'tamed', but conceptually they are still regarded as wild animals, whereas in terms of the perception of members of the audience at the *corrida*, there is a change in the nature of the bull as it passes through the various acts of the event. To quote from Gines Serran Pagan again, 'without wildness', the quality removed by the various impositions of man, 'the bull was no longer a true bull' (1979: 127).

The nature of the relation between the man and the bull presents some problems for definition, especially so because it occupies such a short time. It is certainly a taming (although not in the sense of making docile prior to developing a performance) in that the man brings a wild animal under control. What is peculiar is that he does this in public as a performance. The only other event in this culture in which a man confronts a wild animal has already been mentioned, and that is in certain acts in the circus, but here the relationship between man and animal has an essential difference.

The animals in the circus are certainly controlled by man, but they are also trained to perform certain actions which are then repeated on different occasions over a considerable time span. What the audience sees at the circus is a finished performance. The animals go through their actions supervised by the trainer, and although they are in fact severely controlled, the trainer may make this control appear threatened and thus add to the drama of the event.[8] The man is called a 'lion tamer', but this 'taming' is not part of the public performance, although the man might make both taming and training *appear* to be part of the act. In the *corrida*, the *matador* does not perform as a trainer; the event is about the taming of a wild animal in the sense of bringing it under control. Once this state has been achieved the animal is killed; there is no second level of training and the animal certainly does not perform tricks. The audience at a *corrida* sees what the audience at a circus does not see; they see the *process* of taming. In terms of this culture, the transformation of the bull occurs as its *bravura* (wildness), which is closely linked to its will, is removed.

Desbravando and *domando* are clearly seen as two processes in the context of breaking horses, but in the *corrida* it is not really possible to isolate them as separate in time. The two occur concurrently, and the *torero* may be more or less successful in imposing his will on the animals. Members of the audience are certainly aware of the process and will talk at length about how it ought to be developed with regard to each individual bull. They talk of *rompiendo* (breaking) the bull, a term associated with *desbravando* (although *desbravando* as a term is not actually used), and *mandando* (ordering), *templando* (moderating), *ensenando* and *educando* (teaching and educating) which are associated with *domando*, a term which is used to refer to the effect of the man on the bull. Hemingway, describing a performance of the great Ronda *matador* Antonio Ordoñez, captures exactly this sense of the man imposing his will on the bull and modifying its character and behaviour:

> His first bull was worthless. He was hesitant with the horses and did not want to charge frankly but Antonio picked him up with the cape delicately and suavely, fixed him, taught him, encouraged him by letting him pass closer and closer. He fabricated him into a fighting bull before your eyes. Antonio in his own enjoyment and knowledge of the bull seemed to be working the bull's head until the bull understood what was wanted of him. If the bull had a worthless idea Antonio would change it for him subtly and firmly. (1985: 26)

The *matador* kills the bull once it has been dominated, but this killing is not a simple process, and it is worth comparing it for a moment with the killing of other animals in this culture. The slaughter of animals for domestic consumption is largely unproblematic and, apart from the domestic slaughter of the pigs or poultry which some families raise, it si nowadays an industrial process carried out by specialists working in factory-like buildings, out of public view. Death here is certain, regulated, unelaborated culturally and involves no challenge or risk to human beings. The killing of animals in the hunt has already been mentioned. Here an essential feature is that the death is uncertain because of the possibility that the animal might escape. Although there is a challenge there is usually no risk to the hunter, either because the animals which are hunted are wild but not dangerous, or because there is a considerable distance between the hunter and the hunted. The killing of the animal is also non-public in that, although there may be several people in a hunting party, it takes place outside human habitation. The death of the fighting bull is rather special because it is a public spectacle, and it is the subject of great cultural elaboration. Although it is known that the bull will die, that death is made uncertain in the sense that it is not known how the *matador* will bring it about, or, indeed, whether the bull will be able to reverse the proper relationship and kill or injure the man. The uncertainty comes from the difficulty and danger of the challenge to kill correctly and from the risk to his own life which the *matador* must accept.

There are special rules which stipulate how the killing must be performed and the types of implements to be used (see chapter 1 and Gilpérez García and Fraile Sanz 1972: article 131). The *matador* must approach the bull from the front and the sword must pass through the lower part of the neck of the bull. This means that at the moment the sword goes in, the body of the *matador* ought to pass over the bull's horns (or to be more precise, over the right horn), a movement which involves great risk because if the bull lifts its head at this moment the man is almost certain to be gored. The potential for failure, in the sense of killing properly, if the man is unable to control or dominate his fear is therefore built into the event until the last moment. If the *matador* gives in to his fear and approaches the bull in a less dangerous manner, if he is incompetent in producing a kill because of this unwillingness to risk himself, the audience is likely to shout '*¡asesino!*' ('murderer!'), a term which suggests an unacceptable killer, someone who, because he kills another is, in one sense, dehumanized. It is not that the audience is attributing humanity to the bull and suggesting that the man is immoral, but rather that they are denying the proper humanity of the man – denying the very quality which he is attempting to emphasize. If the *matador* kills successfully he shows that he has not succumbed to the threat posed by the animal; he has dominated it and, through his mastery of it, triumphantly asserted his humanity.

A *matador* can fail in several ways. If he is unable to bring the bull under control because he has not mastered his own fear, then his failure is total. If, on the other hand, he has demonstrated his courage and been willing to commit himself, but has been unable to perform well either because the bull was simply impossible to work with or because he did not have sufficient knowledge or technical resources with which to resolve the problems, then he will probably be criticized but forgiven. Similarly, for the man to be caught and injured by the bull is not necessarily a sign of total failure. Although in one sense it does indicate that the bull has imposed itself on the man, this can also be accepted as the result of an error of judgement on the part of the man, or the result of a completely unpredictable piece of behaviour on the part of the bull. In other words, it is regarded as bad luck and evokes a sympathetic response. In the world of *los toros* there is no great emphasis on the idea of being wounded and having scars as an indication of masculinity. Press and television reports dealing with a particular *torero* might mention the bad scars he has, but the emphasis is that these are the price one has to pay to be a *torero* rather than indicative of his great courage. Scars are not borne proudly in the way that they were by duelists of the last century.

The *corrida* is a cultural event which puts the definition of humanity, especially male humanity (something which will be dealt with more fully in the following chapter), in jeopardy precisely so that it may be dramatically reaffirmed in the most difficult of circumstances. To be an adult human male in this culture is to be an active agent, to be capable of control, and yet the *matador* risks his ability to control when he enters the arena. It is an audacious act, a supreme folly, for a man voluntarily to put himself in this precarious position, where the public can observe him attempting to prove himself and where he risks not being able to master the situation. In this culture, neither men nor women are normally willing to present themselves in uncertain circumstances and in such a way as to allow fellow humans to publicly comment on and critically evaluate their character and behaviour. In the *corrida*, however, the *torero* does just that; he offers himself to the public for them to judge whether or not he justifies his claim that he is this very special person, a *matador*. Anyone in the *plaza* is free to comment loudly about his behaviour and character and to abuse him publicly, and yet the *matador* may not respond to such attacks (except by improving his performance so that they may cease), and indeed can be fined if he argues with the public. This is a very odd position for a man in this culture to be in, for such an attack and such abuse would provoke an immediate response in any other public place (Brandes 1980 and Driessen 1983).

At the beginning of the afternoon, by his presence in the arena, the man asserts his claim to be a man worthy of the title *matador*. The event them progresses, through a period of doubt and the necessary demonstrations of his character and skill to support the claim, to a final acceptance of the claim by the audience. The *corrida*, however, also allows for the possibility of failure, a possibility which gives the event an element of uncertainty and dramatic tension. The arena contains sets of relationships which are loaded with peril for the human performers as they attempt to establish a proper order. Members of the audience are aware of the difficulties of the situation and they are there to watch the performers overcome these, for that is what the *matador*'s artistry consists of – the elegant and stylish resolution of both the difficulty of mastering himself and his fear and the dangerous process of bringing the bull under his control. In a sense the *matador*, although performing as and judged as an individual, is a representative of humanity; he is a figure in whom key human qualities valued by this culture are epitomized, and it is those qualities the audience comes to see asserted.

Although these are human qualities and the fundamental distinction in the arena is between human and animal, one cannot fully understand the *corrida* without understanding that it is a totally male-orientated event, and that the values which underlie it and give cultural sense to it are essentially masculine values – that is, they are values which are held by men concerning proper and expected behaviour both of themselves and other men. It is therefore necessary to focus on that particular aspect of humanity, and on how the *corrida* may be interpreted as a statement in a dramatic form of what it means to be a human male in this culture.

9

On being male

It was emphasized in the previous chapter that the assertion and maintenance of the state of being fully human is a fundamental concern of Andalusians. Although they understand human beings to be creatures which have certain elements in common with other animals as well as having a spiritual aspect, these are not given equal weight. The animal element is subhuman and should be transcended in order for a person to participate fully and successfully in humanity. All humans are subject to their animal natures – all must eat, drink, defecate and sleep, all are likely to experience fear, illness and sexual arousal – but all of these should be controlled by the exercise of human will. Apart from establishing their identities as human beings, Andalusians are concerned with what sort of human beings they are. Here the fundamental cultural distinction is the gender division, the basis of which is how men and women construct, understand and respond differently to their sexual natures, that being the only component of the human animal which is unique to each of them. As Corbin and Corbin write of this culture:

> The biology of sex ensures that women and men experience their bodies differently, not just in the mechanics of copulation but in that women are subject to biological imperatives of menstruation, pregnancy, childbirth and lactation and men are not. Sexual identities elaborate these differences – masculinity is more willed, less natural, than femininity. (1987: 19)

These sexual identities inform social behaviour, and in this culture gender distinctions determine and limit behaviour in most contexts of human interaction. This is a theme about which Andalusians have very clear ideas, and they are extremely concerned with the behaviour proper to the expression of their identity as men or women. In terms of this cultural model, female sexuality is ascribed; it is a given, and women do not have to – indeed, they should not – attempt to demonstrate it. Male sexuality, on the other hand, is achieved and has to be asserted; not to demonstrate it might lead others to suspect that it does not exist. Women should not be wilful in terms of expressing their sexuality, whereas male sexuality is demonstrative and is often given as the reason for actions.[1] Brandes writes that an important part of the Andalusian masculine self-image is that: 'the locus of power and will, of emotions and strength, lies within the male genitals. Men speak as if they are impelled to act according to opinions and desires that originate in their testicles or penis' (1980: 92). What the actual demonstration of male sexuality usually involves is the verbal assertion of proper sexuality and masculinity, and the avoidance of any behaviour which could be interpreted as associated with women, or at least as being non-masculine. Men in this culture ought to be:

> wilful, to seek to assert themselves, to control the course of their lives, to influence others, to be competitive, courageous and persistent in the pursuit of their goals. Manliness is thought to have a physiological basis – strength of character is equated with 'having balls', vital men must be sexually active, but uncontrolled physical aggression or sexuality is brutish and improper to the affairs of men. (J. R. Corbin 1978: 4)

The comment on the importance of 'having balls', together with the view that uncontrolled sexuality is 'brutish', highlight an important difference between human males and male animals; for it is felt that animals are unable to control their sexuality whereas a defining characteristic of men is that they are able to exercise such control. Not to do so is to signal a shift towards the animalistic aspect of human nature. As Campbell and Sherrard comment about manliness in Greece:

> [it] is, in part, a self-assertive courage and to have it a man must be *varvatos*, that is well endowed with testicles and the strength that is drawn from them. This power is not morally distinguished, for it may be ill-employed, lead a man to rape or casual killing. The manliness which is related to honour requires this physical basis, yet it must discipline animal strength and passions to its own ideal ends. (1968: 44–5)

In Andalusian culture, masculine wilfulness and assertiveness become elaborated in another context, that of men contesting verbally against others in the daily rituals of masculinity in bars and other public places (Driessen 1983: 128–9), and it is this which is the driving force behind the *torero*'s performance as he contends with another assertive male in the arena.

An important spatial distinction made in Andalusian culture which must be introduced at this point is that between the *casa* (house) and the *calle* (street). This distinction is very much associated with that between the animal and the essentially human side of human beings and, at another level, with the distinction between women and men. The *casa* is: 'residential space which is the proper place for more biological acts – eating, sleeping, sex, excretion, washing, birth, illness and death. The *casa* encapsulates the irreducible animal aspect of mankind, removing it from public view' (Corbin and Corbin 1987: 22). The *casa*, then, is associated with the non-public side of men and women and with intimate individual and family activities. Furthermore, it is perceived to be the realm of women (see for example Press 1979, pp. 117–29). The *calle* is literally the street, but in general the word can refer to all *plazas* and public places such as bars and cafés. Unlike the *casa*, which is marked by restricted access, the *calle* is open to all. It is the place of public life and socializing, and is generally the place for 'those activities which are quintessentially human'. (Corbin and Corbin 1987: 22), but it is also particularly associated with men.

Traditionally in this culture men spend very little time at home.[2] For most of them it is a place for eating, sleeping and other bodily functions, and when these have been satisfactorily attended to they should be either at work or out socializing with friends. The proper place for men is the *calle*, for it is there that he can engage in the processes by which he establishes his male identity. A man who spends too much time at home, in the domestic realm (the realm serviced by and associated with women), puts his masculinity in jeopardy, for as Brandes notes, most men in this culture 'consider domesticity of whatever kind to be inherently unmasculine' (1980: 185).[3]

In terms of the cultural model being advanced here, the *plaza de toros* pertains to the realm of the *calle*. It is a public area, and the *corrida* held within it can be interpreted as representing key aspects of public life in a highly stylized, focused and concentrated way. Just as the earlier quotation from John Corbin mentions the male qualities of courage, assertiveness, desire to influence and competitiveness which are worked out in everyday circumstances, so these are worked out in public in the special circumstances of the *corrida*. These are *male* qualities, they inform *male* behaviour and the *torero* in this culture has traditionally been seen as the epitome of masculinity; the character who most obviously and dramatically demonstrates the qualities of courage, dominance, control and assertiveness. Audiences have long admired the audacity and bravery of *toreros*, and from the earliest treatises on *toreo* they have been emphasized as essential qualities for a *torero*. Pedro Romero, one of the earliest professional *toreros* in the eighteenth century, wrote a series of rules for *toreo*, among which are included the following points: 'The coward is not a man and for *toreo* men are needed. More can be done in the *plaza de toros* with an *arroba* [11·5 kilos.] of courage and a pound of intelligence than the other way round' (quoted in *Sur Oeste* 24 August 1981). This courage, of course, is a quality of men, and is linked with having *cojones*.

These qualities are still demanded today, and all those with whom I spoke emphasized the essential maleness (the sexual identity of men) which underpinned the masculinity of the *torero*. There are, however, ambiguities about this role, and I would suggest there is a particularly heavy insistence on the norm of the masculinity of the *torero* because of these ambiguities; this is particularly centred on the fact that there is a high degree of non-normal masculine behaviour associated with this role, a fact which has often been commented on. For example, although the epitome of masculinity, the *torero* performs the role in a costume which in comparison with other male attire in this culture is non-masculine; moreover, he makes use of actions and postures, particularly the gyrating in front of the bull and the thrusting of the pelvis towards it to encourage it to charge, which are certainly not the normal movements of a man towards another male. The wearing of a similar costume or the use of similar gestures by a man in the street, the realm of men, would not lead to the interpretation 'valiant male', but would be commented on as inappropriate behaviour for a normal male, with the further comment that such a person was probably a homosexual. While in the *plaza* the ambiguity is reduced, because here it is emphasized that the person thus dressed and using these actions is a *torero* performing a special role, set apart from 'ordinary' men and subject to special rules.

Despite the insistence on the masculinity of the *torero*, there were enough comments about homosexuality and *toreros* for me to take an interest and ask questions about this. The very fact that it could be believed and stated that a man could be both homosexual and a *torero*, when there was such an insistence of the *torero* being a valiant male, struck me as problematic. Some whom I tackled on this issue dismissed the matter as an impossible conjunction; for example, one said, 'It is absolutely impossible, a *torero* has to be a "true" male.' This was the comment of many, but there were others who told me of *toreros* who were reputed to be homosexuals. One particular well-known *torero* is regarded as a great classical artist of *torero*, a maestro, and yet many people told me that he is a homosexual. There is, of course, an ambiguity here, in that homosexuals are regarded by the majority as not 'true' men, and yet some who are reputed to be homosexuals are able to perform in this most male of events. In one sense the very fact that *aficionados* would say that a particular person is a good *torero*, *and yet* he is a homosexual, emphasizes the normal necessity for masculinity in this event, even though they were unable to explain the courage of a *torero* who is also homosexual. One afternoon I watched a *corrida* on the television in a bar with a group of men in which a *matador* who is reputed to be a homosexual gave an exceptionally courageous performance. In the discussion around the table afterwards this was commented on, marvelled at and the inconsistency pointed out, but it was not something anyone could explain to me except to say that it was unusual.

One tentative explanation which I offer is that once someone is dressed in the suit of lights, a symbol of the 'truly male' male, that person of necessity is regarded as a man and the public's expectation of that person is that he be a man. It is significant that a commentator has written in the context of women as performers that the *torero* 'was a man, is a man and will be a man (even though a woman performs the role)' (Guirado Rodriguez-Mora 1969: 204). Even though this explicitly refers to women, a general gloss can be given: once dressed in the suit of lights and for the time in the arena, that person is a representative of male virtues even though not a man or regarded as not being a 'true' man in some other sense.

I will discuss later how the masculinity of a *torero* can be threatened if he fails to perform well in the *plaza*; but generally speaking, when he is dressed in the suit of lights and is in the *plaza* he can be safely labelled '*torero*'. Prior to this, however, there are times of ambiguity. I was struck by the amount of teasing and joking using sexual references in the dressing room of young *toreros*. On the occasions on which have seen *toreros* changing, the room has been full of male friends. This in itself is unusual and fraught with possible ambiguities, in that a group of men have come together in a bedroom to watch another man dress. Men do not normally go into the bedroom of another and wait with him while he carries out his toilet and dresses, activities which are usually conducted in private, within the restricted zone of the house. In front of this group the *torero* has to groom himself carefully; he is dressed by another man; he is concerned about wrinkles in his silk stockings (items which are very definitely not part of normal men's clothing), about the way his tie is tied, about whether the waistcoat is tied well at the back, whether his hair is combed just right; all of which might well be regarded as non-masculine behaviour or even effeminate out of this context. Not only is the normally private bedroom turned into a semi-public arena in terms of dressing, but also the man cannot express the fears and doubts that he might have as he prepared for the danger which is waiting for him in the *plaza*; even in this private zone he must operate in terms of a public persona.

Most of the joking and teasing takes place early in the process of dressing. The *torero* has only just woken up and is still in bed when the first group of friends arrive; again, it is an unusual event for men to be sitting around the bed, some actually on it, of another man. The atmosphere of joviality continues during the early stages of dressing, and gradually tails off as the *torero* puts on the main parts of the suit of lights, which announces that he is now definitely the special kind of man called a *torero* who will shortly go into a public arena to demonstrate this.

The suit of lights is a peculiar costume for this event, for as one Spanish writer comments, it: 'offers no greater protection than any other; it is heavy and impedes movement; it is too thick for the season, latitude and time of day in which bullfights take place. In fact it is quite unfit for its purpose, from a practical point of view' (Acquaroni 1958: 16). What is of particular interest in this study is not how such a costume came to be the prescribed wear for *toreros*,[4] but the fact that it is perceived as the costume of the truly male, and as such it needs further consideration because here too there is an important ambiguity.

The suit of lights is a costume of 'ritual artifice' (Corbin and Corbin 1987: 110), and in this sense it is in direct contrast both with the naked animal and the dress of ordinary men. As mentioned earlier, humans are dressed animals who alter their natural appearance with clothes, personal grooming, jewellery and cosmetics in order to stress their removal from nature (Corbin and Corbin 1987: 28). The bull comes into the arena as undressed, unadorned maleness whereas the man, in terms of his dress, is exaggeratedly cultural. Both man and bull have the quality of maleness, but in the bull this remains natural whereas in the man it becomes reshaped as the cultural quality – 'masculinity'. If clothing in general sets the human apart from the animal, so the exaggerated dress of the *torero* sets him apart from ordinary men. Once in this costume he is clearly marked as someone special, and the ornateness, complexity and richness of the decoration of this costume is entirely fitting in its suggestiveness of the general richness of the cultural process in which he is involved. It is also entirely appropriate for those who figure in presentational roles of any kind, all of whom are generally dressed especially lavishly for ceremonial occasions this is immediately apparent for example at religious, civic and military celebrations. In this sense, the costume of the *torero* relates to copes and ecclesiastical finery of priests saying Mass, and the special forms of decoration of statues of the saints, of Jesus Christ and of the Virgin Mary, in that these are all forms of dress which are set apart from everyday wear. The use of such dress emphasizes that something important and significant is taking place.

The comparison with the dress of the priest should not be read as -implying a similarity between him and the *torero*, despite the fact that the former is also involved in cultural events which centre on the definition and assertion (and, unlike the *corrida*, the transcendence) of humanity. Although not denied their humanity, priests are certainly not regarded as true men in the sense of being properly masculine. They are celibate (or at least there is a norm to that effect), they do not spend much time in male meeting places, they concern themselves with unmasculine things and in fact spend much of their time with women in the domestic realm.

Self-control has been mentioned as an important male quality, and priests exhibit or are expected to exhibit qualities of self-control beyond the normal, particularly so in the sense of remaining celibate. This too adds to their ambiguous male status, because while self-control is an admired quality, celibacy is not (men with whom I spoke could not understand why anyone would *want* to be celibate or *how* they were able to maintain that state), in that one of the ways of demonstrating or asserting masculinity is through sexual activity. Self-control, control over one's own nature is a quality admired in *toreros* and has positive value, yet in other circumstances it has negative values. Although self-control is an essential and expected human quality, total control is, in a certain sense, inhuman. It is understood that human beings have an animal/ natural side which is thought of as powerful and often difficult to control. The occasional failure of self-control reveals that a person is essentially human and suffers the problems of a 'normal' human being, while the successful exercise of it, which is difficult in many circumstances, indicates an ability to keep the animal/natural side in check or to rise above it. Constant self-control is regarded as impossible for 'normal' human beings. As will be mentioned later in this chapter, it is felt that to indulge in sexual activity is a threat to a *torero*, in that it saps his strength and will thus result in a poor performance in the arena. It is known that a *torero* must often abstain from sexual activity, that is to say, that he must exercise control over desire. Such abstention is regarded as a difficult but necessary evil if he is going to be a good *torero*. It is also felt that this is merely a temporary measure (usually only immediately prior to a *corrida*) in order to succeed on another level of masculinity. To dedicate one's life to celibacy, and thus totally deny an aspect of the defining feature of one's particular humanity, as priests must do, is a very different matter.

The suit of lights, although remarkably similar in the sense of design, (although not shape), ornateness and colour combinations to those of these church-related figures, is the costume of the person who is regarded as the epitome of masculinity. All my informants told me that to wear such a costume one had to be *'un hombre de verdad'* ('a real man'), and yet this costume bears no relation to normal attire for men. It can be argued that the costume is a continuation of costumes worn in the infancy of the event in the late eighteenth and early nineteenth centuries, but unlike military uniforms, for example, there is no sense that the costume links the modern *corrida* to a long and glorious tradition – it has no historical resonances. The continued use of the costume today does, however, have important cultural implications and it is certainly regarded as a very special form of dress. It is a costume which has no relation to modern Spanish male dress, and yet it stands for masculinity. In fact, with its bright colours, its elaborate gold embroidery of floral designs with artificial jewellery worked into it, its pink silk stockings and light slipper-like ballet-style shoes, it is a costume which suggests exactly the opposite.

The fact that there is a potentially ambiguous response to it is emphasized by the way in which its use is controlled. Once dressed in the suit of lights, the *torero* cannot appear in the bars, cafés or the street places where ordinary men normally meet. This contrasts with the other type of dress worn by *toreros*, the *traje corto* used in *festivales*, whose use in the street, because it is only a refined version of country dress, is perfectly acceptable. A *torero* never walks to the *plaza* even if it is very near; once he is dressed a car comes to collect him and takes him close to the door of it. All those I spoke to said that it would be entirely inappropriate for a *torero* to walk through the street in his suit of lights, and the image of it seemed to jar with them.[5]

This costume is inappropriate for the street because of its eye-catching designs and colour and its shape, which draws attention to the man's body. In that sense it is similar to the effect of women's dress on men. To dress elegantly, to dress up and display oneself in public, is to *lucirse* and is quite appropriate (within certain limits) for women, but to draw attention to oneself in this way, to *lucirse* in the street, is inappropriate for men and certainly a man should not attempt to attract the attention of other men in this way. Although there may seem to be an inconsistency here in the argument put forward about the assertion of masculinity in the *calle* and in particular in the *plaza de toros* (which, it has been argued, pertains to the *calle*), it is also important to point out that the *plaza de toros* is not 'public' in exactly the same sense as the street or an ordinary *plaza*. Special rules and expectations apply to the activities (and dress) associated with the *plaza de toros* which do not apply to other parts of the public domain.

It has been suggested that the dress of the *torero*, rather than being non-masculine dress, could be interpreted as emphasizing masculinity. The costume has a jacket with bulky shoulders and skin-tight trousers which emphasise the genitalia, thus stressing that this is a male body.[6] Taken in this sense it would be similar to the equipment and clothing worn by American football players, which Dundes, following Arens, suggests: "'accents the male physique" through the enlarged head and shoulders coupled with a narrow waist. With the lower torso "poured into skintight pants accentuated only by a metal codpiece", Arens contends that the result "is not an expression but an exaggeration of maleness"' (Dundes 1978: 77). While the jacket of the suit of lights does indeed make the *torero*'s shoulders appear wide and the rest of the costume is body-accentuating, it is difficult to relate this to any sense of his thereby exphasising his maleness in terms of physical attributes, because the idea of having a large, well-formed and muscular body is not one associated with being a *torero*. There is no sense of a required physique for a *torero* and certainly his masculinity is not expressed in terms of any such notion. The body type associated with American football players, rugby players or boxers is not associated with a *torero*, and the physicality associated with these sports is not to be found in *toreo*. I never heard any comments about the need for a particular sort of body or there being an ideal type of body for a *torero*, although there were comments about slenderness being attractive, and there were often jokes made in the *plaza* about how ridiculous some of the older and fatter *banderilleros* looked in their suits of lights.

The tight trousers do obviously emphasize the genitalia and could perhaps be interpreted as expressing the maleness of the *torero*. Although it is important 'to have balls' because this is the source of a man's strength and valour, and although a truly brave man has '*mucho cojones*' (literally, 'a lot of balls'), this is a conceptual matter rather than an expression of the requirement actually to have large testicles; the *toreo* demonstrates his masculinity by his actions rather than by showing off his anatomy. I certainly gained no sense that the emphasis of the genitalia was a significant aspect of the costume (although I agree that it is open to such an interpretation), and I heard no comments about what is called *el bulto* the shape, the mass, the form) which is visible in the trousers – indeed, there seems to be as much attention given to it as those who go to the ballet in England might give to the similarly indistinct shape in the tights of a male ballet dancer.[7]

It is the context which controls any ambiguous response to or interpretation of the suit of lights. Such a costume can only be used within the very clearly delineated sphere of the *corrida*; an event in which those thus dressed actually assert their masculinity. If worn in the street, the oddness and inappropriateness of the costume would be highlighted in comparison with the normal dress of men. Certainly any man wearing tight-fitting, colourfully embroidered clothes in the street would have his masculinity called into question. In the *plaza de toros*, although surrounded by other men in everyday clothing, the ambiguity of the *torero*'s costume is reduced because, together with the other performers similarly dressed, he is set apart in an arena which constitutes a framing device, and the costume is seen in its proper context. There is no problem in classifying a person dressed in a suit of lights in the *plaza de toros* as a *torero*, and thus as a true man, whereas by contrast it would be difficult to classify someone similarly dressed walking through the streets.

Despite the apparent connotations of feminity or at least non-masculinity in the *torero*'s costume, the majority of those with whom I spoke were emphatic that it was inappropriate dress for a woman and that women should not even be in the arena as performers. Part of this objection can be interpreted as a result of many ambiguities and confusions of classification which arise from a woman being dressed in such a costume. On the one hand, a woman thus dressed draws attention to the feminity of the costume, and thus increases the ambiguity between the role and the costume in which it is performed. She threatens the fragile 'suspension of disbelief' which allows a man to wear such a non-masculine costume and yet to be a 'superman': by stressing the feminine elements (colour, embroidery, attention-attracting glitter, body-emphasizing fabrics and style) she tips the balance to the weighting of female factors, and thereby in a sense reduces the ambiguity. However, by being a woman in the costume of a superman and performing in an event associated with men, she yet again increases the ambiguity in a different dimension. Something which is immediately wrong with this costume as female attire is the fact that it has trousers – items of clothing which are traditionally male. Although many women in this culture now wear trousers, this is fairly recent, and even the majority of those who do would not wear them for a formal occasion. Whereas the tightness of the trousers around a male performer's body is not commented on by members of the public, the tightness around the groin and buttocks of female performers is; the costume becomes the focus of erotic interest and the performer an object of sexual rather than artistic interest.

Although a costume with many non-masculine elements, the suit of lights can only be worn by 'true' men, and the man thus dressed performs in an event in which masculinity is asserted. A woman wearing this male costume makes herself closer to being a man, which of course she is not, and men are uncertain how to respond to her. For example: by what standards should her performance be judged? Are the expectations for the fulfilment of the role to be the same as they would be for a man? Can insults be shouted at her, as they would be at a male, even though she is a woman and men do not normally insult women in public? All of these points raise many questions about women in *toreras*, and they will be taken up later in this chapter.

It was mentioned earlier in this chapter that men in Andalusia are expected to be sexually assertive and sexually active, and in the previous chapter reference was made to the popular image of the *torero* as that of the playboy or rake. Although *toreros* demonstrate their masculinity in the *plaza*, there is also a threat to this public demonstration of their masculinity if they do indeed attempt to be sexually active, that is to say, fully masculine in another context. From the comments made by many *toreros* it is clear that women are seen as a considerable threat, because sexual activity is seen as debilitating and thus many feel that it is dangerous to take too much sexual interest in women. An ex-*torero* told me how difficult it was for him during the season when he was young. He saw many women with whom he wanted sex and because of his profession there were many interested in him, and yet he knew that he dare not give in to his desires because women and sex were the worst things for sapping a *torero*'s strength. He said that all the physical preparation of a *torero* could be quickly lost if he indulged himself, and he described how he spent the season taking regular cold showers to rid himself of his desire. I was also told stories of a still-famous *torero* who would book two separate hotel rooms for his wife and himself when he went on tour in South America, because he dare not sleep with her for fear that sexual intercourse would weaken him (Brandes 1981, pp. 84–7 and 106–10). Association with women can also threaten at another level. *Toreros* have often been criticized for not committing themselves (which involves risking themselves), and thus not giving good performances; something which has often been blamed on having a woman in their lives and putting her before their responsibilities as a *torero*. For example, in a *corrida* in Teruel, Paquirri, who was normally an extremely valiant performer, was performing badly, doing none of the things which excite the audience and for which he is famous, and really looked as though he had no interest in being in the arena. My neighbour commented angrily, 'He's looking after himself for La Pantoja'; La Pantoja being a famous singer with whom Paquirri was having a well-publicized affair (this incident was before they married). I was also told a story about a famous *matador* in Seville during the time he was reputedly having an affair with a Hollywood star. On the first day of the three he was booked to perform in the fair he was bad and was booed; on the second day he was even worse and was booed again; on the third day there had been no improvement, and the audience turned and booed the actress who was sitting in the front row.

Just as the ordinary man risks his masculinity by associating too much with women, such association being feminizing, so with a *torero*, but the latter is caught in a double bind. There is a 'playboy' or 'sex symbol' image which is associated with *toreros*, an image which many feel they ought to or want to keep up, and anyway as men they ought to be sexually assertive. On the other hand, there is the idea that sexual activity is debilitating and therefore as a *torero* one ought to abstain from sex in order to conserve one's strength to be able to perform well in the *plaza*, for in not performing well there is the danger of being destroyed as a *torero*, something which, as has been shown, is usually associated with a denial of masculinity.

Not only are women felt to pose a threat at the individual level, but some *aficionados* and commentators see women as having an influence over the whole event. Some of the older *aficionados* with whom I spoke even bewailed the fact that women are allowed in the *plaza* as members of the audience, where it is felt that their presence has had the effect of attenuating the virile, masculine spirit of the event – what Luis Bollain has called a 'sweetening' effect, and he goes on to say: 'our fiesta, because of its great intensity, its vigorous and robust appearance is, and has to be, of and for men; women are not needed in the *plazas*' (1953: 167). Tomás Leon, an ex-president of the *plaza* in Seville, told me that the *corrida* was a 'virile, masculine celebration' and that women detracted from this. Díaz Cañabate blamed, to a large extent, the attendance of women at the *corrida* for the change in the atmosphere of the event since his youth, a change which he described like this: 'the sensibility has become effeminate, evened out, weakened. It will be difficult for there to remain scope or atmosphere for what was in its best moments strictly virile, consciously dangerous and enormously thrilling, truthful and completely without falsity' (1980: 39). Part of this complaint is that prior to the 1930s the event was certainly not considered suitable for women to watch. It was a more basic and savage spectacle with larger, less manageable bulls which had to be treated roughly in order to dominate them, and because *picadores'* horses did not have padding, dozens of horses were killed in the arena. Since then there has been a gradual refinement of the event with more emphasis being laid on its aesthetics and beauty rather than the basic struggle of man and beast; a movement which many regret.

Commentators also complain about the presence of women because it is felt that men deal with each other differently and moderate their behaviour and language when women are present; not to do so would be regarded as improper behaviour indicating a *falta de educación* (lack of education). As the shouting of abuse and criticism is part of male participation at the *corrida*, it is felt by many that to have women present is inhibiting. Men mix more easily with other men in public and if women are present this often causes problems. One Sunday I was at a cockfight (a more exclusively male preserve than the *corrida*) near Seville, and there were two young women in the audience, something which is extremely rare. An old man who had his back to them started cursing and shouting, using sexual references, about what was going on in the ring. One of the men in front turned, hissed at him and told him that there were women behind him, and the man stopped immediately but grumbled about the fact that they had been allowed in. His complaint was that he was restricting his behaviour because women were present. It is interesting that the day-to-day construction of masculinity, part of which involves the assertion of the superiority of men over women, is a thing which can only easily be expressed when women are not present.

Despite the fact that the *corrida* is indeed a male-dominated event, there have been cases of *toreras* (female performers) throughout its history.[8] their existence and the comments I heard about them sheds some interesting light on the nature of the *corrida*. The answers I received to my questions about *toreras* pointed up the central concern in this event, which is a definition of male humanity.

The *corrida* is a *public* event dealing with the control and domination of a wild animal by a man. In terms of the cultural model being proposed here, public events are male-dominated events, and women should not attempt to exercise control in public. The basis of this particular event is that one male attempts to control another male, to dominate it and finally to kill it. The maleness of the bull is as important a quality as its wildness; although *vacas bravas* (wild cows) are fierce and will attack as well as males, they are never used. When I asked about this, no one was able to give me any technical reason (for example, that cows were too weak, too slow or unaggressive) for not using them. The reaction against the idea of using them was an instinctive one of it not being right; it jarred with a sense of what was correct and appropriate. The *torero* must dominate the animal and on a behavioural level take away its assertive maleness before he kills it. The emasculation of anything male in a public event is certainly regarded as an inappropriate activity for a woman. Most Spaniards referred to this, in conversations with me, not so much in terms of women being technically incapable of performing with and killing a bull (although some did), but in terms of it being *fea*, ugly. This use of *fea* is more than an aesthetic comment; it implies something which is inappropriate, unsuitable or unseemly. For a woman to perform as a *torera*, something which is normally a male role, she would have to take on the behaviour, gestures and actions of a male, and this was regarded as inappropriate for a woman.

Not only is it culturally wrong for a woman to dominate a powerful male 'other' in public, but there is a second major problem, associated with the word *fea*, caused by women performing. This is that, as mentioned before, a *torero* must be willing to get so close to the bull that he is willing to risk injury or ultimately death, and yet this is *fea*, inappropriate, if done by a woman. The idea that a woman could be injured while performing in front of an audience was felt to be extremely distasteful. Whereas it would be expected that a male *torero* should be willing to risk injury, it was regarded as incompatible with the male role not only to stand by and allow a woman to risk herself in this way but also to take pleasure in it. It is bad enough for a man to be injured, but it is felt to be part of the price he has to pay to be a *torero*; this, however, is an unacceptable price to expect a woman to pay. In *toreo*, the performer is required to risk himself, something which is unacceptable for a woman, and yet if she does not she cannot *torear*. The problem or the confusion comes from the mixing of what are felt to be incompatible male and female roles.

Given the fact that there are female performers and men do go to see them, the response to them as performers is problematic. One of the important aspects of the *corrida* is that if the *torero* does not live up to the expected standards the audience is very quick to abuse and insult him. This would be inappropriate behaviour with regard to a *torera* even though she were performing badly, because, once again, for men to insult a woman in public would be unseemly and 'ugly' behaviour. Here again there is a source of confusion; men not being able to respond as they would normally do because of the presence of women. I was particularly interested to see the audience reaction on the two occasions I was able to see a woman perform in Seville, and I must confess that I went with the hope that on at least one occasion she would perform badly so that I could hear what they would say, and particularly whether they would indeed shout insults as they would at a *torero*. Unfortunately for me, and fortunately for her, she performed well on both occasions, and the only comments I heard were those of praise.

Most of my informants were unwilling to accept that women could be *toreras* because, they said, women did not have the necessary qualities. All those with whom I spoke told me that before skill, art or any other quality, a man had to have the courage to be able to put himself in front of a bull and not run away. The source of this courage, as mentioned before, is the testicles of the man: to be a *torero* one must *tener cojones* (have balls). The reason I was usually given why women could not be *toreros* was that they lacked this anatomical prerequisite for courage. One *matador* friend of mine, having explained that *toreros* had to have *cojones*, dismissed the idea of the possibility of *toreras* by simply saying 'They don't have...', pointing to his groin. A radio commentator, when asked the same question, told me that 'there is a biological discrimination against women, and for a woman to become a *torera* she would have to change her essential nature, for a woman to be a *torera* she has to be a man' (see also the quotation from Carmen Guirado Rodriguez-Mora in this chapter). These comments emphasize how closely the idea of being a *torero* is associated with being a true man, which in turn is largely defined by sexual characteristics.

Not only should women not be publicly assertive in their dealings with men, they should not be seen to compete with men. In the *corrida* there is a considerable degree of competitiveness as each *torero* strives to do better than the other two on the programme. Most *toreros* find it unacceptable to be in a position of competing with women, and state that they would not be willing to appear on the same programme as a woman. The *matador* El Viti, in an interview, told how he had been greeted as a 'colleague' by a *torera* in front of a *plaza de toros*, and he complained that a woman should have the audacity to think that she was a colleague of his.

Once in Colombia, a *torera* – I don't say *torero* because they are not – came up to me and greeted me, 'Good luck, colleague'. I thought that was wrong. 'You, a colleague of mine? No. That's wrong, you are a woman and I am a man. You will be a colleague of your other female companions who *torear* but you are not a colleague of mine'. (*Blanco y Negro* 6–12 June 1979)

Those commentators who complain about *toreras* put the blame for this not so much on the female performers themselves as on the *toreros* who are willing to perform with them. They feel that if men refused to perform with women then the impresarios would have to make up programmes composed solely of women performers, and the whole event could be reclassified and thus viewed in a different light. It would not be regarded as a 'true' *corrida*, which would mean that it would not have to be treated seriously, and it would solve the problem of having to consider men and women in the same light. It is the mixing of men and women in the context of a 'true' *corrida* which causes the confusion. The *toreros* who are willing to perform with *toreras* are usually relatively unknown and so, because of a shortage of opportunities, welcome any chance to perform. Those who performed on the same programme as the woman I saw in Seville only performed once or twice that season.

Most *toreros* with whom I spoke said that they would not appear alongside women performers, and even those who had done so denied that women could 'really' *torear*. One young *torero* who had taken part in a *novillada sin picadores* with women said he was disgusted and ashamed when he saw that they were dressed in 'mini-suits of lights', for their dress, in combination with their style of performance, turned the whole thing into a degrading and farcical entertainment. '*No toreo en plan de cachondero*' (I don't *toreo* in a lighthearted or unserious manner') was his comment, and yet it was impossible for him to generate what he considered proper response from the public when their attention was absorbed by the antics of a group of women.

In the summer of 1979, Maribel Atienza, an extremely good *novillera*, appeared on a programme with two *novilleros* in Seville. During the afternoon one of the *novilleros* was gored and had to retire to the infirmary. This meant that the senior *novillero* had to kill the two bulls allotted to him, plus the remaining bull of his companion. By agreement with the *novillera* and the president the order of performance was changed, so that he did not have to work two bulls consecutively. Such a change occurs frequently enough in such cases for it to be nothing extraordinary, but in the report of this *novillada* in the press the following comment was made: 'what a disgrace for a man and even more for one who would consider himself a *torero*, that a woman had to fill a space in the obligatory order of performance in order to give him a chance to breathe' (*Sur Oeste* 11 September 1979). This sort of adverse comment is the risk a *torero* faces when performing on the same programme as a *torera*. Being unfavourably compared with another *torero* is bad enough, but to suffer adversely in comparison with a woman is a severe blow to his honour.

There is one form of *corrida* in which it is acceptable for a woman to participate, the mounted event, *rejoneo*. Women can take part in this event (although there are actually very few *rejoneadoras*) without exciting the adverse comments which are brought about when referring to *toreras*. It seems that the essential difference lies in the fact that the elements of domination and control are different in this event. In *rejoneo*, the mounted performer must exert and exhibit a high degree of control over the horse in order to be able to work close to the bull; in the *corrida*, the confrontation between the bull and the *torero* is direct, whereas in *rejoneo* it is mediated by the horse. Although the horse might fall, exposing the thrown rider to danger, the physical proximity of the man and bull which excites emotion in the performance on foot is missing in this event. The risk is less obvious and less immediate, and so for many *rejoneo* does not rise above the level of a dexterous and elaborate display of horsemanship, albeit in a difficult and potentially dangerous situation.

Those with whom I spoke about the relationship between the *torero* and the bull emphasized their closeness. They spoke of the two being *compenetrado*, a term which means to be fused or interpenetrated, but also, figuratively, to undergo mutual influence or to share another's feelings. The idea of *compenetrado* in the context of the *corrida* refers, at one level, to the closeness of the body of the man with that of the bull and the attendant risk, which generates emotion. But it also refers to the emotional response of the man who has built up such an understanding of the animal and who is in such tight control of the situation that it appears that the two of them are working together, with the bull as a willing partner, helping the man to develop his performance.

I also received many comments from *toreros*, critics and *aficionados* about the sensuality and even the sexuality of the event from the *torero*'s point of view. The sensuousness is emphasized by the postures and gestures of the *torero* in front of the bull. McCormick and Mascareñas refer explicitly to the sexual referent of the movements used to encourage a bull to charge. Their ficticious *matador* says to his apprentice: 'All *toreo* begins with the '*cojones*', the testicles. This is the true machismo of *toreo*. You must have *cojones* for valor, but more important, every *lance*, every pass begins with the movement as you cite the bull with your *cojones*. In polite words we say the *cintura* [waist] but we mean the *cojones*' (1967: 80–1). It has been suggested that the *toreo*, because he puts himself in a very difficult position in which to assert his masculinity, is in danger of losing it, in that if he fails to live up to the expectations associated with *toreros* he will be denied his masculinity by the audience. Associated with this, it is possible to see the postures and movements which involve thrusting the pelvis forward as an audacious taunting of the bull, in which the *torero* is publicly risking his masculinity. In that such postures involve such an implicit sexual referent, it is inappropriate behaviour for a woman in public.

Unlike the *torero*, the *rejoneador* is never referred to as being *compenetrado* with the bull; the physical and hence the emotional distance is much greater. The rider *is* referred to as being *compenetrado* with the horse – there must be a oneness between them. It is this which emphasises that the most important relationship here is that between the rider and the horse, and that the display of equestrianism predominates over any other aspect of the event. In *rejoneo* the important element is the control of the horse, a domestic rather than a wild animal.

In this culture it is perfectly acceptable for a woman to exert this sort of control, that is, control over a domestic animal, and therefore *rejoneo* is an acceptable activity for women. It is an event which does not depend on peculiarly male qualities. As was mentioned in the earlier section on *rejoneo*, horsemanship has always been associated with the aristocracy or landowning class, and within this class there has been a long tradition of female equestrianism. It is also quite acceptable for a woman to ride in public; indeed, as mentioned before, one of the important aspects of the morning activities in the fair is for men and women to parade on horseback through the streets of the fair ground.

Although women are supposed to be unassertive in public, it is acceptable for them to *lucirse*, display themselves or show themselves off (within certain limits), in public, and this display is in the main associated with dressing well. *Rejoneo*, with its riders showing off their skills on exquisitely groomed and decorated horses, has many aspects of public display. Indeed, many *aficionados* think that *rejoneo* is no more than that – display. For them it is an event which is *bonita*, pretty (a word they would never use for the *corrida*), but without the emotional substance and drama of the *corrida*. Lolita Muñoz, a *rejoneadora* herself, suggested that: 'female equestrianism is a beautiful and graceful spectacle, as well as being feminine; *rejoneo* is very appropriate for a woman' (*El Mundo de los Toros* 1978, no. 656: 24).

It is also important to note that, because there exists this tradition of female equestrianism in the aristocratic and landowning classes, there is a female versiuon of the *traje corto*, the equestrian dress worn by *rejoneadores*, whereas there is no female version of the suit of lights. The female *traje corto* substitutes a skirt for the high-waisted trousers of the male, and this too is important. Apart from the general problem posed by women dressed in the suit of lights dealt with earlier in this chapter, there is also, particularly among older people, an objection to women wearing trousers, an item of clothing which is regarded as essentially male, and when dressed in the suit of lights the woman of necessity must wear trousers. The objection to women wearing trousers seems to be because it emphasizes the division between the legs and therefore has a sexual connotation. Although some women wear trousers as part of their *traje corto* and ride like a man with their legs apart on either side of the horse, the correct form is to wear a skirt and to ride side-saddle so that the legs are neither apart nor seen.

The relationship between the *rejoneadora* and the bull is further reduced, in that according to the regulations if she does not kill from horseback she is forbidden, unlike her male counterpart, to dismount and kill the bull using the sword and *muleta*;[9] this is left to a *sobresaliente* (understudy).

The people with whom I spoke thought it perfectly acceptable for a woman to perform with calves (and events with calves, wherever they occur, are never regarded as serious) in private *plazas* on ranches, because in this setting there was no element of public display. The *plaza* on the bull-breeding ranch does not occupy the same structural position as the *plaza* in the city. It is not part of the public realm and thus events held there do not have the same significance. The private *plaza* is, in conceptual terms, an extension of the *casa*, the private residence, and access is restricted to those invited by the family. The only exception to this is that if there is a *tentadero* (the testing described in chapter 2) uninvited outsiders are tolerated. To *torear* in a small private *plaza* is to take part in a private celebration, and such occasions are essentially an extension of domestic activities.

The discussion of the concepts of wildness, maleness and domesticity in Andalusian culture presented the argument that an essential element in the definition of humanness, and especially of masculinity, is the asertion of control. In the *corrida*, the bull's essential wild nature is gradually removed and the animal is, on a behavioural level, emasculated because the man refuses to allow it to exercise its wilful maleness. During the event the *torero* emphasizes his masculinity as he slowly reduces that of the bull, and yet in order to emphasize that masculinity he must put it in jeopardy and allow for the possibility that the bull may emasculate him. The arena of the *plaza de toros* is the place for truly male animals and truly masculine men, and the highest standards are expected of those who willingly put themselves there in the case of men and which are forcibly put there in the case of the bulls. The *torero* must believe that he has this quality of masculinity before be puts himself in such a precarious position, because if he fails to display these qualities not only does he risk injury from the bull but he will be insulted and judged to be inadequate by the audience. If he fails to dominate the bull because he will not get close, or if he steps back to avoid the animal when it charges, the audience will jeer him and he will be told that he has no *cojones*. It is significant that the imagery of the insults against a cowardly *torero* is usually sexual; the man is denied his sexuality and thus his masculinity.

Cabrón is a common epithet for a cowardly *torero*. *Cabrón*, literally, the 'he-goat', refers to the image of the horns associated with the cuckold in Mediterranean cultures, and emphasizes that he who is wearing the horns must be inadequate as a man – particularly that he must be sexually inadequate because his wife has a lover (or if not married then the woman with whom he is associated has another lover), and also that he is unable to control his wife and prevent her from responding to the sexual advances of other men. The horns are therefore symbols of a man who, because of his inadequacy, has been dominated by another.[10] Whereas it is normally one man who makes a cuckold of another, here it is as though the bull were making a cuckold of the man. The image does not make reference, as it normally does, to the woman in the man's life, but simply to the fact that a more powerful male 'other' has caused the man to reveal his inadequacy as a true man through his inability to dominate the situation. In terms of an event where the central concern is the successful demonstration of humanness and masculinity, it is also inappropriate for a man to be animalized by wearing horns, items which are appropriate for beasts, not for true men.

The imagery of the horns and the cuckold is humorously elaborated in the insults which are enjoyed by all in the *plaza*, all, that is, except the *torero* who is performing badly. For example, in one *corrida* I heard a man shout at a famous *torero* who was making no effort whatsoever, 'You have more horns than the bull'; a remark which was double-edged, in that it used the imagery of sexual inadequacy, plus the insult that as a famous *torero* he could choose to perform with bulls which had small horns and which were less dangerous. In terms of the imagery the man was not a true man because he was wearing horns, and the bull was not a true bull because its horns, part of its proper identity, were inadequate. On another occasion, after a particularly bad performance when the *torero* was so nervous that the could hardly get the sword into the bull, a man yelled 'Cut the horns off the bull and give them to the *torero*, he deserves them', a remark which delighted the audience because it was said at the point when the assistants would have cut the ears had the performance been a good one. What this man was suggesting was that the horns be cut for exactly the opposite reasons, and that the man be forced to carry them to show his inadequacy. A cowardly *torero* has his masculinity denied, or at least brought into question, by the audience, and they thus deny his fitness to be in the arena at all.

A further point needs to be added here with reference to insults. I never once heard the simple term *cobarde*, used of a *matador*, nor did the term figure in the more elaborate insults. Members of the audience know that the *torero* is braver than they are to be in the arena at all, and so he cannot be an ordinary coward. The problem for him is that he has claimed, by being willing to take part in this event, that he is more than an ordinary man, and he must live up to this claim. As a character in a novel said 'there are many ordinary bullfighters but ordinary people don't fight bulls' (Lea 1953: 41). A scared and incompetent *matador* will be destroyed by the bull, in that it is through his relationship with the animal that he reveals his inadequacy and suffers a loss of reputation, but there is no sense that such a *matador* deserves to be physically destroyed by the bull. On only one occasion did I hear a Spaniard utter such a comment – the *matador* had been performing abysmally and seemed to be suffering a particularly bad attack of nerves and all around furious members of the audience were hurling abuse at him, until one man in an angry outburst yelled 'I hope the bull catches you', at which point those nearest turned their attack on him. My immediate neighbour, who had been as insulting to the *matador* as anybody, said in a horrified voice 'What the hell are you thinking of, don't you realize that that man is risking his life?'. Under such an attack a very shamefaced man sat down. However bad the *matador* is as a performer there is never any sense that it is acceptable for a human being to become a victim of an animal attack; still less is it acceptable for anyone to suggest that he deserves to suffer in this way. It is improper to wish for the triumph of animal over human.

If 'having balls' is an essential quality for a *torero*, then the *torera* who does not have the anatomical requisites for performing presents a conceptual or classificatory problem. Most *aficionados*, commentators and members of the public deal with the anomaly by denying the *torera* her femininity. Just as the man who performs badly is liable to lose his *cojones*, so the woman who attempts to perform at all is liable to gain them, at least in the eyes of the public. Vincente Zabala, a critic for the newspaper *ABC* wrote that: 'the history of *toreo* is dotted with the appearance of *toreras* whose femininity, according to contemporaries, was somewhat more than doubtful, although naturally there were exceptions' (1971: 96).

Similarly, many of my friends and informants cast doubts on the femininity of *toreras*. They considered that they must be lesbians, *marimachas* (a masculine woman) or *machotas* (a female equivalent of a *machote*, meaning a 'he-man' or 'tough guy'). Both of these terms incorporate *macho*, which signifies the male element. It seemed that if they denied *toreras* the true attributes of 'true' women they could cope with the anomaly of women actually performing in what is essentially a male profession.

During one of my seasons in Spain I carefully followed the career of a young *novillera*, Maribel Atienza, who was performing in the most important *plazas* in the country. The treatment of her case in the press and among my acquaintances was most interesting. Both the general Spanish press and the specialized taurine press were interested in her. The tone of most of the articles stressed that although she was a good *torera* she was also a normal young woman, a most unusual combination of qualities. It was emphasized that she originally wanted to be a nun, that she had a large collection of dolls, that she took her favourite cuddly toys to bed with her (photographs were usually included), and that she had many friends outside the taurine world with whom she talked about anything except bulls. All of this was to show that in every respect, except that of being a *torera* she was a normal seventeen-year-old Spanish girl. The articles appeared to be an attempt to deal with the difficulty that in order to be a good *torero* one must have masculine qualities, and yet here was a demonstrably good performer who also possessed the attributes of a feminine young woman.

In the arena, Maribel was very astute in the presentation of herself and in her dealings with the audience. In her general behaviour she did not act as a *torero* normally acts, and she did not copy their swaggering movements. When she received an ear from the *alguacil* after a fine performance, instead of embracing him in the way that men greet one another she kissed him on both cheeks, a woman's 'thank you', an action which delighted the audience. On the lap of honour she blew kisses to the audience. In fact, rather than suppressing her femininity she emphasized it and played on it. Her style was much approved of and one report had this to say. 'Nothing of the vulgar imitation of masculine postures. Even less of the repetitions of unsightly gestures. Without losing a jot of her femininity Maribel has made her mark on *toreo*' (*Mundo de los Toros* 14 August 1979, no. 714).

All the comments I received about *toreras* stated that a good *torera* was an exception. Even Maribel admitted to the same view in an interview:

'Toreo, a thing for men and for women?'
'Unfailingly for men and for real men. My case, even though I feel capable, must be taken as an exception.' (*Mundo de los Toros* 19 June 1979, no. 706)

In conversations with *aficionados*, the fact that the *corrida* was an event necessitating masculine qualities was emphasized by the fact that they always said to me that such and such a woman was a good *torera*, *but* (they went on to say) she was a rare individual who did not lose her femininity. They thus revealed that she was in a position where she might easily have done so. In one particular conversation with a friend about the qualities necessary for a good *torero*, he told me that a *torero* had to be *muy macho* (extremely masculine) both in and out of the *plaza*. The role of *torero* was something he ought to follow at all times. We then came on to discuss Cochita Citrón, the great Peruvian *rejoneadora*. He told me that she was a great *rejoneadora* in the arena but that out of the *plaza* she was '*una grande hembra*', 'a great female', 'very feminine' and 'she was neither butch nor a lesbian'. If she had carried the qualities which made her a great *rejoneadora* in the *plaza* out into everyday life, he would have criticized her as he did other *toreras* he had seen and whom he had thought very masculine. Alicia Tomás, a one time aspiring *torera*, was well aware of this threat to her femininity, and she was able to refer to it in a delightfully ironic way when she commented: 'I've been at this business very little time but I am the same shape as before. I promise you that my biceps haven't grown nor have I sprouted a beard since I began to perform' (*Boado and Cebolla* 1976: 369).

10

Form and performance

The theme of the assertion and affirmation of masculinity in Andalusia
and its encapsulation in the *corrida* was dealt with in earlier chapters;
how this theme is worked out in the *corrida* must now be considered in
more detail. In a famous essay, Geertz (1971) interprets the Balinese
cockfight as an expressive cultural form which catches up significant
themes of that culture, an event, he argues, which 'says something of
something' and uses a 'vocabulary of sentiment' (p. 27) to say it to
someone. In a similar way I would claim that the *corrida* is an essentially
expressive cultural event of great significance, which uses a 'vocabulary
of sentiment' to transmit something of cultural significance to both
performers and public. The *corrida* is an event some of whose elements
suggest a ritual, others a game or contest; it is clearly a spectacle and
involves drama, and yet it is not simply any one of these. It is not the
intention of this chapter to attempt to subsume the event under any one
heading and claim that it *is* a ritual or that it *is* a drama, for such a
procrustean categorization would do an injustice to the complexity of the
event. The examination of the form and functioning of the *corrida* is
made difficult by the interrelationship between the elements of ritual,
spectacle, drama, contest and game, for one cannot easily talk about one
aspect without reference to the others. However, for the ease of
presentation and explication, the major elements will be set out and
considered, as far as possible, on their own.

The *corrida* as a ritual performance

Gilbert Lewis has suggested that there are certain 'alerting qualities',
certain 'conspicuous kinds of behaviour', which lead the anthropologist

who is watching a particular event to say: 'This is odd. This is ritual. Why do they do it like that? There is more to this than meets the eye. I must try to find out what' (1980: 8). These 'alerting qualities' involve:

> the peculiar fixity of ritual, that it is bound by rules which govern the order and sequence of performance. These are clear and explicit to the people who perform it. It is a form of custom. The fixity, the public attention, the colour and excitement or solemnity that go with such performances are what catch the anthropologist's attention. He responds to this peculiar quality in ritual performances. (p. 7)

The *corrida* exhibits such characteristics, which arrest the anthropological observer's attention. It is a public event which either takes place in an arena especially constructed for the purpose or in a section of the town closed off for the occasion and which, for the duration of the event, becomes a realm set apart and governed by special rules. Not only does it take place in such a realm but it is often used to celebrate a festive occasion, and thus has a further aspect of being removed from ordinary life (this does not apply to the performers, for whom it *is* their everyday life) and marked out as a special event. Only certain people are allowed to participate as performers and these performers must wear the prescribed costumes and act according to prescribed rules. Use is made of colour, decoration, light, noise and silence. The sequence of actions is ordered and the times at which and during which these actions occur are strictly controlled. The ordering of the event remains the same for every *corrida*, even though the individual performances of the *toreros* vary. It is these elements of separateness, formality, repetition, standardization of action, evocative presentational style and an exaggerated emphasis on means rather than ends (in the sense that this is an extremely elaborate and complicated way to go about the killing of six bulls) which constitute the 'alerting quality' of the *corrida* and signal the presence of ritual.

To suggest that the *corrida* is a ritual performance is to suggest that it's very structure and formal characteristics shape what is expressed in it and influence what is communicated through it. This notion of meaning being ordered and shaped by the structuring quality of ritual is an important one for understanding the *corrida*, for this is not simply a confrontation of a man and a bull but a particular, highly structured, controlled and rule-bound confrontation conducted in special circumstances. It is the form of the event, the fact that the bull is a wild animal which is brought into the city, that the event takes place in a special bounded setting at a special time, that a special procedure must be followed, that the procedure is governed by a complex set of rules and that the event is witnessed by a public which gives it at least part of its meaning. There are other occasions on which men and fighting bulls confront each other in this culture: for example, on the ranches men work with and are in close contact with bulls, aspiring *matadores* go to the fields at night to cape bulls illegally, there are *tentaderos* and training sessions of *matadores* in private arenas in the country, and there are occasions when people run with bulls in the street; but none of these events have the same cultural significance as the *corrida* because they lack its combination of elements and its particular structure.

Although the *corrida* involves initial disorder in that the bull, once in the arena, is uncontrolled, the *matador* must impose order and control, and the whole event turns on a thorough imposition of order through form and formality. The working out of the relationship between man and animal is far from indeterminate – the two are not simply put in an arena to sort things out; there is a set process which must be followed through. Ritual, suggest Moore and Myerhoff, involves a 'cultural statement about cultural order against a cultural void' (1977: 17), a 'declaration of form *against* indeterminacy' (p. 17 – their emphasis). The rules and the process which are set out for all *toreros* provide the outer framework of order, of the imposition of culture, but within this framework the man must impose order directly on the bull and actually take it through this process. The man must transform the wild, erratic and random charges of the bull governed by its inclination into smooth, controlled charges governed by his wishes. The demonstration of control and hence cultural order is in the patterning of the linked series of passes which describe the relationship of the man, cape and bull. It is at this level that the imposition of cultural order on natural indeterminancy is most problematic, and it is the movement through the prescribed sequence which generates interest in the audience.

The formal structuring provides the framework for the event; it tells us what must happen for the event to be a *corrida*. It tells us *what* must happen, but it does not tell us *how* in the sense of what 'style' must be used) it must happen. There are therefore two interrelated aspects of performance in the *corrida*. First, there is 'a certain sequence of actions [which] are held to constitute the performance of an act' (Harré and Secord 1972: 185), that is to say, those actions which are basic to the *corrida*. Secondly, there is the question of 'how' such actions are to be performed; this is decided by the individual *torero* and it is this which constitutes his performance.

Harré and Secord claim that in the case of ceremonies, provided that: 'it is performed according to the rule and role conventions, the thought and feelings of the individuals concerned...have no bearing upon the episode' (p. 190). Although this might well be true for many rituals, it is not so for the *corrida*. It is not enough that the bull goes through the necessary stages set out in the rule book; the event should be a *dramatic* working through of these stages. The mental state of the *matador* is considered to be important, because he must create emotion in the members of the audience, and this he generates through his courage, inspiration and emotional commitment to his performance, which governs his style and the choice and execution of the passes. His performance involves expressive acts, the expressiveness coming from a particular emotional state of commitment in the performer. In the sense used by Susanne Langer, the acts should be 'self-expressive' rather than mere 'gestures':

> as soon as an expressive act is performed without inner momentary compulsion it is no longer self-expressive; it is expressive in the logical sense. It is not a sign of the emotion it conveys, but a symbol of it; instead of completing the natural history of a feeling, it denotes the feeling; and may merely bring it to mind, even for the actor. When an action acquires such a meaning it becomes a gesture. (1942: 152)

All the *toreros* with whom I spoke about style, rather than talking about the need to *create* emotion in the audience talked about *transmitting* emotion. This transmission, it is felt, depends on the successful expression of their emotional response, and so a *torero* who is not emotionally engaged could not give a complete performance. Obviously the audience cannot tell what a *torero* is thinking or feeling, but it is believed that this is registered by his stance, his style of movement and his general demeanour. Technically brilliantly executed passes are not enough to move an audience; unless they convey a sense of emotional involvement they have a vital element missing and become mere gestures. The performance of a *torero* is not like that of a priest saying Mass, or some other ritual specialist when officiating, who by performing the necessary actions or repeating the necessary formulae, can bring about the successful completion of a ritual or ceremony. The *torero* is performing in a ritual setting but his performance is judged in terms of efficacy, aesthetics and the emotional atmosphere. To have a successful end to the event his performance must move people. Within ritual there is a process of communication which involves both the active participants and those who participate as witnesses, but that communication takes place, to use Geertz's phrase again, in a 'vocabulary of sentiment' (1971: 27). There is a cultural message being communicated in any performance of a *corrida*, but it is not communicated in the same way as a bald, verbal statement of how men should be, or what it means to be a human being: it is communicated through sentiment and emotion and it depends for its effect on an emotional response.

Men in their everyday life are able to make statements about what men should be like and how they should behave, but the *corrida* goes beyond that, in that these themes are caught up and actually asserted and demonstrated by the *torero*; to put it crudely, in this case 'actions speak louder than words', or at least have more of a dramatic impact. As Rappaport has argued about formal postures and gestures in rituals, 'how may information concerning some state of a transmitter better be signalled than by displaying that state itself?' (1974: 40). Men should be courageous, exercise self-control and be dominant, but rather than merely stating that he has these characteristics the *torero* in the *corrida* must demonstrate them in a particularly difficult situation; a situation which tests whether he is worthy of the title '*torero*' or '*matador*', a title which is almost synonymous with 'true man'. What the audience is presented with, therefore, is the dramatic enactment, rather than the mere statement, of certain key aspects of their cultural ethos.

An essential aspect of ritual is that it is a public act, and if its centre is the transmission of a particular cultural message then there must be people to witness it and receive that message. Most rituals involve a public recognition of the fact that it has been performed, and that it has been performed in a certain way. The presence of an audience to respond actively to the demonstration or assertion of the masculinity of the *torero* is essential for the *corrida*. Although many writers have referred to and treated the *corrida* as an art, the distinctive role of the public here points to a difference between the *corrida* and other arts. An audience at the theatre, concert, opera, ballet, or even cinema might applaud, and might be expected to applaud at certain points in the proceeding, but the audience at the *corrida* is much more participative than that; without their active response much of the atmosphere looked for in a successful *corrida* is missing. *Corridas* are never staged or filmed without an audience for a cinema or television audience as a concert, opera, ballet or play might be recorded. It is for this reason that films of *corridas* which are shown on television are made during the course of an ordinary *corrida*.

I watched many such televised *corridas* in the *Peña Taurina* (the club of *aficionados*), but the response of those watching was very different from their normal response in the *plaza*. There were no excited comments, no cheers, no applause and no arguments between themselves as there would have been in the *plaza*; there was very much the sense that this was not the real thing. The contrast between the reactions of the people at the *corrida* and the same people watching a *corrida* on television was even clearer when contrasted with their reactions to a televised football match, when they did shout, cheer, clap and make excited comments. There was an emotional atmosphere of involvement during the watching of televised football matches which was completely absent when watching televised *corridas*. One can be a football fan without ever going to a football match; it is something one can quite happily watch in the comfort of one's own home, but no one who did not actually go to the *plaza de toros* would ever be regarded as an *aficionado*. It is something one *must* attend in person. This emphasizes that those watching a *corrida* on the television are passive viewers of a spectacle from which they are divorced, a divorce which is qualitatively more radical than that experienced by someone watching sport on the television or someone listening to a concert or opera via the radio. To watch a *corrida* on the television is very much a second-hand experience, and the impact of the event is very much reduced. The reduction of the impact is further tied up with a notion of the 'inappropriateness' mentioned earlier (see chapter 5) when discussing the reaction to night *corridas* and *plazas de toros* with roofs. Just as these two are regarded as inappropriate or unnatural, so there is a sense of unnaturalness when watching a *corrida* on the television. It is not something which should come into one's living-room; one should go out to it. Somehow the experience is not a real one – it is flat, there is no 'atmosphere', the immediacy of the event has gone and it is very much the case that people are watching a spectacle or show. It is also important that the audience in the *plaza* has an important participative role, especially in terms of the expression of judgement, praise and criticism, and this is lost when watching the *corrida* on television; and therefore not only is the experience second-hand but also the public watching the television is an impotent public – they can achieve nothing by their response.

It is essential for a *torero* to be able to move an audience emotionally to respond outwardly to his performance. The relationship between audience and performer then becomes a two-way process: as the *torero* performs well the audience reacts, and this reaction, in the form of clapping, cheering and shouting *olé*, and with the band playing, provides an emotional charge which spurs the performer on to greater things. *Toreros* told me that even worse than being booed and whistled by an audience for performing badly was to provoke absolutely no response. I have often been told stories of *toreros* almost at the point of tears because of the frustration of provoking no response from the public. To have performed '*Sin pena ni gloria*' ('Without pain or glory') is almost the equivalent of not having been there at all, to have wasted one's time as a *torero* and wasted everyone else's in attending. A *corrida* which generates no emotional response is dull and uninteresting, and has failed in that the *torero* has not achieved public recognition for his claims; from the audience's point of view it is a failure because the *torero* has not exerted himself enough or has nothing to demonstrate.

Apart from the response of the audience to the *torero*'s performance forming part of the atmosphere of the event, the public is also important because, although it is the president who has the power to reward or punish, it is they who are the guardians of propriety; they are very quick to comment vociferously if anything is done wrongly or if there is something not to their liking. As Kehoe has argued, the audience view the *corrida* 'not merely as passive spectators but as an integral part of its every phase in the role of active agents of judgement and progression' (1961: 14). He goes on to say that the bull 'comes out on the sand of the arena to meet *los toreros* and *el público*' (p. 14). If the bull is not in perfect physical condition, if it is lame or in any way damaged, if the *matador* or his assistants resort to malpractice or if the event does not follow the correct procedure, there will be shouts of indignation from the public. In that the public acts as a guardian of propriety in the *corrida*, it is following the same role which it has in daily life, and in this way the *corrida* can be interpreted as a microcosm of Andalusian public life. Just as an individual's behaviour, dress and general public presentation are commented on and evaluated, and character assessment is made in everyday public life, so they are in this special context of the *corrida*.

Games and play

Before going on to consider in more detail the nature of performance, and what this performance is based on in the *corrida*, I want to move from the field of ritual to consider another element which is particularly significant in the *corrida*, that is, the 'game' and 'play' element. The notion of game is an element which it is important to consider both in terms of the structure of the event, especially in that it is a rule-bound formal episode (something which was explored above in terms of ritual) which involves a contest, and in terms of the creation of emotion generated within that structure.

It·is not the intention of this section to attempt to classify the *corrida* as a game, although the *corrida* does have elements in common with games, and an examination of these is helpful in coming to an understanding of the nature of the *corrida*. It is important at the outset to make it clear that although sports can be classified as a particular subset of play and games, Spaniards do not perceive the *corrida* as a sport. The Spanish word for 'sport' is *deporte*, a word which is never used in connection with the *corrida*. Newspaper reports and information about the *corrida* usually appear on a page headed *La Fiesta Nacional* (The National Fiesta), *La Fiesta Brava* (The Wild Fiesta), *Los Toros* (The Bulls) or *La Lidia* (literally, 'The Contest' or 'The Struggle' – for a discussion of this term see appendix). If, for reasons of shortage of space, reports of *corridas* have to be printed on the same page as something else, then the page is clearly divided and one of the headings shown above will be used for that section dealing with reports of *corridas*. Apart from referring to the event as an art or a celebration, there is no sense in which Spaniards perceive the *corrida* as being a subcategory of some other event.

When discussing the nature of the *corrida* with friends and informants, I tried to explain to them the English concept of 'blood sport' (there is no direct equivalent Spanish term), to see if they considered the *corrida* to be a similar event. While they were willing to admit that it was an event which was in some way based on *una salvajada* (a piece of barbarity) or something *cruento* (bloody), they were unable to link this with the idea of sport because the term *deporte* did not make sense in this context. The word *juego* (play) is used, although it is usually used as a verb, *jugar* (to play) and usually in the sense of the *matador's jugando* (playing) with his life or 'playing' with death.

Apart from the importance of the elements of play and game in the *corrida*, the notion of 'play' is particularly illuminating in two other ways. As has been mentioned elsewhere in this study (see appendix), the English term 'bullfight' is an inappropriate and misleading term for this event, because the *matador* does not 'fight' the bull. The image which was chosen as being closest to what the *matador* does is that of the angler, who, when he has hooked the fish, must then play it, something which involves giving it limited freedom of movement, in order to bring it under control and land it. In a similar way, the *matador* must manage the bull in such a way that it is slowly brought under control. Related to this is another sense of play, drawn particularly from the realm of technology and engineering, where 'play' is used to describe a limited amount of free movement within prescribed 'tolerances'. In the context of the *corrida*, the prescribed limits are set by the rules which govern the process of the event, but within these limits there is freedom; although the sort of actions which must be performed are stipulated, the *way* they are to be performed is not, and it is how the *matador* makes use of this freedom which constitutes his performance. This aspect of performance will be considered in more detail later in this chapter.

One of the most significant aspects of games is that excitement and emotion are generated because the outcome is uncertain. This uncertainty is created because, although there are goals which the players wish to achieve and which the audience (if there is one) wish to see them achieve, there are always restrictions on the means of achieving those goals. Miller suggests that: 'Play is not means without the end: it is a crooked line to the end: it circumnavigates obstacles put there by the player or voluntarily accepted by him' (1973: 93). He also suggests that the working with the restrictions or obstacles is a: 'patterned, voluntary elaboration or complication of process, where the pattern is not under the dominant control of goals' (p. 92 – see also Miller 1975: 31–5). In the *corrida*, the goal is the domination (if possible in a graceful and aesthetically pleasing manner) of the bull by the man, the final point in the demonstration of this domination being that the man kills the bull and is not killed by it. Although the *matador*'s performance must lead up to this moment, and although a dead bull is the result of the process, the event must not simply be interpreted as one which has the production of dead bulls as its *raison d'être*.

Emotion, tension and interest are generated because of the restrictions and difficulties built into the structure of the event, and it is because the performers are willing to work within the restrictive rules that the outcome can remain in doubt. It is the process the performers have to go through in order to achieve their goals which makes those goals significant. For example, it is a significant achievement to stand on the summit of Everest because of what the climber must go through to get there; it is the 'what he must go through' which constitutes the sport of mountaineering. If the climber could be lowered onto the summit by helicopter his being there would not have the same significance, because the process of getting there would be different. To get a football between two goal posts would be a relatively easy matter if the eleven men on one side in a football match got together as a group, picked up the ball and ran towards the goal, using indiscriminate violence to remove anyone who came in their way. Such actions would get the ball between the posts, the ostensible aim in football, but it would miss the point of the game. In a similar way, the *matador* must kill a bull and it would be a relatively easy and safe task simply to kill a *toro bravo* in the arena – he could lean over the barrier and shoot it or he and his team could even go into the arena and attack it with machetes and spears – but that would not be a *corrida*. The rules make it difficult and dangerous for the *matador* and the other *toreros* to interact with the bull and finally kill it, but it is because they are willing to expose themselves to the difficulties and dangers, and, within the context of these conditions, to resolve the problems of diminating this wild animal, that interest is created and emotion is generated.

Although the rules set out what will happen and in what order, there is an important element of uncertainty. It is known that six bulls will be prepared for their deaths by a process with fixed rules, but what is not known is exactly how each *matador* will work through this process or whether he will be successful in his task. Uncertainty is extremely important because it keeps the interest of the audience, who wish to have the sense of the man struggling to overcome difficulties. Certain great *matadores*, for example, Rafael El Gallo, Belmonte, and Manolete, at times lost the sympathy of the public in the *plaza* because they reached such a point in the perfection of their art that their domination of the bull no longer appeared difficult or problematic, and the public reacted against them. They became bored with such apparently effortless performances and because the task no longer appeared a difficult one, there was no sense of the *matador* struggling to impose his will and no sense that he was producing anything special. The *matador* must remain a fallible man who might produce something extraordinary or who might fail; there must be some connection between him and the normal human condition of those who watch him.

Uncertainty in the *corrida* is partly created by the rules which limit the means available to the *matador*; this limitation can be interpreted as a movement towards bringing the uneven contest towards a state of balance, even though an equilibrium cannot be achieved. Caillois, in his classification of games, produces the category 'agon', which he defines thus: 'A whole group of games appears in the form of competition, as a struggle in which equality of chance is artificially created in order to make sure that the antagonists confront each other under ideal circumstances' (1969: 47). In many ways the *corrida* is similar to those games of the 'agon' type, which involve competition and struggle between two individuals or teams. There are, however, difficulties in analysing the *corrida* in such terms, in that it is impossible to produce a state of balance through equality of chance, because, unlike other games of this type, the two main figures of the struggle are a man and a bull – two very different entities. The bull has all the strength and physical power on its side and the man has most of the knowledge, intelligence and experience: a true balance between these cannot be struck.

It ought to be pointed out that although there is a contest in the *corrida*, that contest is asymmetrical: although it might appear to be the case, the bull is not actually *contesting* against the *matador*. Whatever it is which produces its aggressive charging, it is certain that it is not attempting to triumph over the man in the same way that the man is attempting to triumph over the bull. The bull merely wants to remove an aggravation; it is certainly not following a set of rules about how to behave. The most important contest is the one within the man, the one between the man and himself; a contest which is worked out through the medium of the bull, with the animal acting as a foil against which the *matador* tests himself. As Homer Casteel puts it:

> The mistake most people make about the bullfight is that they assume it is a contest between the man and the bull. It is not. It is a contest within the man himself. He pits his bravery and his training, which dictates that he must plant his feet and pass the horns as closely past his body as possible, against the innate human impulse to get the hell out. (1954: 11)

In order to approximate to a balance between the man and the bull, the rules and the accepted codes of performance make it deliberately difficult for the man. They force him to base his performance on risk. The excitement for the audience is generated by the experience of watching how much risk he is willing to accept and how well he handles it. Goffman has suggested that risk to physical safety is an important element in certain sorts of game, an element which generates emotion because the players are willing to risk themselves and to accept the challenge to attempt to remain in control in difficult and potentially dangerous circumstances. He writes of children's games (and these comments can be applied beyond this context) in which 'risk to the physical integrity of the body is introduced...on a carefully graded not-too-much-not-too-little basis' (1961: 70). So, for example, a children's slide must be steep enough to be exciting but not so steep as to make an accident inevitable, a rockface must be potentially climbable and a skydiver needs to be fairly certain that his parachute will open. A man who participates in the *corrida* risks the possibility of injury or death, and there must be this sensation in the arena. The man must demonstrate his control, but he must do so in a context of risk; he must place himself in such a position with regard to the bull that only his skill and control can save him. He must survive increasingly difficult tests which he sets himself. Bouissac emphasizes a similar element in lion-taming acts:

Each further segment consists of a different situation in which the disturbing factor is increased, i.e. the distance between the man and the animal is progressively reduced. The man puts himself in certain positions from which control is more and more difficult to maintain and, consequently the feats become more and more valorised. (1971: 852)

In a similar way, *matadores* who bring the bull ever closer to their bodies, who stand their ground even when it looks as though the bull might catch them, who move slowly across the face of the bull to force it to charge, who put in *banderillas* from a position close to the fence where it is difficult to escape, or who kneel in front of the gate to the bullpen when the animal is first released into the arena, are all likely to be vigorously applauded.

Although excitement and emotion are generated by the *torero*'s being willing to risk himself, there is a point beyond which he is not expected to go; indeed, he is regarded as foolish if he goes beyond what is considered to be a 'normal' level of risk, because injury then becomes certain. An example of this occurred in the last *corrida* of the *feria* in Seville in 1980. At the moment of entering to kill the bull, the *matador* threw away his *muleta*, an action which made it almost certain that he would be caught by the bull, as indeed he was. To kill the bull using both the sword and *muleta* is regarded as a difficult and dangerous process if done properly; to throw away the *muleta* is therefore regarded as a foolishness which adds nothing to the drama – in fact the near-certainty of a goring detracts from the drama. The *matador* concerned on that afternoon certainly gained no admiration for his action. Although the *torero* should risk physical injury, it is not expected that he should actually suffer such injury. His risk should be a calculated one, so that he remains in control and is not actually caught by the bull. The audience do not want to see a *torero* gored and there is no merit in being gored; indeed, to be gored usually indicates that the bull is dominating the man or at least that the man has made a misjudgement. The risk should be enough to create tension and yet be manageable.

Although the *corrida* is certainly an event in which there is a contest or struggle, there is no sense in which there is a winner or a loser. The bull does not 'lose' because it is killed, neither does it 'win' if it injures or kills the *matador*. Despite the fact that the *matador* does not 'win', he is either successful or unsuccessful in terms of the different levels of competition which take place within the *corrida*. As has been mentioned before, the *matador* must compete with himself in that he must overcome his own natural instincts, particularly that of fear, in order to carry out his task of the domination of the bull. This in turn is related to competition, in the sense of a struggle to achieve some ideal standard of performance, a standard which may well be shared by members of the audience; although each *matador* will define his ideal standard of performance slightly differently, as will each member of the audience. Finally, there can be competition between the three *matadores*, as each attempts to produce a better performance than that of his colleagues. Such competitiveness is particularly exploited in the *mano a mano* (literally, 'hand to hand') *corridas* when there are only two *matadores* on the programme. Such programmes are set up because the two *matadores* have different but complementary styles, or because there is a particular rivalry between them; a rivalry which it is hoped will provoke or stimulate each into attempting to outdo the other, and thus produce an exciting *corrida*.

Performance – the *torero* as actor?

The first part of this chapter suggested that ritual is an essentially expressive event which is often responded to, both by the participants and the audience, through an effect on emotions. In that section performance was mentioned, but mainly in the context of there being certain actions which must be performed. It is now necessary to consider the nature of performance and style in the *corrida* in more detail.

It was claimed at the outset of the chapter that the *corrida* not only had elements of ritual, game, contest and spectacle but that it also had elements of drama. The notions of drama and performance are obviously linked, and *toreros* are similar to actors or other performance artists in that they produce performances which are judged, in terms of interpretation and presentation, by an audience and by professional critics according to certain aesthetic standards. There is, however, an important and significant way in which actors and *toreros* differ, a difference which is essential for the understanding of the generation of emotion in the *corrida*.

The role of the *torero* is much more closely tied to the man himself than the role of actor is tied to the person who is an actor. In a sense, the role of *torero* is inseparable from that person as a person, and although an actor may be famous and a 'personality', there is no set of expectations of how that person should behave simply because of being an actor. There is, however, for a *torero*. A man may be an actor by profession, but when he goes on stage he does so as another character and performs as that character. Although he might be expected to 'put himself' into the character, there is a distance between himself as that character and himself as a person. On the other hand, the man who is a *torero* 'goes on stage', that is, he performs in the arena, as a *torero*; but performs as himself – the role of *torero* is not thought to be separable from the man who is a *torero*. It is not 'a part' in the sense that an actor plays a part.

An actor accepts an offer to play a part and thus puts his professional self at risk, a self that can be damaged or 'killed' by the audience and critics if he does not perform well. A *torero* too must risk his professional self, in that if he continually performs badly he will not be hired to perform as a *torero*; but more than that, he must risk his physical self – his role as a *torero depends* on his being willing to risk his physical self in a way that an actor never has to. It may be that an actor has to perform a role in which he must boast about his courage and honour, or he may perform a part in which he has to demonstrate his courage in difficult and dangerous situations, but it is only a prt he is playing. However real things might look, and however dramatic the situation appears, the actor is never physically risking himself to the limit – no one is going to kill him, he is not actually going to die, he is only acting. The excitement and emotion are generated because of the danger, but that danger is only an illusion. The *torero*, on the other hand, is a man who is in real danger; to be a *torero* requires that a man be willing actually to risk his life in a dangerous situation. To a large extent the excitement and drama come from the fact that the audience is watching a man in an authentically dangerous situation. Although the structure of the *corrida* is given, and the audience knows, again to a large extent, how the event is going to unfold, the outcome is uncertain: the *matador* might produce a brilliant performance, but there is also the risk that he will fail to control the bull and he might really die. This is not to suggest that Spaniards attend the *corrida* in the hope of seeing a *matador* gored, but simply that the ever-present risk (and it must be ever-present, a point which will be taken up later) which the *torero* must work with gives the event part of its emotional bite.

Lion-tamers and *toreros*

The only other event in western European countries in which men put themselves into a closed space with wild animals to create a public performance is in certain acts, particularly wild cat acts, in the circus. Both the *corrida* and the wild cat acts involve a human being performing with a wild animal in what appears to be an uncertain and potentially dangerous situation, and an investigation of some of the aspects of performance in such circus acts provides an interesting and illuminating contrast with the nature of performance in the *corrida*.

The emotion engendered by the lion-taming acts (lion-taming acts are taken here as the major type of big cat act in circuses) relies on the image of the lion in western European society. It is a creature which is not native to this society and, apart from the regal image, it is a creature which is perceived as savage, ferocious and dangerous to man. Posters for circuses emphasize this ferocity; lions are drawn with long claws and large teeth and are usually in a posture which indicates imminent danger for the man who is featured with them. The lion tamer, like the *torero* with the bull, bases his act on the audience's perception of the animal he works with as being that of a hostile force which is difficult to control and which threatens his physical safety.[1]

Unlike the circus act, the *corrida* does not use an animal which comes from outside that culture. The bull is an animal which is native to Spain, and its popular image, rather than coming from outside the event, comes from the *corrida* itself, and has been taken up by the culture in which the event is set. The image of the *toro bravo* as an aggressive, forceful, dangerous animal that is difficult to manage comes from its role in the *corrida*, whereas the image of lions necessary for the circus acts is brought *to* the event. Just as the circus posters emphasize the fierce qualities of the lions, so the posters for the *corrida* depict large muscular animals with well-developed horns charging fiercely. In the pictorial posters the bull is never shown on its own or in the country; it is always shown during a moment in the *corrida*, usually at some moment when it is being engaged by the *matador*, and no matter how fierce the bull the man is always shown to be in control. Posters often depict a scene of great confusion in which the *picador* is thrown on the ground; such a scheme is acceptable because it shows the forcefulness of the bull, which has enough power to be able to turn over a horse. In this confusion, the *matador* is shown as a man of control coming to the rescue of the fallen member of his team. Posters never show a *matador* out of control, because such a situation should not occur in the *corrida* and this is the wrong sort of message to transmit about the event. In a similar way, circus posters do not show lion tamers being savaged or trapeze artists falling off, because although these are risks which underlie the events, the performers should be successful in surmounting the difficulties and avoid mishaps.

It has already been mentioned that the type of dress used in the *corrida* is most significant, but here that significance will be considered from a slightly different angle; again, a contrast with the circus is illuminating (see Bouissac 1971 and 1976). The lion tamer has a selection of many different costumes and accessories, the choice depending on the impression he wishes to give. This again involves drawing on different cultural realms of meaning. For example, the tamer can wear a Tarzan costume to emphasize wildness, untamedness and a savage struggle; a gladiator costume exphasizes a connection with the Roman circus and a possible struggle to the death; a Maharaja costume that of exoticism; and evening dress that of ease and high culture. He can also carry various accessories such as a gun, whips and sticks of various kinds, or simply use his bare hands. All of these aspects of style of presentation give a slightly different emphasis to the message conveyed in the act.

The suit of lights of the *torero*, however, does not refer to any other cultural context. It is possible to point to a probable origin of the costume in the use of items of clothing, particularly a sash and cap, to distinguish the professional *matadores* from the others in the arena, and later in the adoption by *matadores* of items of dress of the upper classes in the eighteenth century. Nevertheless, there is no sense in which the understanding of the event depends on a knowledge of the historical origin of the costume. The suit of lights has simply become the costume of *toreros*, the costume of the truly masculine, and is used in no other context. The *torero* is playing no other role than that of *torero* and his costume is never varied other than in colour and in the degree of decoration). What the dress says it says once and for all, for all *toreros* in whatever *corrida*. Unlike the circus act, the structure of the *corrida* always stays the same, although the quality of the message will vary depending on the particular performance.

The big cat acts in the circus involve a performance with tamed and trained animals. The lions (or whatever cats are used) are known as individuals by the tamer, who has experience of each one and has built up a particular relationship with each one. The bulls, however, are an unknown quantity; there is a general expectation that fighting bulls will behave in a certain way once in the arena, but, although each animal has been selected for its aggressiveness and fine appearance, it is impossible to predict with certainty how it will react in the arena. The *matador* receives a report from one of his assistants who has seen the animals in the corrals of the *plaza*, and that report gives him a general impression of the bulls, but this information alone does not enable him to decide on his performance in advance; this has to be worked out while the event is in progress. The performance depends on the quality of the bull, its stamina and willingness to charge and the bravery, skill and inspiration of the *matador*. Unlike the lion tamer, the *torero* is not able to rehearse in advance a performance based on a process of his own choosing.

Performance and style

The *matador* must engage the bull with the *capote* or *muleta*, depending on the section of the *corrida*, but the way he performs with each, the sorts of pass he uses and the way he puts these together, is left to him. It is in his choice of passes, his method of execution of them and in his general style of performance, that the person stands out not just as a *matador* but as a recognized individual with a distinct personality and character. *Toreros* spend many hours practising cape movement, and this constitutes an important part of their training; but these practice passes, however graceful they might be, do not carry any emotional weight and cannot be judged aesthetically, because an essential element – the bull – is missing. It is only at the moment of engaging the bull that these become 'real' passes and the grace and skill of the *matador* can be truly evaluated. In order to execute these passes, the *matador* must be close to the bull, but mere proximity is not enough. A *matador* might well be extremely close to the animal but, instead of being tranquil and stationary, be nervously shifting his ground at every pass. What provokes an approving response from the audience is a combination of factors: a *matador* who remains still and calm and who with slow and well-executed cape movements brings the bull in a controlled and elegant fashion close past his body. It is the ability to be dominant and calm, to exhibit what Hemingway called 'grace under pressure', which is admired.

Although it is acceptable for the *matador* to be inspired and even to perform with panache, that inspiration should be directed, and he should not be so carried away by his own performance that he becomes overtly attention-seeking. Self-control has been discussed as an important aspect of the masculine image, and even in the *plaza* when he is performing well the *matador* should exercise self-restraint – even in the moment of triumph. Generally, overstatement is not a quality which is considered praiseworthy: it is felt that there is enough emotional content in the graceful execution of basic passes,[2] and a *matador* who can produce these is much admired. Similarly it is acceptable for a *matador*, in finishing a good series of passes, to end with a flourish of the cape or to stop the bull and posture slightly arrogantly in front of it. This is known as an *adorno* ('an embellishment') but those *matadores* who kneel in front of the bull and attempt to kiss its muzzle or to bite the end of one of the horns are regarded by the *aficionados* as engaging in elements of showmanship, which add nothing of substance to the performance and which in fact detract from the seriousness of it. It must be said, however, that there are many members of the public who do enjoy seeing this style of performance. I would suggest that this is not an aesthetic pleasure derived from the style of the action itself but rather is a thrill which is generated by the audacity of the *torero* in a situation in which he pares the safety margin to a fragile separation such that it seems impossible that the danger does not overwhelm him.

The *matador* is generally able to perform as he wishes within the structure created by the rules, but he is guided by an aesthetic structure which, although not explicitly written out in the rule book, exists in the expectations of the public. There are various styles of performing, different tastes and different schools of thought about which styles are the most attractive, purest, most efficacious and most satisfactory, but there is general agreement as to what the styles should be based on. The aesthetic basis of the performance is not simply that of the beauty of the cape movements themselves; they should also be technically effective in terms of establishing control, and they should transmit the sensation of being intimately connected with the danger of dominating the bull. Many critics complain that the bulls over the years have become smaller and less dangerous, that *toreros* perform less honestly (that is to say, do not stand close to the bull or resort to tricks which make their performance look more dangerous than it is), and that generally the art of *torero* is becoming no more than a dance-like event with attractive movements but with no emotional substance – the emotional substance coming from the excitement generated by the controlled danger of the event. Eduardo Miura, the breeder of probably the most famous fighting bulls in Spain, said in an interview: 'The *corrida* must transmit emotion, if we only want aesthetics then we go to the ballet. The public go to Formula 1 races because the drivers risk their lives, if they could go at no more than 70 mph nobody would go' (*Toro* April 1979 vol. 1 No. 9: 42). Unlike the movements of ballet or some other forms of dance (with which the art of *toreo* is often compared), for example, cape passes cannot be interpreted because they are not representational; they do not *mean* anything or signify anything other than what they are – more or less elaborate movements of a piece of cloth which attract the attention of a bull and bring it close past the man's body. This is not to suggest that all dance forms are representational, clearly many are not, but here it is worth pointing to a difference between these and *toreo*. The movements involved in such forms tend to have no purpose beyond their appearance whereas those of the *torero* are guided by both style (appearance) and practical purpose. The power of cape passes to move people emotionally comes from the fact that they are part of an act whose beauty arises from the danger which is its basis, and without transmitting that sensation of danger they have no significance and no power to generate emotion.

There are, however, performers who are not content to leave the sensation of danger as present but beneath the surface. Instead they raise it to the level of a central feature of their style. These are *toreros* who base their performance less on graceful style than on a more than average bravery and create an emotional response because of the apparently suicidal style of performing. Such *toreros* are called *tremendistas* (from the Latin *'tremere'*, 'to quake, shake or tremble'). In other contexts the word is usually translated as 'crudeness' or 'coarsely realistic' and, in terms of writing, to 'shock by realism'. In the context of the *corrida*, the word is used for a *torero* who shocks the audience through his style, which is extremely frightening and unnerving because it looks as though it is impossible for him to escape unscathed. There is also the implication of coarseness and roughness here, for the *tremendistas* are at the opposite end of the continuum from the great artistic *toreros*. *Tremendistas* are *toreros* who, rather than arousing the audience with the beauty of their slow, graceful, classically executed passes, use danger to generate an emotional response in the audience. Apart from the daring execution of normal passes, the repertoire of the *tremendista* involves the previously described kneeling passes, making passes while looking at the audience rather than at the bull, turning one's back on the bull, throwing away the *muleta* and confronting the bull with no protection, kneeling in front of the bull and caressing its forehead and generally being so close to the bull that it appears that a goring is certain. Such actions and styles of performance do provoke an excited response and admiration from large numbers in the audience (El Cordobés, for example, built his entire career on such performances), because of the raw excitement of watching a *torero* demonstrating his courage and risking his life in such a carefree manner. The admiration shows an appreciation of basic male qualities revealed and asserted in very difficult circumstances. There are some *toreros* performing in Spain today who make use of many *tremendista* elements in their performance, although none have reached that exceptional level of popularity achieved by El Cordobés. People attend *corridas* when they are performing because they know that they are very likely to see an exciting performance, simply because such *toreros* are willing to risk themselves in a more exaggerated way than the more classical/artistic performers. As El Pipo, one of El Cordobés' managers, said of him:

> He seemed to know about as much about the rules of bullfighting as he did about the rules of cricket. As far as art was concerned he was a sorry spectacle. But don't talk to me about art in the bullring. Art you can get in the Prado. In the bullring you want something else. In the bullring, one thing interests me: it's a kid who can excite a crowd. Show me a kid who can make a crowd's hair stand up in the bullring, and I'll show you a kid who can make money as a *matador*. (quoted in Collins and Lapierre 1970: 306)

The traditionalist *aficionados* remain unmoved by the style of the *tremendistas*, and although they do not explicitly refer to it in such terms (they talk about the unaesthetic quality, the way passes are badly performed, and, more disparagingly, how the basis of such performances is little more than crude sensationalism and how such *toreros* have more in common with clowns in the circus than they have with 'true' *toreros*), I suggest that the underlying reason for the dislike of this style is that they do not want the danger element to be raised to the level of the central feature of the style. It should be there as a necessary underlying element; but what is more important is the gracefulness with which the *torero* is able to perform despite the danger. For them the *tremendista* style involves a rather crude and unnecessarily theatrical emphasis on bravery, in which the theatrical often aims at effect rather than 'true' drama. Associated with this is the important sense of control which should always be present. The *torero* should be in control of himself and the bull: he should be close to the bull and yet still show that he is in command of the situation.

For a traditionalist the performance should not simply depend on daring, so that the *torero* is obviously brave and his actions seem to say, 'Look at me in this dangerous position, I don't care if I get away with it or not, but I am going to scare the hell out of all of you and gain your admiration because of my bravery!'. Luck is always a feature of any performance; the bull might do something unusual (although ideally the *torero* should know his animal so well that he is never surprised by it), but luck is not something which should be openly appealed to, as it appears to be in the case of the *torero* who relies on daring. What the *torero* has to do is dangerous, but what is done should be well controlled, so that there is no sense of surprise that he 'got away with it'. It should be added that, although these comments imply that the *tremendista* is not in control, this is merely from the point of view of how his performance appears to the public. It might well be that the *torero* can build that threat of being injured into his performance because he feels totally confident about what he is doing and has judged that he will be able to perform in an exaggeratedly daring manner and yet survive. To a certain extent this is like some circus acts (for example, some trapeze or big cat acts) in which the ability to survive the test which the performers set for themselves appears almost inconceivable, although in fact the situation is well planned, rehearsed and under control. What underlines the traditionalists' comments on such style is that the *torero* does not *appear* to be in control; the effect created is not one of calmness and command but one of disquiet associated with the ever-present threat of disorder, with the possibility of the man being gored by the bull too much to the fore. García Lorca, voicing the traditionalists' view, emphasized the importance of the *art* of *toreo* rather than the mere risking of one's life, because anyone can do the latter; what is special is to be able to risk one's life and on the basis of this to create an artistic performance, but without making that risk the central feature of the performance. In an essay on the theme of inspiration he writes:

> The *torero* who frightens the public in the plaza by his daring does not *torea* but rather, is in that ridiculous state, within the reach of any man, of *playing with his life*; on the other hand the *torero* bitten by duende [that is inspired] gives a lesson of Pythagorian music and makes one forget that he constantly throws his heart over the horns. (1954: 1077 – emphasis in original)

The basis for a good performance by a *torero* should be a balance between courage, skill and grace, but for him to be able to demonstrate these they must be set against a worthy opponent. Because of its impressive size and physical make-up, aggressiveness, wildness and maleness, the bull is particularly suited for men to use as a foil, to assert and demonstrate their masculinity. The bull should inspire wonder, fear and respect, so that the *torero*'s triumph over it will be greatly admired. If it is not a worthy opponent no emotion will be generated and the quality of the cultural message not conveyed. Henry Schwarz summed up this necessary balance when he wrote: 'the traditionalist *aficionados* all agree that the greatest aesthetic value of the fiesta is reached when the conceptual contrast between grace and power is maximised. A docile bull and a *tremendista torero* destroy the structural form of the rite' (1976: 130).

In concluding this chapter, I want to return to Geertz and his interpretation of the Balinese cockfight, in which he suggests that the Balinese attends this event as a sort of 'sentimental education', for: 'what he learns there is what his culture's ethos and his private sensibility (or, anyway, certain aspects of them) look like when spelled out externally in a collective text' (1971: 27). The *corrida* can similarly be interpreted as a collective text which catches up significant cultural themes and presents them to the audience in a complex, stylized and emotionally charged form and setting. The most important themes which are taken up in the *corrida* in Andalusia are those of male experience in this culture. To change the cultural focus from Bali to Andalusia (see Geertz 1971: 27), the *torero* is essentially an interpretative event; it is an Andalusian male reading of Andalusian male experience, a story they tell about themselves. As Brandes has said of other events in Andalusia, the *corrida* is: 'an expressive form which reflects shared assumptions about masculinity and gives these assumptions a concrete reality' (1980: 7).

Conclusion

In concluding this study I want to return once more the Geertz's essay on the Balinese cockfight. Towards the end of that essay he warns that, although the analysis of a major cultural form leads one to discover much about the values of the society in which it is found, the anthropologist obviously should not expect all to be revealed in one event. He makes an explicit reference to the *corrida* when he writes:

> The cockfight is not the master key to Balinese life, any more than bullfighting is to the Spanish. What it says about life is not unqualified nor even unchallenged by what other equally eloquent cultural statements say about it. But there is nothing more surprising in this than in the fact that Racine and Molière were contemporaries, or that the same people who arrange chrysanthemums cast swords. (1971: 29)

What the *corrida* can 'say' is limited by its form and, although it has been examined here as an event which encapsulates key themes of Andalusian culture in a dramatic and ritual presentation, these themes are also treated and presented in other forms (for example, in dance, song, music, folklore, literature and other arts) in ways which are not possible in the *corrida*. These forms also permit the expression of themes which are not dealt with in the *corrida*. On the positive side, the power of the *corrida* is that it *is* a dramatic ritual event which, because of its nature, is able to present to the audience aspects of their cultural ethos in a more emotionally charged and expressive way than is possible in verbal statements and assertions of that ethos.

Although throughout this work the *corrida de toros* has been described and interpreted as an important celebration in terms of Andalusian culture, I would also argue (although I do not do so here) that many of the general points made about the values underpinning the event are applicable, with due allowance being made for regional variations, throughout Spain; and that this is why, at one level at least, the *corrida* is referred to as *la Fiesta Nacional*. It is necessary, however, to point out that although the *corrida* is enormously popular, not everyone shares the values thus asserted nor with the form in which those values are expressed,[1] and it certainly does not hold the same place in popular consciousness that it did even twenty years ago.

Despite the fact that the commentators and critics might call the *corrida* an art form, it is an unusual art form which depends on the very particular view of the world and on the existence of certain values associated with masculinity, which are perceived as embodied in the figure of the *torero* and as guiding his performance. Without the continuance in society as a whole of the high premium put on the values which have been set out in these chapters as fundamental to the *corrida*, it risks becoming an anachronistic event. Under Franco's rule, traditional gender distinctions were maintained, and, generally, social conditions existed in which the *corrida* could flourish; but there were changes even towards the end of his rule, and now, with a return to democracy, with increasing industrialization, with rapid social change and with the changes in values which are bound to follow, the *corrida* could gradually become a minority interest event. This, combined with the increased cost of mounting *corridas* for diminishing audiences and the availability of a greater range of leisure-time activities, could mean that they are likely to be held only in their traditional context, that of town celebrations. Even in this context they are in danger of being preserved as something 'traditional', 'typical' or 'folkloric', but lacking what is regarded as the true essence and meaning of the *corrida*. Certainly the number of full *corridas de toros* per year has decreased; there were 695 in 1974, 538 in 1978 372 in 1980, and 377 in 1985. Some commentators are already apprehensive of such a change and some see it already in progress. The extremely traditionalist Díaz Cañabate is not very optimistic about the future of the *corrida*:

The cinema, another spectacle and love of the masses, will project its new myths, its bewitchments or its violences, even though most of the time these are without the grandeur of the beauty of the true, noble, vivid and virile emotion of the best moments of the *corrida*. The new sensibility of the young generations born during the period of economic development will prefer the lesser emotion, the stupefication, the escapism or frivolity of the latest, almost always recently imported, 'Travolta' musical. Because of the internationalisation of tastes and the enormous presence of women in the

audience, sensibilities becomes effeminate, levelled out and weakened.
(1980: 39)

He further complains, as do many writers, that the present public shows
a lack of understanding of what this art of *toreo* is, something which
indicates its decline and its lack of place in the rapidly changing modern
Spanish culture. On my most recent visit to Spain, in 1987, some *toreros*
complained that their art is now little appreciated in Spain, but others
were quite positive about their profession and felt that they have not lost
any status as *toreros*, and that it is a role which is still respected. Some
aficionados felt that there was little interest in the event among the young,
while others felt that the *afición* was still there and if tickets were not so
expensive young people would go to *corridas*. There is certainly no lack
of young men who want to become *toreros*, but they need the
opportunities to perform, and some city councils and regional adminis-
trations are now actively supporting the staging of cheaper *novilladas* and
becerradas to help them. Despite the fact that there are other
entertainments such as television, cinema, theatre, discotheques and
sports to attract people, the *corrida* is still an exciting 'live' spectacle and
continues to attract people, because of the intimacy of the event and the
emotional impact of being present at a live and unpredictable drama. It is
also still certain that most *plazas de toros* will be packed for the *corridas*
held during a town's fair, and in 1985 several million people attended
1,339 professional events.

Throughout this study I have attempted to avoid the romanticism,
metaphysics, mysticism and 'moment-of-truthism' so beloved by writers
on the *corrida*, but having dissected the event to examine its nature and
form, I want to conclude with an image from a *corrida* to celebrate
Corpus Christi on 18 June 1981 in Seville. Three great artistic *toreros*,
Manolo Vazquez, Curro Romero and Rafael de Paula, were performing,
and the *corrida* was developing well with each of them achieving
something of note with their first bulls. The fourth bull of the afternoon
had enough strength to be led up to the *picador* three times; Curro
Romero asked to be allowed to perform the *quite*. He led it up to the
horse for the second time and did so with such beautifully executed
passes that there were shouts of delight, and the '*¡olés!*' came in a
deafening barrage. Rafael de Paula produced an even finer performance
on the third *quite*, and the excitement increased. Manolo Vazquez had
retired to the barrier, intending to let his assistants carry on, but having
watched the other two he became inspired, grabbed his cape and let the
bull into the centre of the arena to perform a set of dazzling passes. The

crowd was on its feet and wild with delight – I had never seen such a response from an audience in Seville. Around me the men from the club with whom I had attended the *corrida* and those about us had radiant smiles and many (myself included) had tears in their eyes; some were crying openly. The headlines of the reports the next day were; '*El toreo que hace llorar*' ('The *toreo* which makes one weep') and '*cuando lloraron los tendidos de la Maestranza*' ('when the stands of the Maestranza [the *plaza de toros* in Seville] wept'). Rafael Moreno, writing about the response of the audience, said:

> when there is *toreo* like this everyone must give themselves up to it. The uncontrollable tears which welled up in the stands of the Maestranza were not partisan [that is, for a particular *torero*], affected or even hysterical tears. They were simply and unaffectedly the outward manifestation of a feeling which a *torero*, *toreando*, had been capable of provoking. (*ABC* 19 June 1981)

In this book I have not attempted to deal with the nature of individual emotional responses to the *corrida*, but it is necessary to understand that it has the power to provoke such intense emotional responses; without understanding this one misses something essential about the *corrida*, but in the attempt to describe it one must move into the realm of poetry. Evans-Pritchard said in the conclusion of his analysis of Nuer religion, 'At this point the theologian takes over from the anthropologist' (1970: 322); so here the anthropologist must give way to the poet.

Notes

Introduction

1 For examples of recent anthropological debate about the meaning of the *corrida* see Delgado Ruiz 1986; Douglass 1984; Pitt-Rivers 1984(a), 1984(b) and Marshall 1985.

2 Throughout this book the Spanish terms *toreo*, *corrida* and *torero* or *matador* are used in preference to the English terms 'bullfighting', 'bullfight' and 'bullfighter'. For details of these terms, see appendix.

3 The original research for this study was supported by an ESRC studentship held at University College, Swansea.

Chapter 1 The *corrida* described

1 The book of regulations in use at the moment is that originally published by the government on 15 March 1962 under the title *Reglamento de Espectáculos Taurinos*. For the text and a critical commentary, see Gilpérez García and Fraile Sanz 1972, and Zabala 1971. The most recently published work which has these regulations plus changes to them is the *Reglamentos de Espectáculos Taurinos* 1986 (see bibliography).

2 *Plazas de toros* are divided into three categories in Spain: (*1*) Barcelona, Bilbao, Madrid (Monumental), San Sebastian, Seville, Valencia, Zaragoza; (*2*) *plazas* in the provincial capital towns with the addition of Carabanchel (Madrid), Algeciras, Aranjuez, Cartagena, Gijon, Jerez de la Frontera, Linbares, Merida and Puerto de Santa Maria; (*3*) all others.

3 For full details, see Gilpérez García and Fraile Sanz 1972: articles 45–7.

4 The minimum weight for bulls varies according to the category of the *plaza*. For a *corrida de toros* a first category *plaza*, each bull must weigh at least 460 kg, in a second category *plaza* 435 kg, and in a third category *plaza* 410 kg.

5 The *machos* in the context of the dress of the *torero* are technically the bumps on the hat and any of the tassels on the suit of lights but the term has come

to refer almost exclusively to the tassels on the strings which tie the bottoms of the trousers.

6 For example of styles of *brindis*, see Heras and Lozano (publishing date unknown).

Chapter 2 Related bull events

1 Interestingly, although the performers, through their actions, may make humourous comment on elements of the *corrida* (particularly the performances of 'normal' *toreros*) they are expressly forbidden to use the performance to criticize either the president and his agents of authority or the world outside the *plaza*. Article 130 of the regulations states that:

> It is strictly forbidden to caricature or to be indecorous about any institution or recognisable individual, to make apology for any depravity or offence which might have the tendency to excite hatred or aversion between social classes, which might offend the decorum or reputation of the Authority, its Agents or the Armed Forces. (Gilpérez García and Fraile Sanz 1972, Article 130).

2 Article 129 of the regulations states that the performers 'may not use fireworks on the animals, drag them about, turn them over, pull their tails or use any instruments which might cause damage to the calves' (Gilpérez García and Fraile Sanchez 1972, Article 129).

3 There are usually either four or six *rejoneadores* on one programme. If there are six then each will perform with and kill one bull. If there are four then they will each perform with and kill one, and will divide into pairs and take a bull per pair.

4 For a detailed discussion of the *traje corto*, and more particularly the significance of the hat in terms of a system of communication, see Pitt-Rivers 1967: 25–8.

5 A new set of regulations has been approved by the government in an attempt to control these events and to impose some order over what sorts of animals may be used, what age and sex they must be and how they are to be treated and finally killed. Details of the regulations as set out in the Order of May 10 1982 by the Ministry of the Interior may be found in the *Reglamento de Espectáculos Taurinos* 1986 (see bibliography), a volume which includes many useful notes about changes in regulations.

6 Details of these sorts of celebration can be found in Burillo Mozota 1981 and Marvin 1982, who consider events in the province of Teruel; in Pitt-Rivers 1971: 78 and Serran Pagan 1979 and 1980, who consider Grazalema; and in Mira 1976, for Valencia.

Chapter 3   A historical outline

1   Unfortunately I have not been able to discover when this term was first used.

2   See, for example, de Cossío vol. 4: 765ff; Ortiz Cañavate 1934: 384 ff; and Conrad 1954: 114ff.

3   See Alvarez de Miranda 1962: 40.

4   A comprehensive survey of such cults can be found in Conrad 1954.

5   The best available descriptions and most comprehensive survey of such rituals and ceremonies can be found in Alvarez de Miranda 1962. See also García-Baquero et al. 1980: 13ff.

6   Pérez de Guzman and Isidoro Gomez Quintana in Alvarez de Miranda 1962: 37 and 38; Pérez de Ayala 1925: 177.

7   Pérez Villamelon 1955: 1–33; Romero de Solis 1978; García-Baquero et al. 1980: 27.

8   Most influential here was Nicholás Fernandez de Moratín: his views, published in 1777, had a considerable influence on his friend Goya, who made use of them in his drawings and etchings.

9   See Calderon in Pérez de Ayala 1925: 186.

10   Here the reference is to general community celebrations which featured bulls rather than individual family ceremonies or rituals (see Alvarez de Miranda 1962); for example, those associated with wedding ceremonies, in which a lassoed bull was brought from the country to the door of the bride, as which point *banderillas* were put in it.

11   For a description of the organization and the costs of a celebration in the same *plaza* in the eighteenth century, se Toro Buiza 1947: 56ff.

12   For full details see de Cossío vol. 2: 147.

13   See Vicens Vives 1961 vol. 1: 372 for a description of the festivals of the nobility in the seventeenth century. It is also important to note that at this time books were written about the science and art of performing from horseback. Particularly famous are *Avertencias para torear con el rejón* by Luis de Trejo, Madrid 1634; *Preceptos para torear* by Pedro de Cardenas, Madrid 1651; *Avertencias Preceptos para torear* by Pedro de Cardenas, Madrid 1651; *Avertencias para torear* by Gregoria de Tapia y Salcedo, Madrid 1651. All of these books were written by gentlemen for gentlemen.

14   For details of riding styles and breeds of horses see Aurelio Pérez 1955: 58ff.

15   See García-Baquero et al. 1980: 62ff; Pérez Delgado 1978: 872.

16   Although de Cossío has a section dealing with *plazas de toros* (vol. 1: 475–567) and lists 412, he does not include all the dates of construction, and a complete picture of the sequence of construction cannot be obtained except by checking the local histories of individual towns, something which has not been possible in this study.

17   For a full and detailed survey of the regulations, see the essay by García y

Ramos in Díaz Cañabate 1980, and for details of the additional and changes to the most recent regulations see *Reglamento de Espectaculos Taurinos* 1986.

Chapter 4 *Fiesta taurina* or *espectáculo taurino?*

1 See Romero de Solis 1978; García-Baquero et al. 1980: 85ff; Nestor Luján 1954: 267ff; Toro Buiza 1947: 100ff.

2 This can perhaps be compared with the cheering and shouting of 'bravo' at opera, ballet or the end of a classical concert in this country. It would seem that those who shout and cheer are not simply expressing appreciation but are also participating; they too are performers, and the cheering itself contributes as much to the sense of a special performance or a special occasion as that to which it is ostensibly a response.

Chapter 5 The setting

1 The heading above gives the first lines of Federico García Lorca's poem *Llanto Por Ignacio Sanchez Mejías*, probably the best known poem based on the *corrida*. The repeated refrain, 'At five o'clock in the afternoon', has, like the title of Hemingway's book *Death in the Afternoon*, done much to promote the non-Spanish, popular consciousness of the *corrida* as an essentially afternoon event.

2 There is an exception to this in the Feria de Abril in Seville, in that on the last day of the *feria* there are two *corridas*, one of which starts at twelve noon. It is significant, though, that this is a *corrida de rejoneo* (the *corrida* in the afternoon is a normal one) which, as has been mentioned before (see chapter 2), is regarded by many as an essentially different event from the normal *corrida*. Most of those attracted to *rejoneo* seem to be *aficionados* of horsemanship.

Chapter 6 The fighting bull

1 I have never heard of any other animal categorized as *bravo*. Crominas, in the *Diccionario Etimológico de la Lengua Castellana*, suggests that *bravo* derives from the Latin *Barbarus*, meaning barbarous, fierce or savage, and, when used in the context of animals, is only applied to bulls. This is emphasized in Catalan where the word *brau*, with the same Latin origin, means the non-castrated male of the bovine species (*Diccionari Catala, Valencia, Balear*). *Bravo* can be used as a descriptive term in other contexts; for example, the *corrida* is often referred to as *La Fiesta Brava* (The Wild Celebration), and '*La Costa Brava*' is 'The Wild Coast' or 'The Rugged

Coast', but certainly not 'The Brave Coast'. A person who is described as *bravo* or *brava* would be someone who is either tough and spirited or perhaps angry and bad-tempered.

2   See MacNab 1957: chapter 1; Madariaga 1966P 29–45; de Cossío vol. 1, for fuller details of the early history of bulls in Spain.

3   For an elaborate and detailed technical discussion of the different arguments relating to the development of this animal, see Pablo Paños Marti 1969.

4   For use of these terms in a definition of 'domestication', see Bokonyi 1969: 211, quoted in Ingold 1980: 82, and for an examination of domestication in social/cultural terms see James Downs 1960.

5   The use of Leach's classification is not meant to imply whole-hearted acceptance of his arguments in that essay; indeed, serious criticisms can be levelled against it (see especially Halverson 1976 and Howe 1981). It does, however, (especially when read in conjunction with the two articles referred to here) provide a useful starting point for the consideration of many problems associated with animal classification, particularly those of edibility or non-edibility and the types of killing appropriate for certain animals.

6   The only names I ever heard used were *animales de la caza* (literally, 'animals of the hunt'), and *caza mayor* and *caza menor* ('*mayor*' means 'larger' and '*menor*', 'smaller'); the former would be best translated big game hunting, although the largest animals hunted in Spain are stags, mountain sheep and wild boar; and the latter refers to the hunting of smaller animals.

7   Like most aspects of the world of organizing and staging *corridas*, the process of raising fighting bulls is recorded and registered by government bodies. Records must be kept of births and the animals branded on the ranch; for example, the latter occasion is attended by a government-approved veterinary surgeon and often by the *Guardia Civil* who represent the authority of the state (see Domecq 1986: 38).

8   Bull breeders and those who worked with the animals often commented on 'homosexuality' among bulls – how more powerful ones will mount weaker ones and how sometimes in a herd there will be one which all the others mount, a situation which often leads to fights (see Vavra 1972: 113). This seemed to be regarded as something which was to be expected among a group of males which are forced to live their lives together away from members of the opposite sex. Later in the book it will be necessary to consider the theme of sexual control among men and how excessive control, as in the case of priests who voluntarily live a life of chastity, is regarded as unnatural. The similarity between the sexual life of men in a monastery and the bulls in a herd was graphically drawn for me by a ranch foreman who commented, as we watched two bulls, each licking the penis of the other, *¡Como en un convento!* ('Just like in a monastery!'). All the breeders I spoke to, though, felt that this behaviour on the ranch (behaviour which, as it were, was 'in private') did not alter the public performance of that animal in the arena (see Domecq 1986: 93).

The other point to note here concerns 'naturalness'. On a bull-raising ranch, males and females are kept in separate herds, something which would not happen in the wild. The structure is also different from other ranches in that here the primary aim is to raise sexually intact males which are not used for mating. There are therefore four distinct and separated groups on the ranch – stud bulls, breeding females, young which have not been separated/tested, and bulls for sale to *plazas*.

9 Because of the nature of the breed, such animals are not worth fattening for meat, for they put on very little weight.

10 The traditional method is for the breeder to record his impressions of each animal in a notebook. Some breeders now make use of a video, which gives them a chance to watch each testing more thoroughly and thus form a more carefully considered opinion as to the quality of each animal.

11 Further details in English concerning the process of the selection and naming of cows and bulls can be found in Robert Vavra's photo-history of fighting bulls (1972), and in Spanish in an unpublished PhD thesis by Gerald Guidera (1967).

12 For further details of the naming of wild animals in the context of the zoo, see Mullan and Marvin 1987.

13 In a significant way, branding marks a distinction between wild/not wild in the sense that it establishes ownership; wild animals in their natural habitat, the wild countryside, are not normally thought of as being 'owned' by any particular individual. In this ranching system not only is the ranch insignia burnt into the animal's hide but so is an individual number, and the animals are further marked by having notches cut in their ears. This not only establishes that any animal thus marked belongs to an individual, but the use of branded numbers allows for particular animals to be recognized as individual animals. Atwood, writing about the system of branding in the ranching system of the American Great Plains, comments: 'In a herder's world, sharp differentiation of the tame from the wild is a prime concern; those of the domesticated world must be set apart. The patterns seared and cut into their flesh signify human control and domination, and clearly demonstrate that the marked animals have undergone the nature-to-culture transformation' (1982: 78). The branding of fighting bulls does not signify quite the same process, for although not unambiguously wild they are certainly not domestic, and yet in a sense it does indicate human control and domination; for although human management of the animals is kept to a minimum (in order to avoid any behavioural transformation towards the domesticated), their lives *are* managed on the ranch.

14 In many of the less formal, non-professional events in which bulls are run through the street, cows (of fighting stock) are often substituted because they are considerably cheaper. Many of the breeders who supply animals for such events commented to me that cows are often better, for not only will they attack as readily as bulls but also they are smaller, lighter, swifter and

have more endurance than bulls. Despite this, bulls are preferred and command more respect, because they are more impressive physically, they have more 'presence', and to confront such a creature is more meritorious because the challencge is regarded as being more serious (see Marvin 1982).

15   There are certain *corridas* classified as *Concursos de Ganaderías* (Ranch Competitions), in which six ranches are selected by the organizers and each of the six sends one high quality bull for the *corrida*. The competition is to decide which is the best bull of the afternoon, a decision made by a jury which consists of various experts. If one animal is classified as extraordinarily good the president may grant if an *indulto* (a reprieve), which means that it is not killed. If the *indulto* is awarded, the *matador* takes a *banderilla* instead of the sword when he lines up to 'kill' the bull, and he places the *banderilla* in the position where he would normally attempt to push the sword. The *matador* is awarded two ears, which are cut from a previous bull; the reprieved bull is then returned to the corrals and later to the ranch. The bull may not be used again in a *plaza de toros* but it might well be used for stud purposes.

  A bull can also be granted an *indulto* in an ordinary *corrida* if there is great public acclaim for an extraordinary animal, and if the president also judges it to be extraordinary. The granting of the *indulto* is extremely rare, and in over two hundred bullfights I have never once witnessed it.

16   An often-quoted example of a bull with *nobleza*, which emphasizes this non-treacherous quality, is that of *Civilón*, of the ranch of Don Juan Cobaleda. The bull was so meek and gentle that children could play around it in the open fields, they could stroke it and climb on it and it was even fed by hand by the ranch foreman. The bull was finally sent to a *corrida* in Barcelona because the owner wanted to see if a bull which had been raised by hand would still demonstrate the fierceness of a true *toro bravo*; it did so and fought well. During the performance the foreman called to the bull after it had received several wounds from the *picador* and had *banderillas* in it. It came to him quite quietly and allowed him to step into the arena and caress it. This is regarded as showing *nobleza*; despite the fact that the animal had been ill-treated and was probably suffering pain, it remembered someone who had treated it well and did not attack him.

Chapter 7   The *matador de toros*

1   There is a particularly good account of these activities in English in Henry Higgins's autobiography. (1972)

2   A *matador de toros* who performs in a *festival* will perform with *novillos* (the younger bulls). There have been cases of *toreros* who have taken the *alternativa* and then, because they have had problems as *matadores de toros*, have reverted to the status of *novillero*; it must be emphasized, however, that this is extremely rare.

3 When I first saw an *alternativa*, early in my stay in Spain, I suspected that the cape, *muleta* and sword of the senior performer were used by the junior during the first part of the *corrida* in which the *alternativa* takes place. I thought that there was probably some rule or custom which stated that only the capes and *muletas* of a full *matador* could be used in a *corrida*, a rule or custom which I felt would explain this exchange. I asked many people about this but they assured me that this was not the case, and that the sword and *muleta* are the newly graduating *matador*'s own. In my reading I have been unable to discover any further information about the origin or development of this aspect of the ceremony.

4 For a full discussion of *duende* as the spirit of inspiration in artistic creation, see García Lorca 1954.

5 Although not germane to the argument it should be pointed out, in fairness to Curro Romero, that the public does not have this expectation of him for nothing. He is indeed a great *torero* with a long history of great performances, and he does sometimes perform well even now. On those occasions the public is as quick and vociferous with its praise as on other occasions with its abuse.

Chapter 8   On being human

1 Much of the interpretation in this chapter and the next constitutes a development of ideas developed in Corbin and Corbin 1987, an anthropological work which attempts to construct and interpret an Andalusian cosmology.

2 Writing specifically about Seville, Murphy emphasizes the importance of the concept of *ambiente* in the assessment of the quality of a place or a situation:

> Sevillanos spontaneously make judgements about whether or not a social place or situation has *ambiente*. *Ambiente* is at once a feeling in the air and a quality of human interaction. A lack of *ambiente* means that a place or a situation is colourless and unstimulating and not conducive to interesting or pleasant social interactions. Furthermore, a place or a type of situation may have *ambiente* or character which distinguishes it from other places or situations. (1978: 23)

3 For an elaboration of these arguments, see Corbin and Corbin 1987; chapter 2.

4 Driessen gives several examples of the view that those who live in the town have of the life and character of those who live in the country:

> For Santaellanos their *pueblo* is endowed with positive qualities – *ambiente*, *cultura*, comfort and cleanliness, and all these 'civilised' qualities are lacking in the rural settlements. Life in the country is said to be slow, primitive, uncomfortable and filthy. They consider their counterparts as people of a different *raza* (race). They do not

belong to the same community . . . '*Vivir en el campo*', to live in the country, and '*gente del campo*' are pejorative expressions. (1981: 53)

It should be pointed out that this is a view from the village or the town towards the country. There is also another perspective to this, in that villagers who consider themselves to be urban are considered by those in the city to be rural. Although the urban ethos is important, there is also an ambivalent view of the big city (in this case Cordoba) by villagers or by those in small towns and villages (see Driessen pp. 65ff; Caro Baroja 1963).

5 People should avoid behaviour which indicates the animalistic side of humanity, so, for example, drunkenness, explicit sexuality or violence is inappropriate behaviour in public. They should also dress correctly for being in public; men should wear shoes, trousers and shirts, and women should wear shoes, a dress, or skirt and blouse (nowadays it is also acceptable for them to wear trousers) – in other words they should be decently covered. As Corbin and Corbin write: '"Nakedness" is appropriate to wild beasts, to human beings cavorting in the countryside, to infants, to domesticated animality in the house. Civilized people, when not 'enclosed' within the house, should not allow their bodies to be *abierto al aire* (open to the air) in the street' (1987: 28). Their argument is developed further in the chapter from which the quotation is taken.

6 Howe, in a recent study of the ritual of fox hunting, comments generally that rituals which feature animals have been created by human beings in order to 'make statements about themselves through the medium of those beings' (1981: 282). In the hunt, because of the skills necessary to locate and finally kill a wild animal in its own habitat, people make a statement about the human condition (see also Ortega y Gasset 1968).

7 Driessen points to the gradual removal of rural elements, including animals, from the urban realm, as constituting an aspect of the growth of the urban ethos in Santaella: 'In 1923 municipal decrees tried to ban dunghills from the built up area, prohibited the slaughtering of pigs in private houses and the passage of flocks of sheep and goats through the town . . . Rural elements like animals, dung and mud are increasingly considered unclean and removed to rural space' (1981: 198, 191).

8 For a detailed discussion of the construction of big cat acts in circuses see Bouissac 1971 and 1976.

Chapter 9 On being male

1 It is important to emphasize that women only lack will in terms of their sexuality (see Corbin and Corbin 1987: 19). As Marie Corbin notes, Andalusian women are 'independent in their own spheres. The constraints of femininity, such as they are, are reserved mainly for public interaction with men' (1978: 9–10).

2 There are, though, signs that this is gradually changing, at least in Seville itself – see Press 1980: 141–4, 150.

3 This ideal does vary to some extent with class. Gilmore and Gilmore, writing about Fuenmayor, point out that:

> it is important to note . . . that the rigidity of the *perceptual* divorcement between public and private, between male and female, varies according to class position. The rich land owners are unique in Fuenmayor in that they spend most of their time at home, rather than in the neighbourhood bars . . . Most town people do not view this upper-class domesticity as cause to doubt the man's masculinity (as they would do of the worker). Rather the *señorito* is seen as fulfilling a necessary and not un-masculine role as competent administrator of the conjugal property. When in the secluded home, he is assumed by most townspeople to be 'going over the cash accounts of the farm', and thus performing business – a respectable male occupation. (1979: 288 – emphasis in original)

See also Brandes 1980: 185, 164; Press 1980: 120, for further comments on how men feel they *can* lose their masculinity by staying at home.

4 For the history of the development of each item, see Luis del Campo 1965; Giradillo 1951; Carlson 1977: 106.

5 In a similar way, although a priest can go into a bar in his cassock without exciting attention, if he were dressed for saying Mass his presence would certainly be jarring. Both *toreros* and priests when dressed to officiate can only enter the street under specially controlled circumstances. In the case of the priest such an occasion would be a religious procession, and for the *torero* it would only occur if he were *carried* through the street in a triumphal procession.

6 See Corbin and Corbin 1987: 110 for an elaboration of this argument.

7 The exception to this is a popular joke about a cowardly matador which turns on the image of the importance of having *cojones*. The expression for a man who is extremely afraid is '*tener los cojones en la garganta*' ('to have the balls in the throat'). This carries the implications that the person is unable to function normally, that he is unable to demonstrate even normal courage because the testicles, the repository of courage and will, are misplaced. The joke relies on the image of the importance of *cojones* and misplaced *cojones* in the fear image. A man takes his young son to a *corrida* for the first time. The boy notices the bulge of the genitalia in the trousers of an extremely nervous-looking *matador* who dare not even face the bull. 'Are those the *cojones* of the torero?,' he asks. 'No son,' says his father, 'his cojones are here' (he makes a gesture with one hand around his throat). 'Those' (pointing to the bulge in the trousers), 'are the batteries for his suit of lights!'.

8 For a general survey, see Boado and Cabolla 1976.

9   Although women do perform on foot in *plazas de toros* in Spain this is technically illegal. Article 49c of the *Reglamentación* 1972 states: 'It is absolutely prohibited for women to take part in any taurine celebration; even though they may carry out the *lidia* from horseback as *rejoneadoras* they may not dismount in order to finish the animal off on foot'.

10   The imagery is much more complex than this – see, for example, Pitt-Rivers 1971: 116; Brandes 1980: 110; Blok 1981.

Chapter 10   Form and performance

1   Posters for both the circus and the *corrida* are drawn and painted rather than making use of photographs, and in this way there is considerable artistic freedom in the presentation of the animals (see Bouissac 1971 and 1976 for details of circuses).

2   See McCormick and Mascareñas 1967 for a good account in English of the types of pass and when and how they are used.

Conclusion

1   For a general survey of such views in the twentieth century, see Cambria 1974.

Appendix   Some problems of translation

The event with which this study is concerned is known to the English-speaking world as the 'bullfight'. This is an inadequate and misleading translation of the Spanish name for the event, *la corrida de toros* (literally, 'running the bulls'), and gives an immediate false impression of its character. It is the use of the word 'fight' which causes much misunderstanding, bringing to mind notions which are not helpful in understanding what happens in a *corrida*. Men do not fight bulls; only the bull fights. It is therefore necessary to understand how Spaniards refer to the actions of the men in the *plaza*.

La corrida de toros

There are two verbs in Spanish which can be translated 'to fight'; these are *pelear* and *luchar*, and their associated nouns are *pelea* and *lucha*. *Pelear* would be used to describe two men fighting in the street with fists or knives; similarly a fight between two animals would be described as a *pelea* – a cockfight, for example, is a *pelea de gallos*. *Pelea* can also be used to describe a battle of words. For the verb *luchar*, the dictionary of the Real Academia Española gives *pelear* and *combatir* as possible meanings, and in current usage the verb has the implication of 'struggle'. One could describe a man as *'luchando con los problemas de la vida'* ('struggling with the problems of life'), but *peleando* would not be used in this context; *luchar* has a metaphysical sense which *pelear* does not. *Luchar* also means to dispute or quarrel. The closest that *luchar* comes to *pelear* is in *lucha libre* (wrestling), which the dictionary of the Real Academia Española describes as: 'that in which holds and punches are used within certain rules and which ends when one of the combatants gives in/is defeated.' In this example there is the sense of the activity involved in *lucha* being controlled by or contained within set rules, whereas *pelea* conveys much more the sense of the rough and tumble of street fighting where there are no set rules.

It would be impossible to describe a man as *peleando* (fighting) with a bull. This would give the impression of the two in actual contact, with the man attempting physically to restrain the animal or forcing it into a position where he could kill it. One could, however, describe a man *luchando* with the bull (although this is actually rarely used by Spaniards), and this usage would give the sense that he was struggling to resolve the problems created by the bull, or the idea that he was having to struggle with the difficulties of the situation which involved his own nervousness and fear. What is important is that the word here does not imply a physical fight but rather the metaphysical sense of 'fighting difficulties', as discussed above. It is for this reason that *corrida* is used in this study instead of 'bullfight'.

Torear and *toreo*

Having explained that the word 'fight' is inappropriate to describe both the event and the activities within the *corrida*, it is necessary to examine the Spanish terms which *are* used. The most usual words to describe the action of the man are the verb *torear* and the noun *toreo*, derived from the noun *toro* (bull). These derivatives have no direct English equivalents, but there is a parallel in the English use of the verb 'to fish' in the context of angling. This verb only applies to the human actor: the man fishes. The angler not only 'fishes', but once he has hooked the fish, he 'plays' it. This is a term which describes the series of actual physical movements of the fish in the water – the movement away from the angler when he gives it more line, and the movement towards him when he winds in the line. It also refers to the movement in conceptual terms between the possibilities of the fish escaping or being landed. The 'playing' of the fish, that is to say, allowing it to swim away and then reeling in and thus dragging it towards the angler, is an attempt to bring it under control by exhausting it. In a similar way, the choice of cape passes and the sequence of these passes by the *torero* are designed to tire the bull, a necessary part of the process of bringing it under control. As the angler gives a little more line and then reels in, then gives a little more, so the *torero*, by varying the capework, slowly tires and eases the bull along to a point where he has it under control. It is this sense of the bull's movements backwards and forwards past the *matador*, movements which are controlled, or should be controlled, by the man, which are referred to when it is said that the *torero* is 'playing the bull'; it is this English term which is preferred in this study.

Torear and *lidiar*

The sense of the verb *torear* and the associated noun *toreo* is 'what a man does with respect to a bull in a *corrida*'; it is possible to describe all the actions of the man, the *torero*, as *toreo*, and most Spaniards who do not have a specialist interest in the event would use this term. It is perhaps easier to approach the full meaning of *torear* through the examination of another term, *lidiar*, which is associated with it and often contrasted to it.

The verb *lidiar* comes from the Latin *litigare* (to dispute, quarrel, strive, to sue at law) and conveys a similar sense of struggle to that in *luchar*. The word was originally used in the sense of engaging in legal disputes and litigation, and, after several changes of meaning, today in popular use it means 'to struggle with the bull'. Within the range of personal experience I have not heard the word used in any but this latter sense. The compilers of English/Spanish dictionaries certainly do not expect the foreigner to hear the word in any other context, because the relationship with the *corrida* is the only translation they give.

The dictionary of the Real Academia Española gives a general definition as: 'to outmanoeuvre the bull, struggling with it and avoiding its attacks until killing it.' Again, it should be noted that this is something which the human actors do; as in *torear*, the bull does not *lidiar*. Luis Bollain gives a further definition of *lidiar* as being 'the efficient preparation for the death of the bull' (1968:16). This efficient preparation for the death of the bull is what the performance of the *torero* must minimally consist of; he must control the bull. *Lidiar* therefore involves good craftsmanship; it is a struggle or a contest based on the man's knowledge of the tendencies of the animal and on his possession of courage and the necessary technical competence to correct or make use of these tendencies. It might not be possible to obtain a great performance from a particular animal due to a deficiency on the part of the bull (for example, it might be weak or slow and hesitant to charge; it might refuse to charge at all; it might only attack the man's body rather than the cape), but at least the *torero* can acquit himself honourably by mastering the animal before killing it.

Aficionados say that '*cada toro tiene su lidia*' ('every bull has its *lidia*'). By the use of the noun *lidia* they mean that each bull has certain characteristics and the *torero* must shape his performance to deal with these. It also suggests that the bull has within it a performance which the *matador* must release. In this sense, the *matador* is similar to the sculptor who 'sees' a figure within a block of marble – a figure which he has to release or reveal. There is therefore a necessary process for each bull (a different one for each individual animal) to go through for it to be brought under control and prepared for being killed. Again, it should be noted that the bull does not govern the action in the sense of choosing the process: *lidiar* is what the man does, and it is the process which the bull has to go through.

This 'process' does not refer to the structure of the *corrida* as an event, but to the necessary lance thrusts, *banderillas* or types of pass with cape and *muleta* to bring the animal under control. Some bulls have to be treated gently because they are weak; others have to be worked hard to reduce some of their strength and make them more manageable. A good *aficionado* or *torero* can soon see what sort of *lidia* is necessary to get the most from a particular animal.

In a sense, *lidia* is a preliminary stage to *toreo* (the latter being regarded here as artistic performance), because *toreo* must be based on the control and domination of the bull. Rafael Rios Mozo points to the two aspects when he writes that *lidiar*: 'is to give the animal the passes that it needs in order to *torear* [that is, play the bull artistically] if it is possible or if not to finish with the creature if it doesn't allow anything else' (1974:30). *Lidia*, however, must not be regarded as a stage which is completed and then left, with the *torero* moving on to the stage of *torero*; in fact, it is not easy to distinguish between the two processes during a performance – the two are intermingled. *Lidia* in the sense of control and domination is like a thread running through the whole performance, for the *torero* must have the bull under control in order to be able to perform artistically with it. Gregorio Corrochano, for example, commenting on a performance by the great earlier twentieth-century *torero* Joselito el Gallo, wrote: 'After having dominated it with an adequate *lidia*, valiant and intelligent – two indispensible characteristics of the *torero*, he was then able to *torear* in that more attractive, light and artistic way' (1966:149). It is often said that *lidiar* is something which can be taught to someone. They can be taught to look carefully at the full and to interpret its movements, and they can be taught the passes, the sequence of passes, and the complex question of how to place oneself vis-à-vis the bull. What cannot be taught, however, is how to *torear*; this is regarded as an art which is born with the *torero* and can only be revealed if it is already there.

In general usage in Spanish, the work *toreo* describes the activity of the *torero* with regard to the bull in the *plaza*. It incorporates the concept of *lidia* and is thus a more widely embracing term, and as such it is used in this study in preference to 'bullfighting'.

The performers

The team of human performers (and there are usually three such teams in a *corrida*) is led by the head of the team, the *matador de toros* (literally, 'he who kills bulls', from the verb *'matar'*, 'to kill') who is responsible for the main performance and for killing the bull. The head of the team can be a *matador de novillos* (*novillo* being a young bull), someone who has not taken the graduation cermony to become a *matador de toros* and thus performs with younger, smaller, and lighter bulls. Each *matador* has three *banderilleros* (foot assistants – the name is taken from the *banderillas*, the decorated spiked sticks which they place in the bull) and two *picadores* (from the verb *'picar'*, 'to pick or puncture' but also 'to goad or wound').

The term *torero* is a general one which can be used for *matador de toros*, *matador de novillos* and *banderilleros*, but in general Spanish usage it is equivalent to *matador*. Although *matador* is used as a term of reference, to denote someone's specific role, there is a certain sense in which it is a somewhat basic word (I suspect that this is associated with its direct reference to the killing aspect of the role), and the term *torero* is more frequently used, particularly as a means of address. The term *torero* is also used in preference to *matador* by members of the public when discussing performers and performances. They will say *'¡Que torero!* ('What a *torero!*') or *'Es un buen torero'* ('He is a good *torero'*) rather than, 'He is a good *matador'*; and, when shouting enthusiastically during a good performance, *'¡To-re-ro!'* rather than *'¡Ma-ta-dor! Torero*, because of its obvious link with the term which defines the action, *toreo*, seems to give a most complete sense of the role.

Throughout the book the terms *matador* and *torero* are used in preference to the English terms 'bullfighter' because, as was mentioned before, the *torero* does not 'fight' bulls and so the term is misleading. Although the terms *matador* and *torero* are usually interchangeable, the term *torero* is a more general term in that it refers more explicitly to the total performance involved in *toreo* rather than emphasizing the final part, the killing, emphasized by *matador*. In this book *matador* and *torero* are also used interchangeably and should be understood as referring to the man who heads the team and who is the focus of interest. When it is necessary to emphasize the specific role or the career of this person the terms *matador* or the more precise technical terms *matador de toros* or *matador de novillos* are used. The other members of the team are referred to in this study by their technical names, *banderilleros* and *picadores*.

Castigar

This verb, meaning 'to punish', is used on three occasions during the *corrida*, and refers to punishment given to the bull. It is used to describe the action of the *picador*, the use of a type of *banderilla*, and finally a type of pass made with the *muleta*.

Normally 'punishment' in English and '*castigo*' in Spanish are used in the sense of reprimanding or attempting to correct unacceptable behaviour. Punishment can also be used in a learning process to give a negative award for incorrect answers or behaviour. In the section of the *corrida* associated with the *picador*, *castigar* is indeed associated with learning, but refers to punishment given to the bull for correct behaviour. The argument behind this apparently paradoxical reversal of usual usage is as follows: a good bull reveals its qualities, particularly those of ferocity, under whatever circumstances, and the more difficult the circumstances (from the bull's point of view) the better the bull is revealed to be (from the audience's point of view) if it continues to attack and thus exhibits its ferocity. Of course, it is humans who are creating the sitaution for the possible revelation of the bull's qualities. In a sense, therefore, it is not that the bull reveals itself but that *it is revealed* as being a good fighting bull.

Castigar, referring to the action of the *picador*, occurs early on in the *corrida*. The padded horse offers an easy target for the bull, especially after its previous frustrating experience of charging at capes which disappear as soon as it attacks them. As the bull attacks the horse, the *picador* pushes the spike of the lance into the enlarged hump close to the bull's neck, and the two push against each other. If the bull shies away as soon as it feels the pain from the spike it reveals timidity, its lack of ferocity and generally its lack of the quality of a true fighting bull, which should continue to attack under whatever difficulties. Similarly, a bull which continues to push at the horse but with its head held high, to reduce the effect of the spike, is not of the same quality as one which lowers it head and neck (thus exposing itself more to the pain) to push under the horse.

After the first charge and pic-ing the bull is lined up for a second and then a third charge. The argument is that on the first charge the bull does not associate the pain with attacking the horse. By the second charge it has learnt this, and so if it attacks yet again despite the pain it is indeed a good bull. Instead of responding to the punishment/pain, the animal is expected to ignore it or overcome it.

Castigar is used with regard to the use of *banderillas*, but these are not used in every *corrida*. A bull which continually shies away from the horse and does not receive a single lance thrust will probably have *banderillas negras* (black *banderillas*) placed in it. These are similar to ordinary *banderillas* in that they are sticks covered with coloured paper, but they have much longer spikes and a double harpoon. An un-pic-ed bull is difficlut to work with and the *banderillas negras*, with their longer, more deeply penetrating spikes, do reduce some of the strength of the animal, something which would normally be done by the *picador*. The *banderillas negras* also punish the bull for not having done what it should have done (the normal use of the term 'punishment'), the idea of punishment being emphasized by the fact that the bull is referred to as being *condenado* (condemned) to *banderillas negras*. I only saw one *corrida* in which *banderillas negras* were used, and in both of the major newspaper reports of the *corrida* the notion of being condemned to punishment was emphasized. It is a sign of a great dishonour for the breeder to have black *banderillas* placed in one of his animals, because it shows that the animal has not reached an acceptable standard.

The third occasion on which *castigar* or the noun *castigo* may be used is to describe certain *muleta* passes. *Pases de castigo* (literally, 'punishment passes') are those which are used to attempt to bring the bull quickly under control by sapping its strength. They normally involve making the bull turn sharply in a short distance so that it quickly tires; this is called *doblando* (doubling) the bull. *Castigar* here has the sense of the use of punishment to correct a tendency in the bull which makes it difficult to work, and in this sense is an acceptable part of the performance. If, however, a *torero* resorts to nothing but these passes, on a bull which does not need them, because (it is assumed) he does not want to develop the more difficult artistic passes, he will be severely criticized by the audience.

For a satisfactory bull, in a 'normal' *corrida*, *castigar* is only used on one occasion, that of the picador stage. Ideally the bull reveals its quality at this stage, it 'takes its punishment', as we say in English – the situation must be as it is for the bull to reveal that it is indeed a true fighting bull.

Lance

The movements of the large pink and yellow *capote* (cape) are referred to not as *pases* (passes), as are those with the red *muleta* (the semi-circular cloth draped over a stick), but as *lances*. This word derives from the verb '*lancear*', meaning 'to let go of something' or 'to throw out', in the sense of casting a fishing line or net. The parallel with casting a net in order to trap fish is an interesting one, because *lances* with the *capote* have a similar function; to 'trap' or 'catch' the bull when it is first released. Obviously the aim is not actually to entangle the bull in the *capote*, but to 'capture' it in the sense of stopping it running free in the arena, and to bring it into the orbit of the movement of the cape around the body of the *torero*. It thus represents the first stage of bringing it under control.

Bibliography

Books and journals

Acquaroni, J. L. 1958, *Bulls and Bullfighting*. Barcelona: Noguer S.A.

Alcover, A. and de B. Moll, F. 1968, *Diccionari Catala-Valencia-Balear*. Palma de Mallorca: Editorial Moll.

Alfonso el Sabio 1972, *Las Siete Partidas de Rey Don Alfonso el Sabio*; *cotejadas con varios codices antiguos por la Real Academia de la Historia*. Madrid: Editorial Atlas. First edition 1807.

Alvarez de Miranda, A. 1962, *Ritos y Juegos del Toro*. Madrid: Taurus.

Araúz de Robles, S. 1979, *Sociología del Toreo*. Madrid: Editorial Prensa Española.

Atwood Lawrence, E. 1982, *Rodeo. An Anthropologist Looks at the Wild and the Tame*. Knoxville: The University of Tennessee Press.

Bennaser, B. 1979, *The Spanish Character: Attitudes and Mentalities from the Sixteenth to the Nineteenth Century*. Berkeley: University of California Press.

Blok, A. 1981, 'Rams and billy-goats: a key to the Mediterranean code of honour'. *Man*, 16, 3, 419–40.

Boado, E. and Cebolla, F. 1976, *Las Señoritas Toreras: Historia Erotica y Política del Toreo Femenino*. Madrid: Felmar.

Bollain, L. 1953, *El Decálogo de la Buena Fiesta*. Madrid: Editorial Beltram.

Bollain, L. 1968, *El Toreo*. Seville: Editorial Católica Española.

Bouissac, P. 1971, 'Poetics in the lion's den: the circus act'. *Modern Language Notes*, 86, 845–57.

Bouissac, P. 1973, 'On jugglers and magicians. Some aspects of the semantics of circus performances'. *Journal of Symbolic Anthropology*, 2, 127–45.

Bouissac, P. 1976, *Circus and culture: a semiotic approach*. Bloomington: Indiana University Press.

Brandes, S. 1980, *Metaphors of Masculinity. Sex and Status in Andalusian Folklore*. University of Pennsylvania Press.

Burillo Mozota, F. 1981, 'El toro embolado'. In *Guía Turista de Mora, Gudar, Javalambre, Teruel*, Valencia: Alagnas, 50–4.

Caillois, R. 1969, 'The Structure and Classification of Games'. In J. W. Loy and G. S. Keyon (eds), *Sport, Culture and Society (A Reader in the Sociology of Sport)*, London Macmillan, 44–55.

Cambria, R. 1974, *Los Toros: Tema Polémico en el Ensayo Español del Siglo XX.* Madrid: Biblioteca Romania Hispanica.

Cambell, J. and Sherrard, P. 1968, *Modern Greece.* London: Ernest Benn Ltd.

Del Campo, L. 1965, *El Traje del Toreo de a Pie.* Pamplona: Editorial, La Accion Social.

Delgado Ruiz, M. 1986, *De la Muerte de un Dios.* Barcelona: Nexos Ediciones Península.

Douglass, C. 1984, 'Toro Muerte, Vaca Es: An Interpretation of the Spanish Bullfight'. *American Ethnologist*, vol. 11 242–58.

Campos de España, R. 1969, 'España y los toros'. in Carlos Orellana (ed.), *Los Toros en España*, 3 vols., Madrid: Orel.

Carlson, C. L. 1977, 'The vulgar sort: common people in the Siglo del Oro in Madrid'. Unpublished PhD thesis, University of California, Berkeley.

Caro Baroja, Julio. 1963, 'The city and the country: reflections on some ancient commonplaces'. In J. Pitt-Rivers (ed.), *Mediterranean Countrymen*, Paris: Mouton and Co.

Casteel, H. 1954, *The Running of the Bulls.* London: Faber and Faber.

Chaves, M. 1914, *El Primer Año de Feria en Sevilla, 1847.* Seville: Editorial Angel Saavedra.

Collantes de Teran Delorme, F. 1981, *Cronicas de la Feria 1847–1916.* Seville: Publicaciones del Ayuntamiento de Sevilla.

Collins, L. and Lapierre, D. 1970, *Or I'll Dress You in Mourning.* London: World Books.

Conrad, J. R. 1954, 'The bullfight: the cultural history of an institution'. Unpublished PhD thesis, Duke University, North Carolina.

Corbin, J. R. 1978, *Funerals, Bullfights and the 'Terrors' of 1936: Some Dialectics of Death in Southern Spain.* Unpublished manuscript.

Corbin, J. R. and Corbin, M. D. 1984, *Compromising Relations: Kith, Kin and Class in Andalusia.* Aldershot: Gower Publishing Company Ltd.

Corbin, J. R. and Corbin, M. D. 1987, *Urbane Thought: Culture and Class in an Andalusian City.* Aldershot: Gower Publishing Company Ltd.

Corbin, M. 1978, 'Male and female in Andalusia'. Unpublished lecture from public lecture series, *Understanding Societies*, at University of East Anglia.

Corominas, J. 1954, *Diccionario Crítico Etimológico de la Lengua Castellaña.* Berne: Editorial Francke.

Corrochano, G. 1966, *¿Que es Torear? Introducción a las Tauromaquias de Joselito y de Domingo Ortega.* Madrid: Revista de Occidente.

De Cossío, J. M. 1943, 1943, 1947, 1961, *Los Toros.* 4 vols. Madrid: Espasa Calpe. (Note two additional volumes, published 1980 and 1981, under the authorship of Antonio Díaz Cañabate).

Cuevas Villamañan, T. 1976, *Evolución y Revolución de la Fiesta de Toros (Ensayo Juridico Politico Administrativo de la Fiesta Brava)*. Albacete: Graficas Fuentes.

Días Cañabate, A. 1980, *Los Toros.*. vol. 5. Madrid: Espasa Calpe.

Diccionario de la Lengua Castellana. 1970. Madrid: Real Academia Española. (Decimonovena Edición).

Domecq y Diez, A. 1986, *El Toro Bravo*. Madrid: Espasa Calpe.

Downs, J. R. 1960, 'Domestication: an examination of the changing social relationships between man and animals'. *Kroeber Anthropological Society Papers*, 22, 18–67.

Driessen, H. 1981, *Agro Town and Urban Ethos in Andalusia*. Nijemen: Katholieke Universiteit.

Driessen, H. 1983, 'Male sociability and rituals of masculinity in rural Andalusia'. *Anthropological Quarterly* 56, 3, 125–33.

Dundes, A. 1978, 'Into the endzone for a touchdown: a psychoanalytic consideration of American football'. *Western Folklore*, 37, 75–88.

Evans-Pritchard, E. E. 1970, *Nuer Religion*. Oxford: Oxford University Press. First edition 1956.

Fernandez de Moratín, N. 1777, *Carta Histórica sobre el Origen y Progresos de las Fiestas de Toros en España*. Madrid: private publication.

García-Baquero, G. A., Romero de Solis, P., and Vazquez Parlade, I. 1980, *Sevilla y La Fiesta de Toros*. Seville: Publicaciones del Ayuntamiento de Sevilla.

García Lorca, F. 1954, 'Teoria y juego del duende'. In *Obras Completas*, vol. 1, Madrid: Agwilar S. A., 1067–79.

Garcia-Ramos Y Vazquez, A. 1980, 'Historia de los reglamentos de España y otros paises'. In Antonio Díaz Cañabate, *Los Toros*, vol. 5, Madrid: Espasa Calpe.

Gargantilla, Anastasio. 1978, 'El sexo de los toreros'. *Playlady* 83, June 1978, 46–8.

Gasquoine, H. C. 1911, *Things Seen in Spain*. London: Seeley and Co.

Geertz, C. 1971. 'Deep play: notes on the Balinese cockfight'. In C. Geertz (ed.), *Myth, Symbol and Culture*, New York: Norton and Co., 1–37.

Geertz, C. 1975, *The Interpretation of Cultures*. London: Hutchinson.

Gilmore, D. 1977, 'The social organization of space: class, cognition and residence in a Spanish Town'. *American Ethnologist*, 4, 3, 437–51.

Gilmore, M. M. and Gilmore, D. D. 1979, '"Machismo": a psychodynamic approach (Spain)'. *Journal of Psychological Anthropology*, 2, 3, 281–99.

Gilpérez García, L. and Fraile Sanz, M. 1972, *Reglamentación Taurina Vigente: Diccionario Comentada*. Seville: Graficas del Sur. Second edition.

"Giradillo". 1951, *Filosofía del Toreo*. Madrid: Orel.

Goffman, Erving. 1961, *Two studies in the Sociology of Interaction*. Indianapolis: Bobbs-Merrill Co.

Guidera, G. 1967, 'Implicaciones socio-antropológicas del toro de lidia en la baja

Andalucía. 'Fontanillas', estudio de un cortijo. PhD thesis, Universidad de Sevilla.

Guirado Rodriguez-Mora, C. 1969, 'Los toros en lo feminino'. In Carlos Orellana (ed.), *Los Toros en España*, 3 vols., Madrid: Editorial Orel.

Halverson, J. 1976, 'Animal categories and terms of abuse'. *Man*, 11, 4, 505–16.

Harré, R. and Secord, P. F. 1972, *The Explanation of Social Behaviour*. Oxford: Basil Blackwell.

Hemingway, E. 1985, *The Dangerous Summer*. London: Hamish Hamilton.

Heras and Lozano. Date unknown, *Libro de brindis. Arte de Brindiar*. Madrid: publisher unknown – probably privately published.

Herr, R. *An Historical Essay on Modern Spain*. Berkeley: University of California Press.

Higgins, H. and Myers, J. 1972, *To Be a Matador*. London: William Kimber.

Howe, J. 1981, 'Foxhunting as ritual'. *American Ethnologist*, 8, 2, 278–300.

Huizinga, J. 1955, *Homo Ludens – A Study of the Play-Element in Culture*. Boston: Beacon Press.

Ingold, T. 1980, *Hunters, Pastoralists and Ranchers: Reindeer Economics and their Transformations*. Cambridge: Cambridge University Press.

Jimenez Nuñez, A. 1978, *Biografía de un Campesino Andaluz*. Seville: Publicaciones de la Universidad de Sevilla.

Kany, E. C. 1970, *Life and Manners in Madrid*. New York: AMS Press.

Kehoe, V. J. R. 1961, *Wine, Women and Toros: The Fiesta de Toros in the Culture of Spain*. New York: Hastings.

Langer, S. 1942, *Philosophy in a New Key: A study of the Symbolism of Reason, Rite and Art*. Cambridge, Massachusetts: Harvard University Press.

Lea, T. 1953, *The Brave Bulls*. Harmondsworth: Penguin Books.

Leach, E. R. 1972, 'Anthropological aspects of animal categories and verbal abuse'. In Pierre Maranda (ed.), *Mythology*, Harmondsworth: Penguin Books, 39–67.

Lévi-Strauss, C. 1966, *The Savage Mind*. London: Weidenfeld and Nicolson.

Lewis, G. 1980, *Day of Shining Red: An Essay on Understanding Ritual*. Cambridge: Cambridge University Press.

López Casero, L. 1972, 'La plaza, estructura y procesos en un pueblo de la Mancha'. *Ethnica*, 4, 89–133.

Lozano Rey, L. 1931, *La Fiesta y su Urgente e Inexcusable Dulcificación*. Madrid: publisher unknown.

Luján, Nestor. 1954, *História del Toreo*. Barcelona: Ediciones destino s.i.

Macnab, A. 1957, *Bulls of Iberia*. London: Heineman.

Madariaga, B. 1966, *El Toro de Lidia*. Madrid: Ediciones Alimara.

Martinez-Allier, J. 1971, *Labourers and Landowners in Southern Spain*. London: George Allen and Unwin.

Martinez de Alamo, J. 1979, 'El Viti: el hombre y el miedo'. In *Blanco y Negro*, 3501, 6–13 June 1979.

Martinez Rueda, M. 1838, 'Elogio de las corridas de toros'. *Quarterly Review*, LXII, 385–425.

Marshall, A. G. 1985, 'Is a Bull Female?' *American Ethnologist*, 12, 541–2.

Marvin, G. 1982, 'Una orientación para un estudio antropológico de la fiesta del toro embolado'. *Kalathos – 2*. Revista del Seminario de Arqueología y Etnología Turelense, 157–75.

McCormick, J. and Mascareñas, M. S. 1967, *The Complete Aficionado*. London: Weidenfeld and Nicolson.

Miller, S. 1973, 'Ends, means and galumphing: some leitmotifs of play'. *American Anthropologist*, 75, 87–98.

Miller, (Nachmanovich) S. 1975, 'The playful, the crazy and the nature of pretense'. *Rice University Studies*, vol. 2 31–51.

Mira, J. F. 1976, 'Toros en el Norte Valenciano: notas para un analisis'. In Carmelo Lison Tolosana (ed.), *Temas en Antropología Social*, Madrid: Akal, 107–129.

Moore, S. F. and Myerhoff, B. 1977, 'Secular ritual: forms and meanings' 3–25. In S. F. Moore and B. Myerhoff (eds), *Secular Ritual*, Amsterdam: Van Gorcum.

Muga, J. 1978–9, 'Antropología de cazadores'. *Trofeo*, 101–6, Octubre 1978– Marzo 1979, 50–4; 52–6; 64–8; 66–9.

Mullan, B. and Marvin, G. 1987, *Zoo Culture*. London: Weidenfeld and Nicolson.

Murphy, M. 1978, 'Between the Virgin and the whore: local community and the nuclear family in Seville: Spain'. Unpublished Ph.D. thesis, University of California, San Diego.

Nachmanovitch Miller, S. *see* Miller, S.

Ortega, D. 1950, *El Arte de Torear*. Madrid: Revista de Oriente.

Ortega y Gasset, J. 1965, 'Una interpretación de la historia universal'. In J. Ortega y Gasset, *Obras Completas*, vol. IX, Madrid: Revista de Occidente.

Ortega y Gasset, J. 1968, *La Caza y los Toros*. Madrid: Revista de Occidente.

Ortiz Cañavate, L. 1934, 'El toreo en España'. In F. Carreras y Candi (dir.), *Folklore y Costumbres*, Barcelona: Editorial Alberto Martin, 118–40.

Ortner, S. 1974, 'Is female to male as nature is to culture?'. In M. Z. Rosaldo and L. Lamphere (eds), *Women, Culture and Society*, Stanford, California: Stanford University Press, 67–87.

Paños Marti, P. 1969, *Los Toros en España*. 3 vols. Madrid: Orel.

Pérez de Ayala, R. 1925, *Política y los Toros*. Madrid: Urquijo.

Pérez Delgado, R. 1978, 'Sobre las torridas de toros'. In A. Carreira et al. (eds), *Julio Caro Baroja*, Madrid: Centro de Investigaciones Sociológicos.

Pérez 'Villamelon', A. 1955, *Origenes de la Fiesta Brava*. Mexico: Biblioteca Taurina Mexico.

Pitt-Rivers, J. 1967, 'Contextual analysis and the locus of the model'. *European Journal of Sociology*, VIII, 15–34.

Pitt-Rivers, J. 1971, *People of the Sierra*. Chicago and London: University of Chicago Press. Second edition.

Pitt-Rivers, J. 1984(a) 'El Sacrificio del Toro'. *Revista de Occidente*, 84, 27–49.

Pitt-Rivers, J. 1984 (b) 'El Sacraficio del Héroe' *El País* October 4 1984.

Press, T. 1980, *The City as Context: Urbanism and Behavioural Constraints in Sevilla*. Urbana, Chicago, London: University of Illinois Press.

Reglamentos de Espectáculos Taurinos. 1986, Madrid: Academia Editorial Lamruja.

Rappaport, R. 1974, 'Obvious Aspects of Ritual'. *Cambridge Anthropology*, 2, 1, 3–69.

Rios Mozo, R. 1974, *Tauromaquia Fundamental*. Sevilla: Universidad de Sevilla.

Rios Mozo, R. 1979, *Vibraciones Taurinos (La Seda por el Percal)*. Seville: Ecesa.

Rodriguez-Mora, C. *see* Guirado Rodriguez Mora, C.

Romero de Solis, R. 1978, 'Introducción a la sociología del arte de toreo'. Unpublished manuscript.

Rosaldo, M. Z. 1974, 'Woman, culture and society: a theoretical overview' in M.Z. Rosaldo and L. Lamphere (eds), *Women, Culture and Society*, Stanford University Press, 17–42.

Salas, N. 1973, *Secretos del Mundo de los Toros*. Madrid: Editora Nacional.

Sanz Egaña, C. 1947, 'El toro de lidia y su historia ganadera'. Report to *I Congreso Veterinario de Zootecnica*, unpublished manuscript.

Sanz Egaña, C. 1958, *Historia y Bravura del Toro de Lidia*. Madrid: Colección Astral.

Schwarz, H. F. 1976, 'Modelos dualisticos en la cultura de una comunidad tradicional española'. In Carmelo Lison Tolosana (ed.), *Expresiones Actuales de la Cultura del Pueblo*, Madrid: Centro de Estudios Sociales, 115–39.

Serran Pagan, G. 1979, 'El toro de la Virgen y la industria textil de Grazalema'. *Revista Española de Investigaciones Sociológicas*, 5, 119–35.

Serran Pagan, G. and Muntadas, A. 1980, *Pamplona – Grazalema: From the Public Square to the Bullring*. New York: Enquire Printing.

Steen, M. 1956, *The Bulls of Parral*. London: William Collins and Sons Ltd.

Tax-Freeman, S. 1970, *Neighbours: The Social Contract in a Castilian Hamlet*. Chicago: University of Chicago Press.

Toro Buiza, L. 1947, *Sevilla en la Historia del Toreo*. Seville: Publicaciones del Ayuntamiento.

Vavra, R. 1972, *Bulls of Iberia*. Seville: Imprenta Sevillana S.A.

Vera, A. 1951, *Ganaderia Brava*. Madrid: Librería Beltran.

Vicens Vives, J. (ed.). 1961, *Historia de España y America*, 3 vols. Barcelona: Editorial Vicens Vives.

Zabala, V. 1971, *La Ley de la Fiesta*. Madrid: Editorial Prensa Española.

Newspapers and taurine periodicals

ABC (Seville edition) *El País*	National daily newspapers.
Sur-Oeste	Andulusian daily newspaper, published in Seville
Aplausos *El Mundo de los Toros*	The two most important taurine magazines, published weekly; nationwide.
El Toreo *El Toro*	Taurine magazines, published nationwide.

Index